Rural Women
and State Policy

Series in Political Economy and Economic Development in Latin America

Series Editor
Andrew Zimbalist
Smith College

Through country case studies and regional analyses this series will contribute to a deeper understanding of development issues in Latin America. Shifting political environments, increasing economic interdependence, and the imposing problematic of debt, foreign investment, and trade policy demand novel conceptualizations of development strategies and potentials for the region. Individual volumes in this series will explore the deficiencies in conventional formulations of the Latin American development experience by examining new evidence and material. Topics will include, among others, women and development in Latin America; the impact of IMF interventions; the effects of redemocratization on development; Cubanology and Cuban political economy; Nicaraguan political economy; and individual case studies on development and debt policy in various countries in the region.

About the Book and Editors

The UN Decade for Women coincided with an economic crisis in Latin America comparable only to that of the Great Depression. This text synthesizes what has been learned over the past decade with regard to agricultural development for rural women, taking into account the impact of the economic crisis, models of development in the region, and the scope and consequences of "women in development" projects and policies.

Part 1 consists of country case studies ranging from the neo-liberal model of Chile to socialist Cuba. Each author reviews the growing literature on women's roles in agricultural development and examines how changes in those roles relate to agricultural development initiatives and the changing role of the agricultural sector in national and international economies. They evaluate national programs established during the decade that were designed to benefit rural women and explore the consequences of ignoring rural women in state development initiatives.

Part 2 contains four comparative analyses. Contributors consider the major state agricultural policy initiatives in Latin America during the past decade—agrarian reform and integrated rural development—as well as the effectiveness of income-generating projects, which were the main initiatives targeted at rural women. The rural-to-urban migration of women is analyzed as the outcome of the lack of attention to their productive roles.

Carmen Diana Deere is professor of economics at the University of Massachusetts, Amherst. **Magdalena León** is research director at the Colombian Association of Population Studies (ACEP) in Bogotá, Colombia.

Rural Women and State Policy

Feminist Perspectives on Latin American Agricultural Development

edited by
Carmen Diana Deere
and Magdalena León

Westview Press / Boulder and London

Series in Political Economy and Economic Development in Latin America

Copyright © 1987 by Westview Press, Inc.

Published in 1987 in the United States of America by Westview Press, Inc.; Frederick A. Praeger, Publisher; 5500 Central Avenue, Boulder, Colorado 80301

Library of Congress Cataloging-in-Publication Data
Rural women and state policy.
  (Series in political economy and economic development in Latin America)
  "Papers . . . presented at the Symposium "Agricultural Development Policy and Rural Women in Latin America: an Evaluation of the Decade," convened . . . in conjunction with the 45th International Congress of Americanists [and] hosted by the University of Los Andes in Bogotá, Colombia, in July, 1985"—Acknowledgements.
  Bibliography: p.
  Includes index.
  1. Women in rural development—Latin America—Congresses. 2. Rural development projects—Latin America—Congresses. 3. Women in agriculture—Latin America—Congresses. I. Deere, Carmen Diana. II. León, Magdalena. III. Symposium on "Agricultural Development Policy and Rural Women in Latin America: an Evaluation of the Decade" (1985: University of Los Andes). IV. Series.
  HQ1240.5.L29R87   1987   305.4'2'098   87-8264
  ISBN 0-8133-7391-3
  ISBN 0-8133-7390-5 (If published in paperback)

Printed and bound in the United States of America

(∞) The paper used in this publication meets the requirements of the American National Standard for Permanence of Paper for Printed Library Materials Z39.48-1984.

10   9   8   7   6   5   4   3   2   1

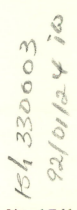

Contents

Tables

Acknowledgments

This book grew out of a collaborative effort by North American, European, and Latin American researchers to synthesize what we have learned about the position of rural women in Latin America over the past decade. The authors benefited from the opportunity to exchange ideas on two occasions during 1985.

The first workshop, on Feminist Theory, State Policy, and Rural Women in Latin America, was convened by María de los Angeles Crummett, Carmen Diana Deere, and Beatriz Schmuckler at the Kellogg Institute of International Studies at the University of Notre Dame in February 1985. The papers presented by Chaney, Crummett, Deere, León, Phillips, and Spindel benefited from the comments and criticisms of the other seminar participants, Alain de Janvry, Ann Kubisch, Marta Roldán, Beatriz Schmuckler, and Alex Wilde. We especially wish to thank María de los Angeles Crummett and Alex Wilde for local arrangements, Shelly Baxter, who served as rapporteur for the workshop, and Ernest Bartell, director of the Kellogg Institute.

All the chapters in this book were presented as papers at the symposium on "Agricultural Development Policy and Rural Women in Latin America: An Evaluation of the Decade," convened by Deere and León in conjunction with the 45th International Congress of Americanists. Participation in the congress, which was hosted by the University of Los Andes in Bogotá, Colombia, in July 1985, was made possible by a grant from the Ford Foundation.

Other invited participants in the Bogotá symposium included Lourdes Benería, Pilar Campaña, Cecilia López, Lidiethe Madden, Marianne Schmink, and Fiona Wilson. Their contributions enriched all the papers. Nancy Castro of the Colombian Association of Population Studies (ACEP) did a superb job of taking care of local arrangements, and we wish to thank both her and ACEP for facilitating our work.

The simultaneous publication of this collection in both English and Spanish was made possible through a prepublication grant from the Ford Foundation. We are most grateful to the foundation for its support of this endeavor. The translation of six of the chapters into English was undertaken by Katherine Pettus of Latin American Scholarly Services. We greatly appreciate her collaboration in bringing this project to fruition. All the chapters benefited from the careful reading of Andrew Zimbalist, editor of this Westview Press series.

Finally, we wish to acknowledge our debt to the rural women of Latin America from whom we have learned so much over the past decade. To them we dedicate this book.

Carmen Diana Deere
Magdalena León

Introduction

Carmen Diana Deere
and Magdalena León

As the UN Decade for Women came to a close at Nairobi in July 1985, Latin America was enmeshed in an economic crisis comparable only to that of the Great Depression. Throughout the region growth rates had been low or negative. In the majority of countries, real per capita income was lower in 1985 than in 1980 and, in several cases, than in 1970 (UN 1985:20). Moreover, staggering debt service requirements and the burden of economic adjustment threatened the very process of development. Yet in the midst of this crisis women had become a development concern.

One of the major accomplishments of the UN Decade for Women was the research effort that made women, particularly poor rural women, visible. Belying census enumerations of the agricultural economically active population, Latin American rural women were shown to be farmers, animal raisers, and traders and a growing component of the rural wage labor force. Nevertheless, most Latin American agricultural development initiatives through the mid-1970s had excluded women as direct beneficiaries.

The UN Decade for Women, initiated at the Mexico City conference in 1975, stimulated not only a concerted research effort but also attempts to "incorporate" women into development, both through state policies favoring sexual equality and specific projects targeted at women. Moreover, the economic crisis of the 1980s directed official attention to women's multiple economic roles: Often women bore the brunt of the crisis, and any solution to the crisis would have to take their participation into account.

The central issue for the authors of this book is on whose terms and under what terms rural women will participate in the solutions to the Latin American economic crisis. Will they be simply a source of cheap labor for renewed export expansion or, as unpaid family workers in smallholder agriculture, providers of cheap foodstuffs to ameliorate the growing urban tensions of the 1980s? Or can rural women be organized and mobilized as a political force with their own vision of development and a different vision of themselves, empowered to challenge their subordinated gender and class position?

In this book, the contributors synthesize what has been learned over the past decade about the meaning of agricultural development for rural women. In the country case studies (of Brazil, Chile, Colombia, Cuba, the Dominican Republic, Ecuador, Mexico, and Nicaragua) and comparative analyses (of agrarian reform, migration processes, integrated rural development, and income generation projects for women), we attempt to synthesize (1) the impact of state intervention in agriculture on rural women, (2) the scope and consequences of "women in development" projects, (3) the impact of the economic crisis of the 1980s on women's productive and reproductive roles, and (4) rural women's responses to agrarian change and economic crisis.

After providing a synthesis of what we now know about women's participation in Latin American agriculture, we present an overview of Latin American development and agricultural policies, highlighting the contribution of the chapters in this book to our understanding of how these policies affect rural women.

What We Now Know

The research agenda for the Decade was greatly influenced by the issues raised in Ester Boserup's (1970) seminal contribution to the field of Women in Development. Boserup argued that not only had women in the Third World been ignored in the development process but also they had been marginalized in both absolute and relative terms. Women had often been deprived of their productive activities or been displaced from the labor force (absolute marginalization), for example, through mechanization. Not infrequently, women had lost out relative to men (relative marginalization) when resources (land, credit, technical assistance) were channeled to only one gender or through unequal opportunities to participate in wage work.

The research effort arising in Latin America differed from that in other parts of the Third World in that these issues were usually framed with respect to the process of capitalist development. Moreover, Latin American researchers asked not only whether women had been marginalized but also whether women's subordination had been exacerbated or ameliorated by the processes leading to the creation of modern farms and industries and a wage labor force. In addition, the degree and context of capitalist development in Latin America were assumed to be related to changes in the world economy and the dependent relationship of the region within the world capitalist system.

To answer the question of how rural women fared in the process of agrarian capitalist development first required an investigation of what work women actually did and how this had changed over time and an analysis of how women's economic participation was related to their class position and social status.

Boserup had distinguished between male and female farming systems across continents, highlighting the fact that farmers were not always men. However, her characterization of Latin America as a male farming system reinforced the biases captured in the national census statistics upon which her analysis had been based. The deficiencies of these, which produced a high degree of underenumeration of women within the agricultural economically active population (EAP), was to be amply demonstrated (Wainerman and Recchini 1981; Deere and León 1982; León 1984). The UN Decade for Women in Latin America could well be called the "decade on measurement" as researchers attempted to make rural women's work visible and to demonstrate its quantitative significance.

What have been the results of this research effort? At the risk of oversimplification, the body of research generated over the past decade suggests twelve facts or tendencies with respect to women's participation in Latin American agriculture.[1]

1. Latin American peasant women are agricultural producers. In all the studies undertaken by feminist researchers it has been found that rural women participate in at least some agricultural task or farm activity.

2. Rather than a male farming system, Latin American peasant agriculture is best characterized as a family farming system. A farming system constitutes an integrated set of activities that involves more than just crop production and participation in field work. Animal husbandry, agricultural processing and product transformation, natural resource management, marketing, and decision-making are all aspects of the work of an agriculturalist. Although women provide an important component of field labor in peasant agricultural production, their participation rates are significantly higher when their participation in all farming activities are taken into account.[2]

3. The significance of women's participation within family farming systems varies widely across Latin America. For instance, it varies with ethnicity and among regions: Women's agricultural participation is much more important in the Andean countries and Central America than in the Southern Cone. Their participation can also vary significantly within

a given country as discussed in Chapter 6 on Ecuador by Lynne Phillips and Chapter 1 on Chile by María Soledad Lago.[3]

This heterogeneity suggests that there is no linear relation between women's participation in family farming systems and the degree and type of capitalist development (Deere and León 1982; Stohlcke 1983; Wilson 1985). Rather, the gender division of labor in agriculture is responsive to a number of technical variables—the specific crops and tasks, the labor intensity of the activity, and the attendant degree of mechanization—and social characteristics of the peasant household and the woman herself—such as class, the family life cycle, kinship position, and age.

4. Although the gender division of labor in productive activities is heterogeneous, that between productive and reproductive activities is homogeneous. Across Latin America, irrespective of their economic contribution, rural women carry the burden of reproductive tasks: housework, child care, care of the elderly and sick, and, of course, child bearing.

5. Domestic labor everywhere has been found to be very time intensive.[4] Moreover, rural women bear a heavier reproductive load than do urban women because the former lack the basic social infrastructure—ready access to potable water, electricity, transportation—and their domestic technology is rudimentary. Women's responsibility for reproduction is also a major source of household inequality, since the working day of rural women is significantly longer than that of rural men.

6. The research effort of the last decade has also confirmed the importance of class analysis in studying the work that women do. Rural women's participation in the family farming system and in the rural wage labor market differs significantly according to the household's access to means of production. As Lourdes Arizpe and Carlota Botey illustrate in Chapter 4 on Mexico, agricultural policy affects households of different classes differently, with varied outcomes for rural women.

Throughout Latin America, rural women's participation in agriculture appears to be greatest among the poorer strata of the peasantry, smallholders and the near landless.[5] In particular, poorer women's greater participation in field work appears to be related to the absence of males from the homestead because of temporary wage migration, the lower opportunity cost of women in the labor market (the result of lower wages), and the fact that in much of Latin America agriculture is a secondary activity among smallholders.[6] The resource base is insufficient for agriculture to be a male occupation, and as wage income becomes an increasingly more significant component of household income, agricultural production becomes increasingly an extension of women's domestic work.

But as Lago argues for Chile, the activities of women from poor, middle, and rich peasant households are differentiated not by whether they work on the farm but by the composition of activities in which they engage. And whether poor women become seasonal wage workers greatly depends on the existence of a local wage labor market.

7. Analyses of women's position in the family farming system must take into account not only women's role in production but also how this role is related to their participation in decision-making and control over the income generated. By determining the relationship between these three variables, we can differentiate between egalitarian and patriarchal family farming systems—a distinction important to an understanding of the mechanisms that reproduce women's subordination (Deere and León 1982). In general, Latin American smallholder agriculture appears much more egalitarian than the family farming systems of the middle and rich peasantry. Nevertheless, a more flexible gender division of labor and of responsibility and authority—particularly in conditions of extreme rural poverty—does not necessarily imply an absolute improvement in women's lives or social position.

8. The argument that women have been marginalized or displaced in the agricultural wage labor force with the development of capitalism is difficult to sustain in the Latin American case. Rather, women have been increasingly employed as seasonal wage workers in the most labor-intensive tasks of export agriculture: the coffee, cotton, and tobacco harvests. This tendency is clearly seen in Chapters 2, 3, and 7 on Brazil, Nicaragua, and the Dominican Republic. Women have also been incorporated into the labor force as new agro-exports are developed, whether strawberries in Mexico, peanuts in Brazil, or flowers in Colombia. As Phillips and Lago argue in Chapters 1 and 6, capitalist development in agriculture and modern technology and mechanization do not necessarily incorporate or displace women—which depends on the specific conditions. Overall, however, rural women's participation in agricultural wage labor appears to be on the rise. This development does not necessarily make them socially visible, as Cheywa Spindel illustrates in Chapter 3 on Brazil.

9. Except in Cuba, the terms under which women have been incorporated into the wage labor force are everywhere unfavorable. Women are always paid lower wages than men. Wages are only potentially equal for those tasks paid as piecework, which require an intensified labor effort. Moreover, few permanent employment opportunities have been created for women. And in most Latin American countries women agricutural workers lack any type of legal protection or benefits. Where these formally exist, such as in Brazil, they have rarely been implemented.

10. The overwhelming majority of female wage workers are from landless or smallholder households. A growing number are household heads who are directly responsible for generating their families' sustenance.[7]

11. The degree of organization of rural women is generally low. However, over the past decade two national peasant women's federations, in Bolivia and Honduras, have been formed. The chapters on Brazil, Chile, and Nicaragua show that at least in these countries rural unions have begun to address the issues posed by the participation of women as wage workers.[8]

12. Finally, in most Latin American countries the majority of rural-urban migrants have been young rural women. As María de los Angeles Crummett argues in Chapter 12, the preponderance of women in the migrant stream has to be understood in the context of the unequal opportunities for men and women in the agricultural sector.

From ISI to the Debt Crisis:
State Policy and Rural Women

The major state agricultural development initiatives of the postwar period generally ignored the participation of rural women. This was partly because of the implicit assumption of developmentalism—that state intervention was gender neutral. Whether in agrarian reform or integrated rural development, it was assumed that by benefiting households, all members within them would benefit as well. The research initiative of the past decade has shown that this is not the case.

Until the 1970s most Latin American countries were pursuing import substitution industrialization (ISI) to the neglect of the agricultural sector. Although agrarian reform was posited as a necessary complement to the industrialization drive—in order to increase agricultural productivity, raise rural incomes, and enlarge the internal market—efforts at reform were often minimal. In the majority of countries that undertook significant reforms (as pointed out by Deere in Chapter 9), women were excluded as beneficiaries of the agrarian reform. Only in Cuba and recently in Nicaragua have significant numbers of women benefited directly from agrarian reform. Women were excluded partly because of legal impediments. In most countries, the beneficiaries were required to be household heads with dependent children; thus female spouses were automatically excluded. It was also caused by structural factors (the seasonal nature of women's labor force participation) and ideological impediments. The implications of rural women's exclusion from the agrarian reform and their response are well detailed for Ecuador in Chapter 6 by Lynne Phillips.

The dominant model of state intervention in agriculture in this period, rural extensionism, was also responsible for the lack of attention to women as agricutural producers. Rural women were perceived only as housewives who were responsible for the domestic realm. The state resources directed toward them focused solely on their roles of wife and mother. Thus home economists were trained throughout Latin America to teach rural women health and nutrition and sewing and handicrafts and at best to introduce home gardens. Programs for agricultural technical assistance and access to credit were directed overwhelmingly toward rural men. Thus, rural extension services reproduced the socially constructed—and idealized—gender division of labor in which men were the agriculturalists and women were the housewives.

As shown in various chapters in this book, neglect of women as agricultural producers had important consequences for women's productivity and their control of farm income and negatively affected their social position. Crummett, in her review of migration trends in Chapter 12, suggests that perhaps an important consequence of this lack of attention to rural women's productive roles is the higher rate of female urban migration characteristic of many Latin American countries.

By the 1970s there was growing awareness of the failure of the industrialization process to bring about both balanced growth and equitable development. Food production had stagnated, and many Latin American countries were experiencing increasing balance of payments difficulties, partly as a result of the stagnation in the agro-export sector and the growth of food imports (de Janvry 1981). Moreover, the failure to institute significant land redistribution in many countries had contributed to increased landlessness and high rates of rural-urban migration. Growing urban problems starkly pointed to the failure of ISI to incorporate the potentially proletarianized workforce. Two very different policy initiatives resulted from these concerns: integrated rural development and economic liberalization.

Integrated rural development in Latin America was a response to both the food crisis and the need to slow down rural/urban migration. It largely focused on the introduction of Green Revolution agricultural technologies in an attempt to make peasants more productive while concurrently improving rural living conditions. But as León argues in Chapter 5 on Colombia, integrated rural development was viewed as an alternative to agrarian reform and was not accompanied by any significant redistribution of resources toward the smallholder sector.

The move toward integrated rural development grew out of the switch in the attention of the international development agencies toward the "poorest of the poor," as signaled by Robert McNamara's 1972 Nairobi speech and the "basic needs" strategy initiated by the International

Labour Organization in 1976. As Cornelia Flora points out, the conditions should have been in place to integrate women into rural development since they are overrepresented among the poor and are generally responsible for meeting the basic needs of the family. Moreover, in 1974, the Percy amendment to the U.S. Foreign Assistance Act required that all U.S.-funded development assistance take into account its effect upon women, a policy subsequently adopted throughout the UN system. However, as in agrarian reform, women were largely ignored in integrated rural development programs. At best, they received increased attention only in their traditional domestic roles. Largely as a result of the Women in Development lobby generated by the Percy amendment, some of the integrated rural development programs had women's components added on.

These women's components, as well as the income generation projects for women, have been the source of considerable controversy, which is reflected in the comparative chapters by Chaney and Flora and the chapters on the Dominican Republic, Mexico, and Colombia. At issue is whether projects aimed at women as beneficiaries should be special projects or part of broader integrated rural development efforts; whether these projects should focus on income generation or income conservation; and the extent to which these projects are paternalistic—embued with a reformist or welfare bias—rather than mechanisms to empower women.

In Chapter 10 Chaney analyzes the women's components of two large-scale integrated rural development projects in Jamaica and the Dominican Republic. These projects were largely focused on subsistence generation or income conservation and attempted to make women more productive in the activities that they currently carry out, such as gardening or small-animal raising. Chaney argues that these projects do lead to improved household welfare, generally by enhancing nutrition. She argues that in many cases they might be preferable to income-generating activities because the return on artisan projects is often abysmally low. In her view a concerted drive is needed to valorize subsistence production and hence women's role in reproduction.

According to other contributors to this book, projects that take the gender division of labor as given simply reproduce women's subordi-nation. This danger is especially evident in projects that serve as women's components of larger efforts, since the most important component of such efforts—that focusing on production—will inevitably be targeted to the men. The argument for income-generating as opposed to sub-sistence-generating projects rests on the assumption that women's access to cash is an important precondition for female autonomy.

The bulk of Women in Development efforts in the 1970s have focused on income generation projects for women. Flora's analysis of these projects in Chapter 11 shows that they too have been problematic. They often tend to be concentrated in low-productivity activities with low remuneration to effort expended. However, many of these projects have multifaceted goals and focus on both income generation and organization. She argues that these organizational goals are key if women are to be empowered.

In Chapter 4 Lourdes Arizpe and Carlota Botey note that the major Mexican state initiative with respect to rural women has been support for women's income-generating projects on the *ejidos*. Although women have responded enthusiastically to these projects, they generally have not been economically viable. Moreover, the rights and benefits that they provide women are not equivalent to having access to ejido land in one's own name or to ejido membership.

Special projects for women have proliferated in the Dominican Republic at the behest of political parties and international agencies. Belkis Mones and Lydia Grant criticize these efforts both for their paternalistic bias and for their lack of focus on the mechanisms of women's subordination. Yet these authors note, as does Flora, that these efforts do provide a forum for organizing rural women around their perceived interests.

Throughout most of the region the limited scope of special projects for rural women and of agricultural development initiatives aimed at smallholders suggests that the more important variable affecting rural women's lives is the model of development and concomitant macroeconomic state policies. The experiences of rural women in countries following the neo-liberal path and of those on the transition to socialism could not differ more.

Neo-liberal economic policy is premised on the supposed superiority of the unencumbered market in resource allocation in which the state refrains from interfering in economic life.[9] The Chilean case analyzed by Lago represents the extreme neo-liberal experiment. For the economy to develop according to comparative advantage, tariffs were removed and Chilean industry and agriculture were expected to compete in the world market. State intervention in price setting was ended as were both consumer and producer subsidies.

The neo-liberal policies have had dramatic regional effects, spurring capitalist development in certain export products and ruining peasant production and thus foodstuff production (see Chapter 1 by María Lago). Rural women have been increasingly drawn into the seasonal labor force of agro-export production in the fruit-producing region of Chile. However, because of the growing immiseration of their households the majority of rural women have been forced to intensify their agricultural work as well as their search for additional income generation opportunities.

The debt crisis of the 1980s brought International Monetary Fund (IMF) stabilization programs to the forefront (Mexico, Brazil, Dominican Republic in 1982, Costa Rica in 1983, Colombia in 1984) and spurred the shift toward neo-liberal economic policies throughout Latin America. Economic adjustment has largely focused on reducing state spending in order to reduce fiscal deficits. In most countries, this strategy has meant the end of basic needs approaches to development and of state subsidies for foodstuffs and other necessities. Across the region, it has meant increasing poverty for the majority of rural households. The authors in this book also show that the increased precariousness of basic reproduction has intensified rural women's labor, in many cases bringing women into social production.[10]

Both Flora, in her analysis of the increasing popularity of income generation projects for women (Chapter 11), and León, in her analysis of why a rural development program for women was recently adopted in Colombia (Chapter 5), see the increased governmental attention to women in the 1980s as partly related to the economic crisis. Flora argues that in the context of reduced fiscal budgets, income-generating projects for women are low-cost programs to augment rural incomes and thus provide a partial solution to the effects of the crisis. Moreover, they strengthen the private sector—a key objective of foreign assistance programs in the Reagan era.

León argues that Colombia's rural women policy—designed to facilitate rural women's access to credit and technical assistance—was adopted in 1984 as a partial and low-cost means of dealing with the stagnation of food production and concomitant increase in food imports and food prices. She notes, however, that the policy ignores a basic condition for increasing peasant foodstuff production—land reform—and that the resources dedicated to implementing the policy are inadequate, resulting in limited coverage of potential women beneficiaries. Moreover, the conceptualization of the women's program leaves much to be desired as a mechanism for female empowerment. As in the Dominican Republic, the issue is whether groups of women organized around production goals can facilitate the formation of gender consciousness.

Despite its shortcomings, Colombia is among the few Latin American countries (along with Mexico, Honduras, and Costa Rica) to attempt to develop a national rural development strategy specifically targeting rural women. The majority of Latin American countries now have national women's bureaus of some sort, and a number have detailed five-year plans for incorporating women into development; yet few have developed the mechanisms or channeled the resources to translate abstract goals into concrete policies and programs benefiting rural women as a whole.

(These limitations are well illustrated in Chapter 6 on Ecuador and Chapter 3 on Brazil.)

The export diversification drive motivated by the financial crisis has tended to increase the demand for cheap labor throughout Latin America. Moreover, the rising cost of living (partly the result of the end of state subsidies for basic goods and services) has forced increasing numbers of women into the rural labor market, as seen in the chapters on Brazil, Chile, and Mexico. The increased need of rural women to earn wage income has not always resulted in their finding employment in agriculture, however, as shown by Mones and Grant in Chapter 2 on the Dominican Republic. The specific effect of the crisis on women's agricultural employment opportunities is closely related to such factors as the gender division of labor in specific crops and tasks and whether the crops that employ significant numbers of women face favorable or unfavorable international market conditions as well as state policy support.

In Chapter 3 on Brazil, Spindel shows that the increased participation of women in the agricultural wage labor force has been accompanied by the organization of women agricultural workers. For the first time, women's issues are being voiced within the rural unions, even if they are not yet fully addressed. Likewise, in the case of Chile, Lago shows that women wage workers are being incorporated into the newly emerging rural organizations and that as a result of the agrarian crisis rural women are participating in community organizations as never before. It is thus ironic that the very dimensions of the crisis in Latin America have created some important preconditions for women's collective action. We consider the implications of this fact in the concluding chapter of this book.

The socialist experiment of Cuba and the transition process initiated in Nicaragua in 1979 differ significantly from the other Latin American development processes. Rather than the forces of the marketplace determining the demand for rural labor, direct state intervention in the form of state farms and support to cooperative development partially account for women's greater participation in agriculture. Moreover, in both countries the incorporation of women as beneficiaries of the agrarian reform has been an explicit objective of state policy. The result of this approach in Cuba, as Jean Stubbs and Mavis Alvarez show in Chapter 8, is that women have been a major force behind the development of production cooperatives in the late 1970s. In Nicaragua, women's incorporation within the cooperative movement is still incipient; nevertheless, women represent a higher proportion of cooperative members than in other Latin American countries that have not had an explicit state policy favoring women's incorporation. Martha Luz Padilla, Ana Criquillon, and Clara Murguialday in Chapter 7 on Nicaragua analyze how *machismo* and women's responsibility for the reproductive realm continue to be factors limiting women's full participation in production.

In both Cuba and Nicaragua women are guaranteed equal pay for equal work. But although women's working conditions are superior to those in other Latin American countries, they still tend to be concentrated in the low-paying and low-skilled jobs. Nevertheless, in Cuba women have gradually entered the full-time agricultural labor force, often assuming tasks and occupations traditionally defined as male. In the Nicaraguan case, Padilla, Criquillon, and Murguialday report that although rural women are now finding more employment than previously, this gain is largely the result of the shortage of male labor caused by the war effort against the Reagan administration–backed contras.

The Cuban and Nicaraguan experiences show how a positive state policy and an ideology of equality are necessary but not sufficient conditions to ensure women's incorporation into social production on the same terms as men. If the other mechanisms that reproduce women's subordination are not also challenged, the socially defined role of women will hold back and limit their productive role. Moreover, as both experiences illustrate, women's participation in social production does not automatically produce gender consciousness. Stubbs and Alvarez's analysis, however, shows that women's participation in social production does increase the tensions in gender relations and that Cuban women, particularly the younger generation, are slowly beginning to challenge traditional patriarchal attitudes and structures. An autonomous or at least explicitly feminist women's movement may be the necessary mechanism to link a positive state policy with fundamental changes in gender relations.

Organization of the Book

In Part 1 of this book we present country case studies of different models of development and the effect of agrarian policy and the economic crisis on the position of rural women. The chapters are arranged according to the predominant model of development and agrarian policy.

Chapter 1 begins with Chile because it represents the extreme case of neo-liberal economic policies guiding the model of development. The focus of this chapter is rural women's response to the agrarian crisis and the uneven regional development prompted by neo-liberal policies. Chapter 2, on the Dominican Republic, also highlights the economic crisis of the 1980s and the multiple income-generating strategies of rural women required to deal with the crisis.

The next two chapters focus on the two major industrialized countries of Latin America, Brazil and Mexico. In both, the agricultural sector was called upon to support industrial development and state policies favored the development of agrarian capitalist firms. But whereas a major agrarian reform characterized Mexican economic development, a comparable reform was not carried out in Brazil. Chapter 3 focuses on the dominant trend of the decade in Brazil—the growing labor force participation of the peasantry, particularly that of rural women. In Chapter 4 on Mexico, Arizpe and Botey show how agrarian reform may be a precondition for more equitable rural development, but if not followed up by supportive state policies, it can also lead to agrarian crisis, growing rural immiseration, and dependence on wage labor among the peasantry—all of which impact upon the productive and reproductive roles of rural women.

Colombia, analyzed in Chapter 5, was characterized by ISI policies accompanied by a minimal agrarian reform. In the 1970s it gave more attention than other countries in the region to integrated rural development, and in the 1980s, along with Mexico, it was among the few countries to develop a national-level policy with regard to rural women. The focus of this chapter is on the limitations of such a strategy when it ignores both agrarian reform and other preconditions for women's emancipation.

The subsequent three chapters focus on women's experience in the Latin American agrarian reforms. In Chapter 6 on Ecuador, Phillips describes how women were excluded from the country's major reform of land tenure relationships and what the implications were for women's productive and reproductive roles. In contrast, in Nicaragua, analyzed in Chapter 7, the incorporation of women into the new cooperatives and state farms fostered by the agrarian reform was an explicit objective of state policy. This chapter highlights the problems of integrating women under the same terms as men even during revolutionary processes of change.

In Chapter 8 on Cuba, Stubbs and Alvarez consider recent agrarian policy in the only socialist country of the region. They show how a deliberate state policy to incorporate women into production cooperatives can be successful once certain preconditions are established. Women's participation has strengthened the cooperative movement and challenged many of the structures that reproduce women's subordination.

In Part 2 of this book we turn to comparative analyses of rural women in agricultural development initiatives. In Chapter 9 Deere presents a synthesis of the Latin American agrarian reforms with respect to women's participation. In Chapter 10 Chaney focuses on how integrated rural development projects were placed on the development agenda and analyzes women's components that attempted to make women more productive in their traditional roles. In Chapter 11, Flora presents an analysis of the strengths and weaknesses of income generation projects for women. Finally, in Chapter 12 Crummett considers why many rural women in the region find that their principal alternative is migration to urban centers.

In the conclusion Deere and León look toward the future and consider how the goals of the UN Decade for Women of "equality, development, and peace" might be translated into policy if Latin American rural women were to become a political force.

Acknowledgments

An earlier version of this chapter was presented as the Keynote Address at the Conference on Gender Issues in Farming Systems Research and Extension, University of Florida, Gainesville, February 1986. We are grateful to Andy Zimbalist, as well as several anonymous reviewers, for helpful comments.

Notes

1. Other overviews of the literature on women's role in Latin American agriculture include Arriagada and Noordam (1982); Jaquette (1983); Stohlke (1983); CEPAL (1984); FAO (1984); Spindel, Jacquette, and Cordini (1984); Wilson (1985); and Flora and Santos (1986). Much of the recent research on rural women is presented in the collection by León (1982).

2. For example, according to the ACEP survey of rural households in Garcia Rovira, Colombia, in only 18 percent did a woman participate in field work, but in 24 percent a woman participated in marketing; in 53 percent, in processing farm products; in 88 percent, in animal care; and in 95 percent a woman carried out agricultural service activities such as cooking for fieldhands (Deere and León 1982:119). In the Dominican Republic, a national survey of 2,152 rural households revealed that according to a broad definition of participation in a farming system, the economically active female participation rate was 84 percent; in contrast, according to the 1981 census only 21 percent of rural women were economically active (CIPAF 1985:162). The definition of what constitutes agricultural work has thus been an important source of underenumeration in census measures of the female agricultural economically active population. Also see Wainerman and Recchini de Lattes (1981).

3. The regional variation stood out in the comparative analysis of three regions of Colombia and Peru (Deere and León 1982:54). In the Colombian cases, in the region characterized by advanced capitalist development a woman participated in at least one agricultural activity in 29 percent of the households; in contrast, in the region characterized by a predominantly peasant economy, a woman participated in agriculture in 40 percent. The participation rate of women was significantly lower than in the Peruvian region where a woman participated in agricultural activities in 86 percent of the households. See Sautu (1982) for the differences in women's agricultural participation in Argentina,

Bolivia, and Paraguay. The intracountry regional differences stand out sharply in recent surveys undertaken in the Dominican Republic (CIPAF 1985) and Nicaragua (CIERA et al. 1985).

4. A not uncommon finding is the typical day of a woman in rural Nicaragua reported in CIERA (1984). Her working day consisted of eighteen hours and twenty minutes of which 52.5 percent was dedicated to reproductive tasks. A maximum of 19 percent was dedicated to leisure, but this component included the time she spent tending her country store and visiting with neighbors. The rest of her working day was spent on directly productive activities. See Campaña (1982) and CIPAF (1985) for detailed analysis of the multiple productive and reproductive activities in which women engage.

5. For analyses of how the sexual division of labor in agriculture varies according to peasant social differentiation see Deere and León (1982) on Colombia and Peru, Aranda (1982) on Chile, and CIPAF (1985) on the Dominican Republic.

6. A comparative analysis of peasant household incomes, based on the major rural household income surveys of the last decade, is found in Deere and Wasserstrom (1981). In most of these surveys, off-farm income represented from 40 percent to 60 percent of total household income for the smallholder strata.

7. For example, in the national-level survey of 800 female wage workers in Nicaragua, it was found that 80 percent of the women were from landless households and 20 percent from the smallholder sector. Female household heads accounted for 23 percent of the female wage workers; in addition, another 15 percent were unmarried mothers residing with their parents or older relatives (CIERA et al. 1985). The CIPAF (1985) study found that women constituted 22 percent of the rural heads of households in the Dominican Republic. See Buvinic and Youssef (1978) on the general phenomenon of female-headed households in Latin America.

8. See Hisbol (1984) and Ardaya (1986) on the Bolivian National Peasant Women's Federation "Bartolina Sisa" and Callejas (1983) on the Honduran Peasant Women's Federation. On the difficulties of organizing rural women wage workers, even when the political will exists to do so, see CIERA et al. (1985).

9. See de Janvry (1985) for an in-depth analysis of the effect of the neo-liberal model on the Latin American agricultural sector.

10. A detailed analysis of the effects of the economic crisis on women is provided by Barbieri and Oliveira (1985). They note that one important effect of the economic crisis in Mexico has been the increase in acts of violence committed against women. Also see SID/ACEP/PIEM (1985) and DAWN (1985).

References

Aranda, Ximena, "El díptico campesina-asalariada agrícola," in M. León, ed., *Las Trabajadoras del Agro* (Bogotá: ACEP, 1982).

Ardaya, Gloria, "La Mujer Boliviana ante la Crisis: Avances y Perspectivas," La Paz, FLACSO (Facultad LatinoAmericana de Ciencias Sociales), 1986, mimeo.

Arriagada, Irma, and Johanna Noordam, "Las mujeres rurales latinoamericanas y la división del trabajo," in M. León, ed., *Las Trabajadoras del Agro* (Bogotá: ACEP, 1982).

Barbieri, Teresita, and Orlandina de Oliveira, "La Presencia de las Mujeres en America Latina en una Decada de Crisis," paper presented to the panel on "The Global Political Economic and Cultural Crisis," UN Conference on the Decade for Women, Nairobi, July 1985.

Boserup, Ester, *Women's Role in Economic Development* (New York: St. Martin's Press, 1970).

Buvinic, Mayra, and Nadia Youssef, "Women Headed Households: The Ignored Factor in Development Planning" (Washington, D.C.: International Center for Research on Women, 1978).

Callejas, Cecilia, "Examination of Factors Limiting the Organization of Rural Women in Honduras," M.A. thesis, University of Florida, 1983.

Campaña, Pilar, "Mujer, trabajo y subordinación en la Sierra Central del Peru," in M. León, ed., *Las Trabajadoras del Agro* (Bogotá: ACEP, 1982).

CEPAL (Comisión Económica para América Latina), "La Mujer Rural de América Latina: Un Actor Social del Ultimo Decenio (1975–1985)," LC/L. 312 (Conf.73/3), October 1984.

CIERA (Centro de Investigación e Estudio de la Reforma Agraria), *La Mujer en las Cooperativas Agropecuarias en Nicaragua* (Managua: CIERA, 1984).

_____ , CETRA-MITRAB (Centro de Estudio sobre el Trabajo del Ministerio 188 Trabajo), and ATC (Asociación de los Trabajadores del Campo), "La Femenización de la Fuerza de Trabajo Asalariada en el Agro y Sus Implicaciones en la Producción y la Organización Sindical," Managua, October 1985, mimeo.

CIPAF (Centro de Investigación para la Acción Femenina), "La Mujer Rural Dominicana," Santo Domingo, preliminary version of the final report of the Study on the Dominican Rural Woman, October 1985, mimeo.

DAWN (Development Alternatives with Women for a New Era), *Development, Crises, and Alternative Visions: Third World Women's Perspectives*, Norway, 1985.

Deere, Carmen Diana, and Magdalena León, *Women in Andean Agriculture: Peasant Production and Rural Wage Employment in Colombia and Peru* (Geneva: ILO, 1982).

_____ , and Robert Wasserstrom, "Ingreso Familiar y Trabajo No Agrícola entre los Pequeños Productores de America Latina y el Caribe," in A. Novoa and J. Posner, eds., *Seminario Internacional sobre Producción Agropecuaria y Forestal en Zonas de Ladera de America Tropical* (Turrialba: CATIE (Centro Agronómico Tropical de Investigación y Enseñanza), 1981), pp. 151–167.

de Janvry, Alain, *The Agrarian Question and Reformism in Latin America* (Baltimore: Johns Hopkins University Press, 1981).

_____ , "Latin American Agriculture from Import Substitution Industrialization to Debt Crisis," paper presented at the conference on "Food Security and the International Political Economy," Utah State University, Logan, May 1985.

FAO (Food and Agriculture Organization [UN]), "Informe de la Mesa Redonda sobre Estratégias de Sobrevivencia en Economías Campesinas: el Rol de la Mujer," Bogotá, 1984.

Flora, Cornelia, and Blas Santos, "Women in Farming Systems in Latin America," in J. Nash and H. Safa, eds., *Women and Change in Latin America* (South Hadley, Mass.: Bergin and Garvey, 1986).

Hisbol, J., *Las Hijas de Bartolina Sisa* (La Paz: Instituto de Historia Social Boliviana, 1984).

Jaquette, Jane, "The Impact of Modernization on Women in Agriculture," Washington, D.C., Equity Policy Center, 1983, mimeo.

León, Magdalena, *Mujer y Capitalismo Agrario* (Bogotá: ACEP, 1979).

———, ed., *Las Trabajadoras del Agro*, vol. 3 of *Debate sobre la Mujer en América Latina y el Caribe* (Bogotá: ACEP, 1982).

———, "Measuring Women's Work: Methodological and Conceptual Issues in Latin America," *IDS Bulletin* (Institute of Development Studies, Sussex), 15, no. 1, 1984.

Sautu, Ruth, "El trabajo femenino en el sector agrícola: Analisis comparativo de Argentina, Bolivia y Paraguay," in M. León, ed., *Las Trabajadoras del Agro* (Bogotá: CIPAF, 1982).

SID (Sociedad Internacional para el Desarrollo)/ACEP/PIEM (Programa Interdisciplinario de Estudios de la Mujer), *Las Mujeres Frente a la Crisis de America Latina y el Caribe* (Bogotá: SID/ACEP/PIEM, 1985).

Spindel, Cheywa, Jane Jacquette, and Mabel Cordini, "A Mulher Rural e Mudanças no Processo de Produçao Agrícola," Brazil, Instituto Interamericano de Cooperación para la Agricultura, 1984, mimeo.

Stolhke, Verena, Position paper for the Social Science Research Council (SSRC) workshop on "Social Inequality and Gender Hierarchy in Latin America," Mexico City, 1983, mimeo.

United Nations, Economic Commission for Latin America and the Caribbean, *Preliminary Overview of the Latin American Economy During 1985*, Document No. LC/G.1383, Santiago, Chile, 1985.

Wainerman, Catalina, and Zulma Recchini de Lattes, *El Trabajo Domestico Femenino en el Banquillo de los Acusados: Medición Censal en America Latina* (Mexico: Terra Nova, 1981).

Wilson, Fiona, "Women and Agricultural Change in Latin America: Some Concepts Guiding Research," *World Development* 13, no. 9 (1985):1017–1035.

Part 1
Models of Development, Agrarian Policy, and the Economic Crisis

1

Rural Women and the Neo-Liberal Model in Chile

María Soledad Lago

Chile has never had an explicit policy that recognizes rural women as workers. The progressive Frei and Allende administrations, in power for almost a decade (1964–1973), were no exception: Women were excluded as beneficiaries of the agrarian reform implemented during that period. Government policy toward urban and rural women, to the extent that it has existed at all, has focused on either the social welfare ministries or the mothers' centers designed to improve women's domestic skills. The mothers' centers have always been organized locally and have never formed part of a national organization, and because the centers were closely tied to the various regimes, the women could not present grievances or organize politically. Even in their better moments, the mothers' centers did not constitute the basis for a social movement.

Although rural women have always engaged in productive activities, the neo-liberal model of development is now forcing them to intensify their participation in both peasant and capitalist production. Nevertheless, neither the state nor the society acknowledges that women are workers whose contributions to the household and to the country are important.

Research on rural women carried out over the past six years shows that their participation in agriculture varies according to regional dynamic, social class, and predominant local agricultural activity.[1] The possibility for women to organize depends on the degree to which they are incorporated as wage labor, the level of poverty, and whether the local rural support institutions and organizations are receptive to women.

This chapter considers how the neo-liberal model of development has affected rural women's productive work, social participation, and living conditions. The first section summarizes the principal theoretical premises underlying the neo-liberal model, the steps taken to implement it, and its effect upon the rural sector. The second section describes how the model has affected rural women in the five different regions of the country. The final section examines the extent of rural women's social participation and their potential for organization.

The Neo-Liberal Model
and Chilean Agriculture

The neo-liberal model has guided the Chilean economy for twelve years. By minimizing state intervention and allowing comparative advantage to orient growth, it has produced significant social and economic changes. According to its proponents, the underlying theory may be summarized in the following tenets (Tironi 1982):

1. Efficient resource allocation ensures a high economic growth rate.
2. In a small country like Chile, resource allocation must conform to international demand, which implies free trade and specialization according to the law of comparative advantage.
3. Productive resources are most efficiently allocated in a free market economy.
4. Economic growth will eventually benefit all social groups, including the poorest.
5. Private enterprises are always more efficient than state enterprises.
6. Economic freedom is the foundation of political freedom.

The basic features of the new model as applied in Chile included the liberalization of prices and markets, free trade and foreign financing, and reduced state intervention to enable capitalist enterprises to become the motor force of the economy. The application of the model passed through three distinct phases. The initial phase was characterized by economic expansion. The new policies generated a climate of confidence among the private sector, accompanied by high levels of foreign investment; however, by 1980 the economy was in crisis (especially agriculture and industry), ushering in the second phase. The government was forced to respond, and a third phase began in March of 1983, with the modification of a number of the neo-liberal policies.

Three policies implemented in the initial phase had broad reaching consequences for the agricultural sector (Crispi 1981). First, the state withdrew from its traditional role of promoting, developing, and managing agricultural production. In the new model, the state plays a subsidiary role, intervening indirectly, rather than directly, to create the conditions facilitating private sector production. Second, the liberalization of markets removed protective tariffs to national production, transferred the allocation of agricultural credit to private banks, and facilitated the opening up of new land and labor markets. And third, the institutional structure was reorganized to support private enterprise while restricting trade union rights.

Producer confidence in the model lasted from 1973 to 1979, and agricultural production expanded for those products having a comparative advantage in international markets. Private enterprise was indeed strengthened, particularly in the regions suitable for fruit, lumber, and cattle production, which experienced a rapid process of capitalist development. In contrast, those located in the regions specializing in basic foodstuff production stagnated.

The weakness of the first phase of the model was that growth was based on external financing and high interest rates. Although investment soared, the level of demand was subsequently insufficient to generate a profit level adequate to allow enterprises to make interest payments. High unemployment levels had slowed domestic demand for certain types of foodstuffs, and the prices of sugar, cereals, and dairy products fell as the market was flooded with cheap imported substitutes. As a result, the rural economy fell into a spiraling crisis that forced the government to modify and relax the model's rules for the agricultural sector.

The 1980–1983 period was one of agricultural crisis because the success of the agro-export sectors did not begin to compensate for the crisis in the production of basic foodstuffs. Relatively few firms were involved in fruit and lumber production, and the vast majority of capitalist and peasant producers were located in regions without comparative advantage as internationally defined and/or farmed marginal lands. They had few prospects of integrating themselves into the agro-export model or of outlasting the crisis. The crisis thus had serious socioeconomic repercussions. Moreover, the low production costs, which accounted in part for the success of Chile's exports in the world market, were reflected in the low wages and rapidly deteriorating living conditions of workers in the agro-export sector.

In 1983, the government responded to the crisis by controlling prices and raising protective tariffs on the basic foodstuffs that were produced primarily by peasant households. By 1985, the situation had begun to stabilize, allowing the sector to recover somewhat. Particularly benefited was wheat, beet, grape, and sunflower production, which represented 57 percent of total agricultural output in 1985. In addition, barley, corn, and rice production received some state protection. Of total agricultural production, 78 percent eventually benefited from state intervention (Carreno and Fu 1986).

Government policies have had different effects on the various rural social sectors. Economically viable peasant units (only 15 percent of the total) and capitalist enterprises in the depressed zones have managed to integrate themselves into the model, producing basic foodstuffs. Landless laborers have seen their prospects for finding seasonal wage work improve, as have their income levels. Data for 1985 showed that daily agricultural wages, especially in the fruit and cattle regions, increased at a more rapid rate than the consumer price index. This increase is largely attributed to higher producer profit margins, increased demand for labor, and a greater degree of union organization.

Overall, however, application of the neo-liberal model in agriculture and the partial undoing of the agrarian reform have largely impoverished the peasantry and enlarged the sector of landless, seasonal wage laborers. The reformed sector was subdivided into individual private plots, but almost half of the new "owners" have been forced to sell their parcels because the state failed to supply the necessary credit and technology (Crispi 1984). As a result, certain rural groups have lost the capacity to generate adequate income levels and are increasingly becoming proletarianized. The peasantry was forced to reduce its cultivated land area and cut down on pesticide and fertilizer use (because of the lack of credit), lowering both its productivity and its income. Rural wage laborers are increasingly dependent upon temporary, seasonal work, because the number of permanent employment opportunities has decreased; as a result, their incomes overall have fallen. Both groups—the peasantry and landless wage laborers—have had to devise new survival strategies, from enrolling in the government's minimal employment program to gathering wild foodstuffs and to placing the entire family, including children, into the labor market.

Although the conditions in the agricultural sector have fluctuated considerably in response to state policy, resulting in varying degrees of pauperization among the peasantry and even among capitalist enterprises, a constant factor has been sharp regional differentiation. In the past, the state played a compensatory role, ameliorating regional differences in income and productive activity. State withdrawal from economic activity under the neo-liberal model required the regions to depend on their own resources. The interregional imbalance is mainly between those zones with a comparative advantage in the world market and those with none. For example, the area between the Talca and Cautín provinces, a multicrop and grain-producing region, does not have the natural conditions to produce the profitable export crops and, as a result, is forced to produce for domestic consumption. This factor has resulted in a reduction of the cultivated land area and of production volumes, prompting decapitalization of the farm sector. In these zones, capitalist profit margins and hence employment opportunities have decreased.

In contrast, in the fruit- and lumber-producing regions, which have a comparative advantage in the profitable export crops, there have been significant capital investments. These zones are very dynamic, and employment opportunities have expanded. The cattle region was also able to successfully integrate itself into the new model even though cattle are produced for the domestic rather than the export market, because of the protectionist measures that have enabled local production to expand over recent years.

Rural Women and Agricultural Production

In the current context of widespread impoverishment, rural households become economic and labor units wherein all family members have complementary responsibilities. As a result of the economic and social changes in the agricultural sector in recent years, rural women's participation—always considerable—has now increased substantially in both foodstuff and export production.

No studies on rural women's work were carried out in Chile prior to the agrarian reform. Research undertaken since 1979, however, shows that women's productive work has traditionally centered on backyard garden cultivation, caring for the smaller livestock, seed selection and cleaning, and a variety of field tasks in agricultural production. Under the hacienda system, women were always "formally marginalized" from farm production on the estates and were subject to the terms of their husbands' contracts.[2] Women's work was considered a form of collaboration or help, even though in 1875 Manuel Balmaceda, in his "Manual of the Chilean Hacienda," detailed the large number of tasks considered suitable for women. "Women are just as useful as men for many tasks and jobs. They should be made to bake bread, cook for the workers, milk the cows, make butter and cheese, shear the sheep, sew and mend sacks, winnow, sweep, plant, and harvest wheat, and do many other things which they not only do as well, but better than men." According to Balmaceda, "women should not be excused from work, or the *patron* will be forced to slow down production when labor is scarce." And he adds, "On the other hand, since tenants earn so little, they benefit from having women earn their livelihood, so that when their incomes are pooled, they can improve their condition" (Balmaceda 1970:70).

Since the husband was contracted by the patron and was paid for his wife's labor, her work was invisible. In fact, women's work was so invisible that should a woman's husband die, if there was no other adult male to take his place on the hacienda labor force, the widow and children could be expelled from the estate (Oxman 1983).

Tenants' obligations were reduced as the haciendas were modernized, and women's work gradually decreased as wages replaced gratuities and manual agricultural tasks were mechanized. At the moment of the agrarian reform, women's obligations on the estates were limited to performing a few agricultural tasks and preparing food for the workers during the harvest and planting seasons. On their own account, women cultivated gardens and tended the small animals for family consumption.

The agrarian reform dismantled the hacienda system but did not take women's participation into account in the new reformed sector.[3] They were marginalized even from their traditional tasks and were relegated exclusively to the domestic realms (Garret 1982). According to Oxman (1983:38), "the agrarian reform process acted to further inhibit rural women's incorporation into the productive process as workers in their own right. The result of this was to accentuate agricultural employment patterns, increasing women's dependence on men."

Since 1973, the form and the extent to which women have been integrated into agricultural production have been a function of capitalist expansion in agriculture and the effects of the neo-liberal economic model. In the last thirteen years, large numbers of women have entered the labor market as seasonal workers in fruit and horticulture production in the region encompassed between Aconcagua and Curicó. In the southern forestry region, a great many peasants have been displaced from agricultural production and the rural area, swelling the ranks of the marginal population with no means of subsistence who live off state subsidies (Cruz and Rivera 1983). In the other regions and in those undergoing strong capitalist expansion (but where peasant parcels are located on marginal lands), women have had to enter directly into agricultural production on the household plot and to diversify their activities in order to generate sufficient household income.

Analysis of the five Chilean agricultural regions shows that women's participation in agriculture is hardly uniform: It is conditioned by the specific forms of capitalist expansion and by the specific labor requirements of the dominant regional productive industry. As a result, women's participation ranges from exclusive participation in seasonal wage labor to a set of extremely diversified activities within the peasant economy. Between these two extremes, the majority of women engage in reproductive and productive work within the peasant household. The way they are integrated into production depends on the character of the regional economy, farm size, the availability of land rentals, conditions in the labor market, and the availability of employment for other household members. The instability of male employment and their inability to generate sufficient household income condition the way women become integrated into either peasant agricultural production or the labor market.

In the fruit-producing region, women play an important role in capitalist expansion in the temporary, seasonal labor force. The demand for labor is so high that even women from outside the region (from the depressed areas) migrate here during the most labor intensive periods. Since this work is relatively well paid, women help to sustain the rural labor reserve; the combined seasonal incomes of the woman and man are sufficient to cover the subsistence needs of the household throughout the rest of the year when they face unemployment. The pattern of female employment is a function of both the labor requirements of the fruit production cycle and, maybe more important, the high level of male unemployment, one symptom of the consequences of neo-liberal model policies in agriculture. To the extent that male earnings are progressively reduced and men have fewer possibilities of permanent employment, women are forced to accept nontraditional jobs, becoming tied to the labor market. This phenomenon accords with the specific labor needs of the fruit industry as well as those of capitalist expansion.

In regions where capitalist expansion has been less pronounced and where the neo-liberal model has weakened capitalist enterprises, causing unemployment and falling wages, the situation is somewhat different. Women's productive participation in peasant agriculture has increased along with gardening and artisan production. On the farms with the capacity to produce for the internal market, female family members have replaced former wage workers in the fields.

The degree to which women become integrated into the productive process is also related to peasant social differentiation. Rural social differentiation in Chile is based on the amount of land to which a household has access and on access to wage income in certain regions. It is generally assumed that women from the poorer strata of the peasantry participate more in agricultural work. My research indicates, however, that in periods of economic crisis, women of different strata intensify their productive work in similar ways, both in the amount of time they dedicate to productive activities and in their contribution to household income. Cash and in-kind income earned by female small-holders and agrarian reform beneficiaries in the multicrop zone are very similar. Comparisons with female workers in the fruit-growing region show further similarities.

The most important difference by social class and productive region has to do with the type of work in which women engage (Campaña 1985). Women from the upper strata of the peasantry intensify their productive work on their own farms, whereas those from the lower strata diversify their income-generating activities.

Rural Women in the Zones of Capitalist Expansion

In the fruit and lumber regions, where capitalist expansion has been most pronounced, the neo-liberal model has drastically changed rural women's working and living patterns. Rural women's incorporation into the seasonal labor force in the fruit industry has been one of the most significant changes. Because the fruit industry's capacity to compete in the world market depends on its efficiency, complex technologies that demand a skilled labor force have been introduced. Much of this labor force is female and is relatively better paid than the male labor force because the work (especially packing) is considered skilled.

Studies carried out in the area show that the women employed in these capitalist enterprises as seasonal workers come from households that have either lost their land or never owned land. This stratum of landless laborers has grown significantly in recent years, contributing to the growth of new settlements or villages on roadsides or to slum belts around towns and cities near the fruit plantations. A recent study showed that only 18 percent of the total number of household heads owning land in the fruit-growing region and only 7 percent of their family members were employed as seasonal labor (Klein 1985). From this we can deduce that the role of the rural labor reserve, once played by smallholders, has increasingly been taken over by the landless as a consequence of government policies.

A study of female wage workers in the Putaendo Valley showed that (1) the majority have urban or semi-urban origins, (2) the wage workers from rural areas have proletarian or semiproletarian origins, and (3) the tendency of rural women whose households have access to sufficient land is to remain on the farm and participate in agricultural work rather than to work outside the home (Aranda 1982). These conclusions concur with those of my own research on peasant households in the same region (Lago and Olavarria 1981).

Three strata of peasant women were identified as having very tenuous links with wage work.

1. Women whose households were beneficiaries of the agrarian reform and had received land suitable for fruit growing.[4] Family and especially female labor accounted for the success of these fruit-producing farms that responded to the neo-liberal model. Women engaged in the various field tasks while continuing to cultivate their gardens and care for

domestic animals. Married women never sought wage work, although daughters sometimes do if their labor is not required on the family plot.

2. Women on small traditional farms, where the land is of marginal quality suitable only for growing staples such as potatoes, corn, wheat, and beans. Because their land was of such poor quality, this group was least affected by the expansion of fruit production. Women household members perform the same types of tasks as their counterparts in the depressed regions: preparing seedbeds, weeding, and harvesting, and raising small farm animals. The impact of the crisis on both groups has been similar; women have either diversified or intensified their activities.

3. Female smallholders. For households of this stratum, the fruit industry has provided the possibility of wage work for all family members. In this situation, women have two options: to take responsibility for the parcel while other adult household members become seasonal agricultural laborers or to seek wage employment for themselves. Their choice largely depends on the distance between the parcel and the fruit enterprise, household composition, and internalized cultural factors regarding the proper gender division of labor. Although women from this sector carry out the same tasks as women smallholders in other regions if they opt to remain on the family farm, their workload is even heavier because of the absence of the male household members incorporated into the wage labor market.

Beginning in 1973, the expanding lumber industry created a new landless population by forcing many rural families to sell their lands to large companies (Lago 1985). Unlike in the fruit industry, this form of capitalist expansion has not increased employment opportunities for two reasons. First, the labor process was reorganized to increase efficiency, reducing the number of permanent wage workers while increasing the number of workers contracted on a temporary basis. Second, mechanization based on sophisticated technology has made much of the labor force redundant. For example, in cellulose and paper production, the labor force was reduced by more than half between 1973 and 1980 (Díaz 1983).

Lumber, unlike other agro-exports, has not favored a female labor force. Since the technology employed in the lumber industry has always been associated with men, the industry does not offer women the alternative of wage work. The primary way women may contribute to household income is by gathering wild plants for sale. Between February and May, they gather dog roses (Japanese globeflowers), which they then dry and sell. In winter and spring they pick mushrooms, which grow in the damper areas of the pine forests. Some of these are sold to factories to be processed for export whereas the remainder are used for family consumption.

The foregoing analysis indicates that capitalist expansion in agriculture does not necessarily either incorporate or expel the rural female labor force. Rather, the specifics and dynamics of each industry determine whether modern technology marginalizes women or incorporates them into productive work.

The gender division of labor also helps to determine whether a given industry incorporates women into production or expels them. In the two regions that have undergone strong capitalist expansion, the major industries show different employment patterns. In the forestry region, only men engage in lumber production, which is socially defined as "masculine work," whereas women are marginalized from productive work. In the fruit-growing region, because export production demands such traditional "feminine" characteristics as gentleness, delicacy, patience, and dedication the demand for female labor is high. In addition, women workers have no history of political or union experience. Because women are conditioned not to assert themselves politically, they are a particularly attractive labor force to capitalist employers. And because women are acutely aware of how important their contribution is to household income (because they have greater possibilities of employment than do men in this region), they accept exploitative conditions. As a result of all these factors, the labor force for the fruit export industry—which contributes almost 20 percent of national exports—is predominantly female.

To sum up, in the multicrop, grain, and cattle-producing regions, women have intensified their productive activities without significantly changing the activities in which they engage. In the forestry and fruit-growing regions, rural women's participation in production, their domestic roles, and their social participation have undergone great changes as a result of the neo-liberal model.

Rural Women's Social Participation

The rural sector began to organize and confront the state and dominant classes in 1964, when Peasant Union Law 16625 was promulgated. During the nine-year agrarian reform period, tenants and peasants constituted one of the most important national social movements. But this organization and the social effervescence failed to motivate rural women.

Chilean women, particularly rural women, have traditionally had low levels of organization and political participation. Women's organizations have functioned as extensions of their traditional domestic roles, and women's social participation has always taken place in the context of established organizations such as political parties, labor unions, or organizations dependent on state or church. Such organizations conceive of women's role as one of assistance to the organization's general activities or of service to given community activities, always within the framework of a predetermined agenda (Díaz 1984).

The women's organizations have tended to be dominated and directed by outsiders whose agendas bear no relation to the issues and interests of the women themselves. Women members are perceived as clients, open to manipulation by the traditional organizing groups, whether political parties, unions, or church organizations (Lago 1983).

These tendencies persist in the traditional rural women's organizations and account for their low membership. The mothers' centers are the only organizations in which a considerable number of rural women have participated more or less continually. They were founded in 1954, during the presidential term of Carlos Ibáñez del Campo, with the name "Ropero del Pueblo" (People's Wardrobe), and because they were clearly paternalistic, few women joined. They did not flourish until the Frei administration came to power and promoted them as mothers' centers in the mid-1960s. In the context of the rural mobilization of that period, they offered rural women the opportunity for social participation.

Although the mothers' centers retained their paternalistic bias, the last two democratic governments conceived of them as places where women could discuss their problems as mothers and wives and channel their grievances for improved living conditions and services. The centers also served as local credit unions, helping women to purchase equipment such as sewing machines, kitchen utensils, and stoves to modernize and improve conditions in the rural household. Because the mothers' centers did not challenge traditional gender stereotypes and implicitly accepted women's traditional social role, they never became the organizing basis for either feminist or political consciousness-raising activity (Garret 1982).

When the military dictatorship came to power in 1973, the repression in the countryside led to temporary closing of the mothers' centers. Since the centers represented organizations linked to democratic governments, many of their members were targeted for persecution. When the period of generalized repression ended, however, the military government seized upon the centers as potential bulwarks in the defense of regime, homeland, and family. The mothers' centers have been transformed into the "social organization of poor women" and depend directly on the Office of the Secretary General. They have become efficient mechanisms of political-ideological control.

In their analysis of the mothers' centers, Levy and Lechner (1986:86) note that the present government considers "women (to be) a natural category (sex), whose permanent and unchangeable essence is determined (by biology). Women are not subjects, but objects of history." And in the words of General Pinochet, "women are essentially spirit, not flesh; they belong to the world of values, not of necessities, which determines their life project" (Munizaga 1983:43).

Nevertheless, for the first time in Chile, new types of organizations, spawned in reaction to the current authoritarian regime, are springing up in the countryside. Women began to join the rural labor unions in 1982 in conjunction with their massive incorporation into the fruit industry labor force. Moreover, in the new unions, besides work-related problems, women are discussing gender-specific problems. The double workday and the problem of child care are only two of the grievances listed in the petitions presented to the management of the fruit enterprises. Some of the women's sections of the Union Federations have seen how important it is to integrate these new demands of working women into the general union agenda, leading to internal struggles between the overwhelmingly male hierarchies (with their traditional patriarchal schemes) and the new generation of female leaders. This new generation has been significantly influenced by the tenets of the feminist movement and the urban grassroots women's organizations; the informal network between them provides support for the demands of the rural women trade unionists and influences the direction of rural women's politics.

The church-associated women's groups are another significant set of organizations that have sprung up in the rural areas in recent years. The degree of rural poverty and repression has prompted the church to become concerned about issues beyond those considered strictly religious. As a result, many "subsistence maintenance" organizations have been fostered not only to channel material aid but also to engender consciousness about the concrete situation of the poor under the present economic conditions imposed by the neo-liberal model. These groups have organized community gardening projects, children's dining rooms, and sewing projects, among other activities. They are most prevalent in the depressed multicrop and grain-producing regions between Talca and Valdivia.

The type and the degree of rural women's organization depend upon the productive region in which they work and live. In the fruit-growing region, women tend to increasingly participate in union organizations. In the multicrop and grain regions, the two most depressed in the country, women are more likely to participate in church-sponsored women's organizations or women's groups with ties to independent programs. Both kinds combine welfare-type assistance with income-generating projects. Programs of this kind have also been set up for low-income women in the cattle region.

Although the rural women's organizations continue to depend upon external agents, progress has been made in the agendas of these organizations. Although as yet there is little consciousness of gender issues, many agendas now incorporate a broader, more challenging social perspective and no longer consider women's traditional gender role as their main source of interest or activity. Whether gender-related issues are considered by the unions and other organizations largely depends on the women who join them and the degree to which these mostly male-dominated and deeply patriarchal organizations are receptive to another perspective.

Acknowledgments

This chapter was translated by Katherine Pettus.

Notes

1. See Lago and Olavarria (1981); Aranda (1982); Campaña and Lago (1982); Barría et al. (1985); Valenzuela (1985); and Campaña (1985).

2. Dairy farms were the exception since they employed women as milkmaids.

3. The reformed sector was initially composed of *asentamientos* that functioned much the same as production cooperatives but under direct state supervision. The Allende government subsequently transformed these into the agrarian reform centers (CERAS), and the membership was broadened to include not only the former tenants or permanent workers on the estates but also the seasonal workforce.

4. Such farms represent 49 percent of the parcels distributed in 1976.

References

Aranda, Ximena, "Participación de la Mujer en la Agricultura y Sociedad Rural en Areas de Pequeña Propiedad," Santiago, FLACSO (Facultad Latino Americana de Ciencias Sociales), 1982, mimeo.

Balmaceda, Manuel Jose (1875), "El Manual del Hacendado Chileno," in Antonio Corvalan, ed., *Antología de la Tierra* (Santiago: ICIRA [Instituto de Capacitación e Investigación en Reforma Agraria], 1970).

Barría, Liliana, et al., "Participación de la Mujer en la Economía Campesina en Chile" (Santiago: Instituto de Promoción Agraria e Instituto Chileno de Educación Cooperativa, 1985).

Campaña, Pilar, "Peasant Economy, Women's Labor, and Differential Forms of Capitalist Development: A Comparative Study in Three Contrasting Situations in Peru and Chile," Ph.D. thesis, University of Durham, England, 1985.

_____ , and Maria Soledad Lago, "Y las Mujeres Tambien Trabajan," Research Publication No. 10, Grupo de Investigaciones Agrarias, Santiago, 1982.

Carreno, Dora, and Guillermo Fu, "1985: Coyuntura Agraria mas Dolares que Alimentos," Working Paper No. 25, Grupo de Investigaciones Agrarias, Santiago, 1986.

Crispi, Jaime, "Neoliberalismo y Campesinado en Chile," Working Paper No. 5, Grupo de Investigaciones Agrarias, Santiago, 1981.

————, "Nacimiento, Vida Pasion y . . . ? de un Tipo de Propiedad Familiar en Chile: los Parceleros de la Reforma Agraria," paper presented to the Seminar on Medium-sized Agricultural Enterprises, FAO–Cambridge University, Cambridge, England, 1984.

Cruz, Maria Elena, and Rigoberto Rivera, "La Realidad Forestal Chilena," Research Publication No. 15, Grupo de Investigaciones Agrarias, Santiago, 1983.

Díaz, Cecilia, "La Mujer Campesina en Chile," Working Paper No. 15, Grupo de Investigaciones Agrarias, Santiago, 1984.

Díaz, Harry Polo, "Forestry Labor; Neoliberalism and the Authoritarian State. Chile 1973–81," Doctoral Thesis, York University, Toronto, 1983.

Garret, Patricia, "La Reforma Agraria, Organización Popular y Participación de la Mujer en Chile," in M. León, ed., *Las Trabajadoras del Agro* (Bogotá: ACEP, 1982).

Klein, Emilio, "El Impacto Heterogeneo de la Modernización Agrícola sobre el mercado de Trabajo," Working Paper No. 260 (Santiago: PREALC [Programa de Empleo para America Latina y el Caribe], 1985).

Lago, Maria Soledad, "El Participa, Ellos Participan, Participamos Nosotras?" Working Paper No. 5, Grupo de Investigaciones Agrarias, Santiago, 1983.

————, "Buena Esperanza: Una Esperanza Perdida," Working Paper No. 18, Grupo de Investigaciones Agrarias, Santiago, 1985.

————, and Carlota Olavarria, "La Participación de la Mujer en las Economías Campesinas: Un Estudio de Casos en Dos Comunas Frutícolas," Research Paper No. 9, Grupo de Investigaciones Agrarias, Santiago, 1981.

Levy, Susana, and Norbert Lechner, "CEMA Chile y Secretaría Nacional de la Mujer," in M. Angelica Meza, ed., *La Otra Mitad de Chile* (Santiago: CESOC and Instituto para el Nuevo Chile, 1986).

Munizaga, Giselle, "El Discurso Publico de Pinochet, 1973–1976" (Buenos Aires: CLACSO [Comission Latino Americana de Ciencias Sociales], 1983).

Oxman, Veronica, "La Participación de la Mujer Campesina en Organizaciones: Los Centros de Madres Rurales," Research Paper No. 12, Grupo de Investigaciones Agrarias, Santiago, 1983.

Tironi, Ernesto, "El Modelo Neoliberal Chileno y su Implantación," Working Paper No. 1, CED, Santiago, 1982.

Valenzuela, Oscar, "El Papel de la Mujer en la Economía Campesina: El Caso de la Septima Region de Chile" (Santiago: FAO, 1985).

2

Agricultural Development, the Economic Crisis, and Rural Women in the Dominican Republic

Belkis Mones
and Lydia Grant

As the UN Decade for Women officially drew to a close, the world economy was immersed in a serious economic and social crisis. The industrialized countries, which over this period had increased their exports of capital to the Third World through direct multinational investment and financing of chosen economic sectors, were in a recession. This economic climate produced an acute crisis and disarticulation of the financial and monetary systems created at the Bretton Woods Conference in 1944. Growing fiscal deficits spurred increased competition for external capital, which caused sharp fluctuations in interest rates and liberalization of exchange rates.

The crisis was quickly transmitted to the Third World, which is inextricably bound to the advanced capitalist countries through the international division of labor. Unequal exchange and deteriorating terms of trade produced a growing foreign debt and, concomitantly, an accelerated inflationary process. The Latin American economies have been burdened with reduced growth rates, growing unemployment, trade deficits, unmanageable external debts, and alarming decapitalization— a situation aggravated by unsuccessful attempts at regional integration.

The dramatic drop in levels of food self-sufficiency—yet another aspect of the crisis in Latin America—relates directly to the deterioration of rural living standards. This aspect of the crisis particularly affects rural women, who migrate from the countryside to urban areas at a high rate and are overrepresented in low-productivity income-generating activities.

35

The Dominican Republic is not immune to the effects of the world crisis. Its primary export economy, which historically has functioned in response to the processes of capital accumulation of the industrialized countries, is now experiencing a "crisis of integration into the world economy, a crisis of a structural nature" (Ceara 1984). Because of its dependence on the price fluctuations of the external market, the national economy is subject to imbalances and structural maladjustments, which limit prospects for national development.

In this chapter we attempt to evaluate how, in light of this economic crisis, the past decade's agrarian development policies have affected Dominican rural women. We argue that although a wide variety of agrarian development strategies—mostly welfare-style social programs and to a lesser degree small-scale production-oriented programs—were implemented by the three governments in power during the period, no administration promulgated explicit policies toward rural women. Projects aimed at women were primarily designed either to be mechanisms for social and political control or to improve general living conditions for rural families. We also show that, given the gender division of labor, the world economic crisis and the changes in agrarian policy have caused agricultural employment opportunities for women to decline.

We first briefly analyze the development of capitalism in Dominican agriculture, review the effects of the economic crisis, and outline some general features of the past decade's agrarian development policies. In the second section, we describe the sociodemographic characteristics of rural women and suggest how recent agrarian policies have affected female employment in the agricultural sector. In the third section, we examine the state programs for rural women and then conclude with a look at the gains women have made during the decade.

Capitalism in the Dominican Republic

Agriculture—primarily sugar cane, coffee, cacao, and tobacco production—has been the primary source of capital accumulation in the Dominican agro-export model since capitalist development first began in the late nineteenth century. This development reflected the way the Dominican economy—through the prevailing international division of labor—became integrated into the world market, with foreign market price fluctuations determining cycles of economic growth and contraction. The model has become only slightly more diversified over the past decade as a result of the mining activity of foreign capital and the export of gold and nickel.

Under the Trujillo dictatorship (1930–1961), the agricultural sector was oriented toward the internal market and provided wage goods and raw materials for the embryonic 1950s import substitution process. The production of wage goods was necessary to guarantee the low-cost reproduction of the industrial and urban labor force. During this period, land holdings became increasingly concentrated, the agricultural frontier was extended, and evictions of small farmers and/or forced sales of their land resulted in the proletarianization and semiproletarianization of the Dominican peasantry, as well as rural-urban migration.

Five different administrations came to power during the four years (1962–1965) following the fall of the Trujillo dictatorship—a period of great change for the Dominican economy and for the agricultural sector. The expectation of democratization and of wage and employment increases, along with growing class struggle, resulted in the stagnation of exports and an expansion of internal demand and contributed to the steady growth of imports (financed primarily by foreign loans). Nevertheless, the balance of payments was in deficit, and the agricultural sector's share of the gross national product (GNP) had declined.

The 1965 insurrection, followed by U.S. military intervention, erupted amid this economic and political crisis. Supported by the local bourgeoisie and the U.S. government, the Balaguer (1966–1978) administration took power, committed to regaining political control through repression and to capitalizing and revitalizing the economy.

The Agrarian Crisis

The Dominican agrarian structure has been characterized by both growing land concentration and fragmentation. According to the 1970 and 1981 agricultural census, farms consisting of less than 8 *tareas* (one-half hectare) grew in number (by 24 percent), with average size falling from 4 to 3 tareas; farms measuring from 8 to 79 tareas also grew in number (by 37 percent), whereas average size for this group fell from 29 to 20 tareas. In contrast, the number of farms in the 80 to 159 tarea range fell by 4 percent, whereas average size increased from 109 to 113 tareas; the growth in medium-sized properties is also evident in the next category, farms in the 160 to 799 tarea range, where average farm size remained stable. The phenomenon of land concentration, on the other hand, is found in the 8,000 and over tarea stratum where estates increased in average size while total numbers diminished.

Other characteristics of the agrarian structure include the low level of development of the productive forces, accounting for its low productivity, and product specialization, based on potential profitability. Small and medium-sized farms, which use both family and wage labor, produce mainly foodstuffs for subsistence and/or the internal market; they also cultivate coffee and tobacco, export crops monopolized by middlemen and large companies. The agrarian reform sector of cooperatives and independent producers plays an important role in the production of foodstuffs, particularly of rice and tomatoes. Large capitalist estates concentrate on producing for the export market, although they also grow the more profitable crops destined for the internal market.

Against this background, the indications that the agrarian sector had begun to deteriorate by the mid-1970s were the following: (1) drop in food production and increased imports of food and agricultural raw materials; (2) lowered production of certain traditional agricultural exports such as cacao and sugar cane; (3) increase in the relative surplus population, expressed in growing unemployment, underemployment, and rural-urban migration; (4) stalling and, finally, paralysis of the agrarian reform; and (5) systematic soil erosion, deforestation, and deterioration of the fluvial valleys.

These manifestations of the agrarian crisis originate in the particular model of agrarian capitalist development based on an uneven pattern of growth. The crisis is an expression of the relation between the structure of the agrarian sector, the forms of agricultural production, and the way the Dominican economy is integrated into the world capitalist economy.

Agrarian Development Policies and Strategies

The last three administrations in the Dominican Republic have introduced and implemented an entire spectrum of political and economic strategies for the agricultural sector. The Balaguer administration, in power for twelve years, attempted to reorganize government spending by channeling resources toward public investment in order to create external economies for the industrial sector.

The agrarian development strategy adopted in this era was compatible with the import substitution industrialization strategy referred to earlier. The agricultural sector was linked to the development of the industrial sector, through provision of low-cost wage goods, raw materials, and labor, as well as through the transference of its surplus. To promote and develop the small and medium-sized farm sector, the administration implemented credit, technical assistance, and agrarian reform policies.

The aim of the agrarian reform inaugurated in 1972 was to restructure the farm sector to reflect the requirements of capitalist development in agriculture and of capitalist accumulation in the advanced countries. The reform originated, however, in the pressure exerted by peasants demanding land. The agrarian reform was limited, on the one hand, by the content of the law itself and, on the other, by the opposition of certain power groups (medium-sized farmers and landlords) in the countryside (Dore y Cabral 1982, 1984).

During this period, the population growth rate continued to exceed that of food production, leading to a sharp increase in food imports. To guarantee low wage levels, a price policy was initiated through the National Price Stabilization Institute (INESPRE) and the National Office of Price Control. INESPRE controls prices of basic agricultural products and subsidizes such staples as rice, corn, sugar, potatoes, red beans, and edible oils.

In 1978, the first PRD (Partido Revolucionario Dominicano) administration of social democratic tendencies was elected, and it gave high priority to agricultural development. Its development strategy was to raise effective demand by expanding the internal market via increased employment opportunities and income redistribution. The administration assumed that this approach would result in an across the board increase in agricultural production.

Priority was given to agro-industrial production and the export of nontraditional products such as processed foodstuffs.[1] These activities were encouraged through fiscal incentives, tax shelters, and subsidies. Despite the attempt to increase the supply of foodstuffs and to reduce unemployment, the relation between the national economy and the external market resulted in higher domestic food prices, which did not result in higher incomes for farmers (Tejada 1983).

During this period, the agrarian reform was restricted to the consolidation of the already existing reform sector; moreover, individual holdings were favored over production cooperatives, and some of the latter were divided into parcels. Among the factors limiting the economic policy of this administration were the unresponsiveness of private investment, growing internal and external debt, a rigid tax system, and the structural dependence on imports (Ceara 1984).

The second PRD administration (1982–1986) began its term by renegotiating the external debt with the International Monetary Fund (IMF). Both the present government and the IMF have attributed the present crisis, which began in the mid-1970s and worsened during the 1980s, to the budget deficit, which they see as the cause of the balance of payments deficit. Economic policy has thus focused on restricting effective demand and public spending while stimulating and revitalizing foreign exchange generating activities through promotion of exports.

Agricultural development policy has concentrated on selective industrialization of agriculture and incentives for traditional and nontraditional exports. It has sought, by supporting agro-industrial production (mainly vegetables, fruit, legumes, and inputs for edible oils and animal feed) to emphasize modernization of the sector and more efficient farming.

The strategy has been supported by fiscal and exchange incentives benefiting the agro-export sector and by modification of export quotas and tariff concessions for imports of agrochemicals, farm machinery, and equipment. State reduction of effective support—technical and financial assistance—to small producers and relative paralysis of the agrarian reform have accelerated the process of proletarianization.

Foreign and domestic investment in agribusiness enterprises (most are subsidiaries of multinationals producing for the external market) has been considerable. The new IMF strategy has given agribusiness greater control of the productive process, allowing it to monopolize sources of credit and raw materials and to fix prices paid to producers. It has also reduced the production of foodstuffs for internal consumption.

The new fiscal policy has placed a 36 percent surcharge on traditional exports. Although not specifically directed at producers, this tax hurts them. Exporters, as pricetakers in the international market, try to maintain their profits by keeping prices to producers low. The latter group sees their incomes falling as prices of agricultural inputs continue to increase.

To sum up, the agrarian crisis is expressed through a relative paralysis of the agricultural sector and falling production. In response to the shortfall, imports of basic foodstuffs have increased, principally the import of surplus U.S. farm products through subsidized loans under U.S. Public Law 480 and the Commodity Credit Corporation. These transactions directly favor increased public spending and limit development of the national grain industry. During the 1970s, the cost of food imports and agricultural raw materials was approximately equal to the external debt during the same period ($1.2 billion).

The agrarian crisis is a direct function of the way the Dominican economy is integrated into the world market and the pattern of capitalist development in agriculture. Unequal exchange internationally, growing deterioration of the intersectoral terms of trade domestically, and the uneven growth pattern of capitalism in the agricultural sector must all be taken into account (Ceara 1984; Vicens 1984). As a result, the agricultural sector has been unable to meet either the internal market's demand for food or industry's demand for raw materials, and unfavorable conditions for production and growing agrarian decapitalization have precipitated rural-urban migration.

Women's Participation in Agriculture

Up to now, the analysis of Dominican women's participation in agriculture, in both subsistence food production and the agricultural labor market, has been limited by the few existing studies of rural employment in general and women's agricultural work in particular. Information gathered in 1985 by the National Survey of Rural Women (ENMR) and from case studies of firms in five crops employing female labor (coffee, tobacco, cotton, peanut, and tomato) provides the data base for our study.[2]

To analyze women's work in agriculture, it is first necessary to situate rural women in the context of their households, taking into account quality of rural life indicators as well as the social differentiation among rural families. Basic services in the Dominican countryside may be characterized as tenuous. According to ENMR data, well over half (67.2 percent) of the homes surveyed had no access to piped water or electricity and used kerosene lamps for light.[3] The average number of inhabitants per unit was six. The absence of adequate basic services under these conditions increases the domestic workload to an average ten to fifteen hours a day of fixed and monotonous tasks and means that rural women—many of whom work a double day—suffer rapid physical deterioration and permanent stress.[4]

Of the rural population surveyed (12,246 inhabitants) 49 percent were female and 51 percent were male. This population was young: Sixty-nine percent were under the age of twenty-four. The majority of households were constituted of nuclear families (56.2 percent) in the expansion stage of the life-cycle (44 percent); that is, the majority of the children were between eight and nineteen years of age. In almost one-fourth of the rural households (22 percent), women were the household heads.

The analysis of rural women's educational levels reveals high illiteracy rates. Only slightly over half knew how to read or write. Of those who had attended grade school, 21.8 percent had forgotten how to read and write and were now functional illiterates. Only 6.8 percent of the sample had entered secondary school, and of this group only 2.9 percent had graduated or continued on to the university.

Rural households are subject to a permanent process of social differentiation, clearly expressed in terms of land distribution. Forty-one percent of the households sampled were landless. If the number of households with subsistence parcels measuring less than one-half a hectare are added to this figure, the majority of Dominican rural households (65 percent) have access either to no land or to insignificant amounts of land. These statistics reveal how limited the possibilities are for household reproduction through farming activities and largely explain the growing proletarianization of this sector.

The reproduction strategy of the great majority of households (70 percent) includes wage labor. Only 30 percent earn their income solely from farming or nonagricultural activities such as commerce and trade or handicraft production.

The ENMR data on female economic activity show that 84 percent of the rural women studied (over ten years of age) contribute economically to the reproduction of the household unit. Female economic participation has been grossly underestimated in official statistics; according to the 1981 Dominican agricultural census, only 21 percent of rural women were economically active.

The incapacity of the formal labor market to absorb the total available rural labor force and the preference given men in agricultural wage work have meant that women have a relatively low rate of participation in wage labor, only 18 percent. Rural women have thus been forced to find alternative ways to generate income (whether cash or in kind) to ensure their household's survival. The large majority of women (82 percent) carry out economic activities linked to the household, allowing them to integrate their reproductive and productive tasks. These economic activities are very diversified.

Although access to land is quite precarious for either farming or animal-raising activities, the majority of the economically active females (79 percent) contribute to household income through agricultural-related activities. Of these women, slightly more work a garden or contribute labor to the household plot (55 percent) than engage in animal raising (45 percent) as their principal activity.

Alternative income-generating activities available to women outside the domestic unit are very restricted because women must first comply with their reproductive roles. But they are very creative in devising income-generating activities, which range from raffles and lottery ticket sales to neighbors to the production and sale of foodstuffs and sweets on their doorsteps.

Participation in such secondary activities has increased considerably as a result of the acute national economic crisis. The crisis has stimulated the growth of a variety of low-productivity activities, such as small-scale production and vending of clothes, flower arrangements, and so on. Women predominate in these activities because these products have traditionally been made at home and are considered "women's work." These "temporary alternatives" to increase family income continue to favor women's presence in the home; they do not conflict with or limit women's capacity to engage in their assigned social function of reproduction. These cottage industries also symbolize the return of basic food and clothes production to the home at a time when the economic crisis and inflation make acquisition of these articles impossible for the majority of the rural population.

In the face of the crises, the reproduction strategy of rural households with limited access to means of production is to engage in a wide and diverse set of economic activities. But the effects of the crisis and the feasibility of a given productive activity becoming an option vary in accordance with the specific agro-ecologies of the diverse regions of the country.

The agricultural labor market is characterized by the temporary and unstable nature of the work available and by its low absorption of the available labor force. The production of the two most labor intensive crops—sugar cane and coffee—exemplifies how restricted employment opportunities are for both women and men. Sugar cane production employs only Haitian labor for the agricultural field tasks; Dominicans are employed in the industrial, intermediate, and distribution (transport, sale) phases and in management (administration and supervision). Coffee production employs mainly low-wage Haitian workers for the harvest although not in all regions of the country. The participation of Haitians has increased and extended nationally in the last decade although it is most concentrated in the region of Enriquillo (ONAPLAN 1979).

The gender division of labor further restricts women's options, leaving them the unskilled, lowest paying jobs. In the ENMR survey, only 14 percent of the economically active women participated as wage workers in agriculture, indicating the tightness of the agricultural labor market for women. Women participate in agricultural production during the labor intensive phases. The ENMR data indicate that more than half of all women engaged in agricultural wage work are employed during the harvest season (68 percent), whereas the remainder work in husking, destemming or other processing tasks (25 percent) and in planting (5 percent). Crops traditionally employing a female labor force are coffee, cotton, tomatoes, tobacco, and peanuts and to a lesser extent horticultural crops such as potatoes, beans, chickpeas, and melons.[5]

Although women's participation is limited primarily to two phases (harvesting and processing), men compete in a much less restricted and more diversified labor market. Sixty-four percent of the men work in the harvest or in husking and destemming tasks, but they also find employment in field preparation (13 percent), planting (12 percent), and fertilizing (13 percent). Although the productive forces in Dominican agriculture are very underdeveloped as a whole, women are excluded from all the mechanized or skilled activities and are limited to manual tasks.

Women's agricultural wage work is poorly paid and unstable. Rarely are women workers paid on a daily basis. Most of their tasks are remunerated as piecework so that women have little control over their total daily earnings. Their real wages, especially compared with men's, are very low. In 1985, a male farmworker's daily wage averaged between 4 and 7 pesos, whereas women's ranged between 3 and 6 pesos.

Wages paid according to piecework function as a mechanism of overexploitation of the labor force because to achieve high production quotas and higher pay workers must intensify their labor effort and minimize their breaks. Women workers, in effect, are denied the opportunity to rest during the lunch break (from thirty minutes to an hour), which is allowed those workers (generally men) remunerated by the day. Under the piecework system, women supervise and control their own labor. For instance, a woman will perceive talking with her coworkers as a way of reducing her own salary. Strict supervision of the labor process by capital is unnecessary because both the hours and intensity of work can be increased while production costs are considerably reduced.

Women's participation in the wage labor market is conditioned both by the demand for their labor and by their socially assigned role in reproducing household labor (Benería 1984). Notwithstanding, in the current crisis the supply of female labor has increased substantially. Government policies toward crops employing female labor affect women to the extent that they change the demand for labor. An analysis of production trends in the principal crops employing female labor (coffee, cotton, tomatoes, tobacco, and peanuts) suggests how state policy and the crisis have affected women's employment in the short or medium term.

The production of coffee and tobacco—crops that have formed part of the agro-export model of accumulation since the nineteenth century—has traditionally employed a female labor force. Coffee has historically been the crop employing the most women, particularly during the harvest season; recently, as a result of a plantation renewal program, women have also been employed in the nurseries. Coffee production has fluctuated in the past decade owing to climatic disasters (Hurricanes David and Frederick in 1979), which significantly reduced production, and the 36 percent surcharge on exports (1984). This surcharge, price increases for agricultural inputs, poor agricultural practices, and a variety of other unfavorable production conditions have reduced both production and employment in the short and medium term. Production is especially difficult for smallholders (1 to 99 tareas) who represent the majority (94 percent) of the coffee growers. The current problems could in the long run diminish the demand for female labor.

Likewise, tobacco cultivation, predominantly carried out by small and medium-sized producers, has usually employed female labor—both unremunerated family labor and wage workers. Women are employed for the tasks demanding maximum care and dexterity, such as destemming and deveining leaves. Tobacco production has been relatively stable in the last decade, although the 36 percent surcharge on exports indirectly affects small producers and their demand for labor.

Recently, there has been an increase in the area cultivated in blond tobacco, which is gradually replacing the traditional black tobacco variety. This change is altering the demand for labor because harvesting and destemming processes differ for the two kinds of tobacco. Black tobacco is harvested in stages—to take maximum advantage of leaf condition—whereas blond tobacco requires only one harvest. Since blond tobacco requires a smaller labor force and does not need careful destemming—traditionally women's work—women's prospects in the tobacco labor market look grim in the medium term.

Over the last decade, peanut production has declined partially as a result of the favorable credits under PL-480 that have been used to import cotton and soy oils. Agribusiness has also invested heavily in the production of African palm oil, which is gradually replacing peanut oil in the edible oil industry. Peanut production is expected to decline still further, with severe consequences for female farm employment.

The cultivation of industrial tomatoes, a highly labor intensive crop favoring women workers, could maintain its current level of female employment. In the last ten years, because of the demands of the tomato paste and juice processing industries, tomato production has grown at an annual rate of 10 percent. In the short term, this crop could maintain, or even increase, its production levels, depending on the raw material requirements of the processors, who have until now financed and promoted production. The agrarian reform sector is significant in tomato production, representing about one-half of all producers.

Female employment prospects are also favorable in cotton. By providing incentives for local and foreign investment, the government has tried to promote local cotton production to supply the internal textile market and the edible oil and cattle industries. The area under cotton production has also been expanded by the conversion of former state-owned sugar cane plantations to cotton production. The higher levels of cotton production have increased the demand for women workers during the harvest.

Finally, employment opportunities for rural women have increased in the horticultural sector on fruit, legume, and vegetable farms as a result of the policy of export promotion, particularly of nontraditional crops. These new industries pay poorly, however, and are very unstable.

To sum up, although the state has not formulated a specific employment policy toward female farmworkers or regulated their working conditions, government policies and agrarian development strategies directly affect women's employment prospects in the agricultural labor market.

When women are unable to find work in the countryside, they are forced to migrate to urban centers.[6] The move means that the women face new and adverse conditions in the urban labor market; they work mainly in the service and commercial sector and, to a lesser extent, in industry. Although precise data are not available, international migration of Dominican women, a great many of whom become prostitutes, has increased in the past decade.

State Policies Toward Rural Women

State policies aimed at rural women in Latin America in the last decade either have been initiated as part of a strategy to revitalize agriculture or have been the result of growing political pressure by women on the state. State policies toward rural women in the Dominican Republic, in contrast, have been motivated since 1966 by the desire to have political and ideological control over women and, therefore, over the rural family structure. These programs also attempted to improve rural living conditions (access to basic services, health, and education), slow rural-urban migration, lower the cost of reproducing the labor force, and reduce demographic growth.

The main public sector agencies charged with implementing rural women's programs were chartered during the 1960s: the Secretary of State for Agriculture (SEA), the Community Development Office (ODC), the Dominican Development Foundation (FDD), the Institute for Development and Cooperative Credit (IDECOOP), and the Dominican Agrarian Institute (IAD).

The SEA, through the Home Improvement Program, implemented gardening, handicraft, sewing, and health and hygiene projects. The ODC ran similar projects advised by home economists. The IAD opened supplementary maternal-infant feeding centers in 1968 to distribute food to pregnant and lactating women and children under age five. President Balaguer's government also set up sewing centers, which were welfare-type projects based on donations or "gifts" of sewing machines.

When budgetary priorities changed in the early 1970s, many of these programs were either put on hold, dismantled, or adapted to respond to the new "developmentalism." The move away from welfare-type programs was also a response to growing struggles in the countryside and pressures for land. The new programs focused on income-generating activities for women, in particular small-scale agricultural projects that transferred technology through technical and financial assistance. Policies of family planning and birth control, run by the Secretary of State for Public Health and Social Policy and the National Family and Population Council, have also been directed toward rural women in the last decade.

The vast majority of the new women's projects are productive activities linked to the home. Most are characterized by low investment and productivity levels and are not, therefore, very profitable. Moreover, because they maintain the prevailing gender division of labor and its underlying social constructions, the projects have not attempted to change women's subordination.

A series of government projects to integrate women into development were prompted by the 1975 UN International Women's Year Declaration (CEPAL 1975). In 1982, the government created the General Office for the Promotion of Women, whose function is "to integrate women into national development, and to maintain the peace, within the framework of respect for national sovereignty" (Dirección General de Promoción de la Mujer 1985). Nevertheless, the activities promoted and carried out by this office reflect both traditional notions of women's roles and the prevailing gender division of labor.

In sum, state programs and policies aimed at rural women have generally been mechanisms for political control of women; nevertheless, they have attempted to improve rural living standards. Moreover, by bringing issues onto the political agenda, they have helped lay the foundations for the Dominican rural women's movement.

Evaluation of the Decade

The 1975 International Women's Year Declaration and the 1981 Latin American and Caribbean Feminist Congress spurred local debate on women's issues and provided a context for Dominican women to begin organizing. The significant Dominican participation in the first Feminist Congress in Bogotá contributed greatly to the emergence of an embryonic, primarily urban, feminist movement. As a result, rural women for the first time began to be exposed to ideas that challenged traditional concepts of women's "nature" and predestined social subordination and at the same time ascribed value to domestic work.

The decade's most important achievement in rural areas is the growth of women's organizations. As noted, these organizations are byproducts of the development and welfare policies and projects promoted by the 1966–1978 reformist administration. The work of religious groups and the development of the predominantly male peasant movement also helped create the conditions for the growth of independent women's groups. The current crisis, because it affects rural women so directly, will undoubtedly promote greater organization and consciousness of women's issues.

Another important aspect of the decade is the growing public recognition and awareness of women's issues, as reflected in the increase in the number of research programs on women in state and private agencies, education campaigns, seminars, workshops, and so on.[7] The media has also played a very important role in disseminating information on women's problems across the country.

An evaluation of the decade would be incomplete without criticism of the way women's issues are still used by both the political parties and the government. Under pressure from feminist groups, however, some of the left-wing parties, committed to the elimination of all forms of social inequality, have gradually changed. In sum, although there is still a long way to go, we believe that the balance of the decade is positive.

Acknowledgments

The authors would like to thank the Rural Women's Study Team for their assistance in writing this paper, especially Milagros Dottin, and Margarita Cordero. This chapter was translated by Katherine Pettus.

Notes

1. The nontraditional agricultural products include roasted coffee, canned chickpeas, coconut paste and candy, beeswax, chocolate and cocoa, unsweetened chocolate powder, tomato paste, guava paste, jelly and juice, and plaintain chips.

2. The National Survey of Rural Women (ENMR), encompassing 2,152 households, was carried out by the Center for Research for Feminine Action in December 1984–January 1985, as part of the Dominican Rural Women's Study. In addition to the case studies of agricultural enterprises employing female wage workers, five in-depth case studies of rural communities in different regions of the country were conducted. See Arango and Rosado (1984), Fernandez (1984), Grant and Dottin (1984), Mones and Done (1984), and Pou and Hernandez (1984).

3. Fifty-five percent of these homes have only one room, and 45 percent have two.

4. Data from time allocation analyses of women participants in the community case studies conducted by the CIPAF researchers in 1984.

5. Seven of the eight crops (cotton, coffee, chickpeas, peanuts, tobacco, tomatoes, beans, and string beans) that employ significant numbers of women are among the top twelve crops in terms of labor employed per hectare (SEA 1977). The most labor intensive crop is tomatoes.

6. Of each 100 women who migrate, 37 percent go to the capital city of Santo Domingo.

7. See Castillo (1984) and Centro de Estudios Dominicanos de la Educación (1983), for example.

References

Arango, Amparo, and Tarasy Rosado, "Mujer, diferenciación social y subordinación: estudio de una comunidad olvidada de la regional fronteriza—Dajabon," Santo Domingo, CIPAF, 1984, mimeo.

Benería, Lourdes, *Reproducción, producción y división sexual del trabajo* (Santo Domingo: Ediciones Populares Feministas, CIPAF, 1984).

Castillo, Martha, et al., "Antecedentes para un Diagnóstico de la Problemática de la Mujer Rural en la Republica Dominicana" (Santo Domingo: Instituto Interamericano de Cooperación para la Agricultura (IICA), 1984), mimeo.

Ceara Hatton, Miguel, *Tendencias estructurales y coyuntura de la economía dominicana 1968–83* (Santo Domingo: Fundación Freidrich Ebert, 1984).

Centro de Estudios Dominicanos de la Educación (CEDEE), "Historia y Situación de la Organizacion de la Mujer Campesina en Republica Dominicana," Santo Domingo: CEPAL, 1983, mimeo.

CEPAL (Comisión Económica para America Latina), *Mujeres en America Latina. Aportes para una discusión* (Mexico: Fondo de Cultura Económica, 1975).

Dirección General de Promoción de la Mujer, "Documento sobre lineamientos generales y objectivos" (Santo Domingo: Dirección Gral. de Promoción de la Mujer, 1985).

Dore y Cabral, Carlos, "Posibilidades y Límites de la Reforma Agraria," *Forum, Los Problemas del Sector Rural en La Republica Domincana* (Santo Domingo), no. 3, 1982, pp. 155–173.

———, "Clases sociales y políticas agrarias en la Republica Dominicana (notas para la discusion)," *Ciencia y Sociedad* (Santo Domingo) 9, no. 1 (1984):41–62.

Fernandez, Brinella, "Mujer, diferenciación social y subordinación: estudio de una comunidad de mujeres organizadas—Higuey," Santo Domingo, CIPAF, 1984, mimeo.

Grant, Lydia, and Milagros Dottin, "Mujer, diferenciación social y subordinación: estudio de una comunidad tomatera—Azua," Santo Domingo, CIPAF, 1984, mimeo.

Mones, Belkis, and Elsie Done, "Mujer Rural: Diferenciación social, subordinación y división del trabajo por genero," Santo Domingo, CIPAF, 1984, mimeo.

Oficina Nacional de Planficacion (ONAPLAN), *Encuesta Nacional de Mano de Obra Rural* in the magazine of the Technical Ministry of the President, Santo Domingo, 1984.

———, "Partipición de la Mano de Obra Rural," *Revista del Secretariado Técnico de la Presidencia*, Santo Domingo, 1984.

Pou, Francis, and Pastora Hernandez, "Mujer, diferenciación social y subordinación: estudio de una comunidad tabaquera," Santo Domingo, CIPAF, 1984, mimeo.

Secretaría de Estado de Agricultura (SEA), "Aspectos del Empleo Rural en la Republica Dominicana" (Santo Domingo: SEA, 1977).

Tejada, Argelia, "Estado y desarrollo capitalista de la agricultural dominicana 1966–1978," Primer Congreso Latinoamericano de Sociologia Rural, Santo Domingo, 1983.

Vicens, Lucas, *Auge y Receso del Capitalism Dominicano*, Santo Domingo 1984, manuscript.

3

The Social Invisibility
of Women's Work
in Brazilian Agriculture

Cheywa R. Spindel

In this chapter I examine the "invisibility" of working women in Brazil. My subject is not a particular type of magic but rather the historical concealment and undervaluation of the contribution of rural women to agricultural production. Neither Brazilian society nor its institutions recognize rural women as workers in their own right; they are even denied the scant benefits now extended to male workers in rural areas.

The male household head in Brazilian rural areas has traditionally had absolute control over the labor power of family members and over the distribution of the fruits of household production. The man has received full credit for household reproduction—a factor that serves to hide the economic and domestic participation of women and children. Thus the household unit, as a producer of commodities, is an integral part of the process rendering women's contributions to the production of exchange values invisible. Domestic labor, in contrast, is considered the exclusive and natural domain of women and is not classified as work. It is important to understand how the concept of social invisibility is formulated and reproduced and how, as a result, the paradigm of women's supposed nature is sustained. It is hoped that this analysis will lead to a clearer understanding of how Brazilian society manages to hide the economic participation of women who are supposedly free workers in an increasingly capitalist economy.

The Social Relations of
Production and the Household

Household production provided the basis for the development of capitalist agriculture in Brazil. Although women were not included on the coffee plantation payroll lists, they were counted, along with children, as workers in the calculations for the distribution of coffee land to each family of tenant farmers.[1] The success of this system as a source of capital accumulation depended upon the unremunerated participation of women and children, whose labor contribution on the coffee plantations always exceeded that of men.

Women were generally responsible for foodstuff production on the *roca*, the subsistence parcel assigned to a family on the plantation. The productivity level of the roca in many ways determined the possibility for economic emancipation of the tenant farmer household. The roca produce guaranteed a family nutritious, low cost food, and commercialization of the surplus production sometimes allowed tenant farmers to accumulate savings to buy land, thus becoming smallholders, or to migrate to the city.

During the period between the end of World War II and the early 1960s, the growth rate of agricultural production (4.5 percent) exceeded that of the rural population. Not only did agriculture not constitute a drain on national resources; the sector generated a surplus that could be channeled into industrial development, the top priority during this phase of Brazilian capitalist development.

The participation of unremunerated family labor accounts in part for the economic performance of the agricultural sector during this period. Until the early 1960s, the rural household constituted the basic unit of production, whether as tenants, sharecroppers, squatters, or smallholders. The very structure of household production allows for subsistence production, production for the market, and domestic work to be performed either within the same physical space or in close proximity, enabling rural women to combine their productive and reproductive work.

Women played an important role in the development of Brazilian agriculture precisely because household-based production kept costs low, allowing cheap foodstuffs to be the basis for the expansion of capitalism until the mid-1960s. Moreover, subsistence production and women's domestic labor supplied the market with a low-cost labor force, one whose full cost of reproduction need not be borne by capital. The household production unit, therefore, largely guaranteed reproduction of the family labor force during this period and, despite increasing rural-urban migration, ensured that the rural labor market remained relatively elastic.[2]

During the period following the 1964 military coup, the economy was restructured in the function of industry, not only through a transfer of the surplus to this sector but through the enlargement of the internal market for Brazilian-made manufactured goods. The agricultural sector was reoriented to serve two new roles: It was to become a market for the agrochemicals and machinery produced by the industrial sector, and it was to help reduce the balance of payments deficit both directly, by producing export crops such as wheat, and indirectly, by supplying the export-oriented agro-industrial enterprises with raw materials.[3]

In combination with other incentives, rural credit was clearly the most important instrument for the implementation of these new policies. It was institutionalized as part of the National Credit System in 1965, and by 1969, it was financing 40 percent of the value of agricultural production, reaching 102.5 percent in 1975, although it subsequently stabilized at 80 to 90 percent (Quedes Pinto 1981). Between 1969 and 1979, credit increased almost twice as fast as agricultural production.

This enormous expansion of resources, in the context of an accelerated industrial development process favoring the concentration of income and centralization of capital, was directed primarily at large producers, reinforcing these tendencies. Moreover, real interest rates were negative, implying high subsidies, which contributed significantly in recent years to an accelerated inflationary process (Martine 1983).[4]

Moreover, credit was not distributed uniformly, even among the mere 20 percent of rural holdings that had access to it. In 1977, no more than 1 percent had received almost 40 percent of the available credit (Quedes Pinto 1981). A large part of these resources were redirected into the stock market or were used to purchase additional land, resulting in further land concentration. Land prices rose 130 percent between 1956 and 1971 and almost 2,000 percent in the period between 1971 and 1977 (Martine 1983). The Gini land concentration index rose from 0.837 in 1970 to 0.849 in 1980 (Kageyama and Silva 1983).

But subsidized credit and relatively low (and subsidized) prices for modern agrochemicals and farm machinery did stimulate the increased consumption of these products. And a diversified and highly complex agro-industrial sector was developed that was competitive in world markets.

These changes have only aggravated long-standing regional economic and social inequalities. The process has accentuated the disparity in rural living conditions, reflecting the wide range of productive situations in the agricultural sector.

In this stage of agricultural capitalization, the viability of the household unit of production depends on its ability to absorb modern technology, integrated into the circuit of financial and agro-industrial capital. This new confrontation between capital and labor "violently accelerates the process of horizontal differentiation within the peasantry. Survival within the new productive system depends upon the capacity to adapt, which is only possible if the producer generates a surplus or goes into debt.

The producer who wishes to succeed must reinvest in agriculture" (Sorj and Wilkinson 1983).

Some peasant households have been able to make the technological transition and become part of the modern, capitalized smallholder sector. Others, unable to modify their productive structure, have undergone a process of pauperization, eventually becoming proletarianized. The possibilities of survival of the household unit of production largely depend on the available opportunities in the region and the extent to which household composition allows for different combinations of direct production and wage work. Some household members may take up temporary agricultural wage work whereas others seek permanent wage employment in town; others may become sharecroppers or tenants. These alternatives are all grounded in the household as a unit of production, sustaining simple reproduction, even though its level of productivity is much lower than that governing society a whole.

Two other factors help to explain the persistence of household producers: (1) the intensification, at the end of this period, of the articulation between the smallholder sector and agro-industry and (2) the fact that the impact of the new technology on household labor relations, above all of propertyless households (tenant farmers, sharecroppers, squatters), did not occur all at once or with uniform intensity. Moreover, it was not necessarily in the interest of capital to eliminate the smallholder sector altogether. Smallholders still provide 70 percent of basic foodstuff production in addition to raw materials for agro-industry. Agro-industry has restructured, rebuilt, and reintegrated tenant farmers and small family farms into its productive process according to its particular needs. Although this process may guarantee the survival of household production, it is highly exploitative of family labor and makes small producers totally dependent on agro-industry.

As large estates became large enterprises, they expelled their resident labor force of tenant farmers and other workers, and temporary wage work became the norm. The exresidents formed part of the new labor force of temporary wage workers, who now resided in urban areas. They remain dependent upon rural employment largely because there are few other alternatives. Temporary wage workers are also recruited from the smallholder sector, which is in the process of disintegration or stagnation.

As shown in Table 3.1, between 1970 and 1980 women's participation in agricultural wage work increased relative to their participation as family labor in household units of production. The marked difference in the structure of labor relations in São Paulo compared with that in the rest of the country reflects the high degree of regional differentiation in the level of technology and in the degree of capitalist development.

TABLE 3.1
Economically Active Population in Agriculture in Brazil and in São Paulo
by Occupation and Gender (percentages)

	Brazil			São Paulo	
	1970	1976	1980	1976	1980
All Workers					
Wage workers	22.8	36.1	38.2	67.4	68.6
Family workers	77.2	63.9	61.8	32.6	31.4
Economically active population	100.0	100.0	100.0	100.0	100.0
Females					
Wage workers	8.4	20.6	32.8	68.5	76.6
Family workers	91.6	79.4	67.2	31.5	23.4
Economically active population	100.0	100.0	100.0	100.0	100.0
Males					
Wage workers	29.2	36.1	39.0	66.9	67.1
Family workers	70.8	63.9	61.0	33.1	32.9
Economically active population	100.0	100.0	100.0	100.0	100.0

Note: The category "family workers" includes independent producers as well as their nonremunerated kin.

Sources: Brazil data are from Singer (1981:36-37); São Paulo data are from Saffiotti (1984). Both estimates are drawn from PNAD 1976 Household Census published by the Instituto Brasileiro de Geografía e Estatística (IBGE).

The labor market is now absorbing women wage workers at a faster rate than men (see Table 3.1). Two factors help to explain the measured increase in women's agricultural wage employment: (1) There is a growing awareness of women's role in society as a result of the voluminous literature on the topic, leading to greater sensitivity to gender in statistical studies; and (2) women's work is easier to measure when they are employed as wage workers rather than family workers. When women participate in agriculture as temporary wage workers, the unit of commodity production is different from the unit of family reproduction. As a result, women's work is compartmentalized, both in space and in time. The dividing line between production and reproduction sharpens, and it is easier to calculate "time spent in the fields" as compared to "time spent in the home." Furthermore, production for the market is no longer "unremunerated family labor." Women's labor now has a price, although women's wages are very low and do not cover the full cost of reproducing labor power. In statistical terms, however, women's work can no longer be completely ignored. According to official statistics, the proportion of economically active women (aged 10 and older) engaged in agriculture rose from 9 percent in 1970 to 13.2 percent in 1980 and to 21 percent in 1982 (Saffiotti 1984).

Mobilization of Rural Women Workers

Brazilian legislative and executive policies have largely ignored women workers in their role as producers of household goods and services and/ or commodities. Rural women could easily be disregarded since their participation in the household unit of production was invisible, making legislation superfluous. Official discourse reinforced the general belief that a woman's work was only to "help" her husband and was, to a certain extent, "natural"—integral to her role as a woman.

Rural workers were largely at the mercy of landowners until 1963, when the Law for Rural Workers was promulgated. This law officially established a minimum wage and extended to rural areas the benefits and legal rights that urban workers had enjoyed since 1940.[5] Rural workers rarely exercised their legal rights, however, including their right to unionize, and they were neither well organized nor politically assertive.

The military dictatorship cut short the process of politicization of rural workers, which had begun in the early 1960s with the struggle for agrarian reform (particularly in the northeastern section of Brazil). Special decrees promulgated after the 1964 military coup prohibited demonstrations and barred labor unions from any sort of political action. For nearly twenty years, the military government withheld basic democratic freedoms and subjected the population to rigid control and repression.

During this period wage labor became predominant in the countryside—giving rise to the so-called *boia fria* (an urban resident who is a temporary agricultural wage worker), the product of the political and technological processes that ensured the continued expansion of Brazilian agricultural production.

In 1978, the convening of the Third Congress of the National Confederation of Agricultural Workers (CONTAG) signaled the beginning of the *apertura* (period of political liberalization), indicating that the government intended to adopt a more tolerant position toward political mobilizations and public demonstrations organized by the workers. The apertura represented an attempt by the military government, anticipating the economic crisis that was to erode its political bases, to improve its image both inside the country and abroad.

The main theme of the Third Congress was the right of peasants to land. The arguments outlined in the minutes centered on the contribution of smallholders to total agricultural production (Gallano 1984). It was argued that small producers used land more intensively, that they could help increase food production, and that they thus directly contributed to improving the balance of payments and keeping prices stable.

Although the virtues of the household unit of production were amply discussed at the congress, no mention was made of the fact that household production depends on the unremunerated labor of all family members, particularly that of the wife, who works a double or triple shift. Moreover, no attention was given to the legislation denying women legal title to land and access to credit. Neither were the rights of women wage workers discussed in relation to labor legislation.

According to the 1963 law, rural women wage workers as well as men have the following legal rights: They are to be included in the payroll lists and enrolled in social security; they are entitled to the minimum wage (beginning at age sixteen) and to rest with pay on Sundays and national holidays, and work is limited to eight-hour shifts. Job stability is also provided (after sixteen years of service an employee cannot be dismissed without just cause or unless an agreement has been reached); and an employee must be paid compensation if dismissed without just cause after being employed for more than one year. Workers may negotiate wage agreements and work longer shifts (up to two hours' work for 20 percent extra overtime pay) without union assistance.

As a rule, rural female wage workers may not work night shifts (between 10 P.M. and 5 A.M. for work in the fields and between 8 P.M. and 4 A.M. for livestock work). Exceptions can be made during the harvest of perishable products or in extenuating circumstances. Female employees who work night shifts are entitled to overtime pay at a rate 25 percent above the hourly wage.

Wage workers officially registered in "PRO-Rural" have the legal right to retire for reasons of disability or old age and are entitled to a pension equal to 75 percent of the prevailing minimum wage.[6] In the case of peasant producers, only one family member is entitled to retire for old age (at sixty-five) so rural women can potentially benefit from this provision only if they are household heads or officially registered wage workers. Maternity leave, although legally guaranteed, is unpaid, and maternity benefits are not included in general employment benefits.

Mobilizations and public demonstrations demanding that these laws be enforced and that rural women be granted other rights did not begin until the early 1980s. The context for women to begin to engage in this type of political activity as well as unionization was provided by the democratization process, the *apertura*, and Tancredo Neves' campaign for the presidency. Logistical support for the growing political momentum of women was provided by the newly created state women's councils.

The first meeting of rural women took place in October 1984, in the capital of the state of Minas Gerais. It was sponsored by EMATER (the Rural Extension and Technical Assistance Office of the Ministry of Agriculture), the Minas Gerais secretariat, and UNICEF (UN International Children's Emergency Fund). More than 300 women from 250 municipalities in Minas Gerais attended. The summary of the conclusions reached in the group discussions indicates that rural women are well aware of their problems and are able to articulate them clearly. This fact suggests that their traditional silence, rather than resulting from any inherent difficulties in articulating the issues, can be attributed to their past lack of assistance or recognition.

These rural women demonstrated that they were well aware that their status was devalued, that they were not taken seriously, and that they were denied certain rights, such as retirement benefits. They also clearly defined the problems affecting their day-to-day lives, whether with respect to production (prices, interest rates, access to land and fertilizers), their children's needs (schools, food, quality of education, lack of nearby facilities), or the labor market. What they lacked was social recognition of their problems and of their status as citizens, wives, mothers, and workers.

The Minas Gerais meeting was followed, in 1985, by rural women's conferences in the states of São Paulo and Paraná, sponsored by the Ministry of Labor and state agencies. Besides reiterating the need for agrarian reform, these conferences called for policies to ensure the survival of small household producers.

One of the most debated issues on the agenda was the conditions of retirement. Although it was suggested that the retirement age be lowered from sixty-five years to fifty, the demand of most women wage workers was that the criteria for retirement be changed to take into account the length of employment. The demand of peasant women was different: They wanted to be given the legal right to retire on their own account. As noted previously, only one member of the household production unit, usually the male household head, is entitled to retirement benefits. A married woman receives a pension only if she is widowed, in which case she receives the payments that would have accrued to her husband. The implication of this plan, of course, is that society does not consider women's contribution to household production to be work in its own right.

Another issue discussed at these meetings was women's lower wages compared with those of men. The participants recounted a few successful, but isolated, struggles for equal wages in some regions. In Terra Roxa in Paraná state, for example, women previously were paid at the same rate as children until they demanded to be paid at a rate equivalent to men.

Macro-economic questions affecting the agricultural sector, such as price policies, interest rates, and inflation, were also on the agenda of the rural women's meetings. Moreover, the women demanded that they be accorded equal rights in the labor unions, associations, and cooperatives, and they called on the government to provide improved services and public education (more schools, better teachers, school lunches, day care).

The fourth congress of CONTAG, organized by the National Workers Confederation (CNT), took place in 1985, seven years after the Third Congress. In the interim, governmental policy had changed, new parties had come to power, and the women's rights movement had come into being and gathered momentum. With the establishment of the National Council on Women's Rights (linked to the Ministry of Justice) in August 1985 and the state-level women's councils, women's rights organizations had an official forum. The aim of the council is "to promote policies that eliminate discrimination against women, that enable women to be free and have equal rights, and participate fully in national economic and cultural activities."[7]

Despite this favorable political climate, the proposals presented by the work commissions of the Fourth CONTAG Congress are both timid and naive with regard to women's problems.[8] Only five of the 170 proposals presented by the commission on labor issues specifically mention women. Three of these deal with enforcement of the existing legislation (maternity leave, equal opportunities, and equal pay).

The most novel of the proposals called for three days' paid leave of absence per month during menstruation. If this highly controversial proposal were endorsed, it could increase discrimination against women, considering that the labor market is flooded with unskilled workers and is highly elastic, a condition unlikely to change in the foreseeable future.

Another proposal called on women to intensify their participation in union life—in assemblies, strikes, and leadership positions—and asked that the gains women have made be communicated to them. This proposal reflects a lack of awareness of women's participation in demonstrations and strikes for worker's rights, even in the front lines. Once the mobilizations are over, however, women are totally forgotten—as economic, social, or political agents. The proposal's directive to explain to women "the specific gains they have made" is inherently paternalistic and implies that women cannot act for themselves and are essentially passive, apolitical beings.

Of the 250 proposals presented to the commission on agricultural policy, only one—which specifies that women's names should be placed alongside those of their husbands in receipts for the sale of agricultural products—mentions women. The commission on agrarian issues—which debated agrarian reform—made no mention of women's rights with respect to access to land, profits, credit, technology, or marketing channels. In other words, the commission ignored the fact that only equal access to the basic means of production will guarantee the autonomy of women as economic agents.

Considering that CONTAG is the most important confederation of agricultural workers in the country, this analysis suggests a certain indifference toward the defense of women's rights. Only one proposal, forthcoming from the commission on unionization, was on target: "Rural women, whose participation in the household economy is fundamental, must be recognized as workers in their own right; the discrimination that stems from their being regarded as a domestic or dependent worker should be eliminated, and all the benefits provided for in the law must be extended to them."

A recent episode illustrates the urgency of having CONTAG take a stronger position with respect to women's rights. In October 1985, the National Agrarian Reform Program (PRNA) was finally passed (Decree 91766/85). In the months immediately preceding ratification, a group of women mobilized by the Commission for Rural Women's Rights (part of the Rio de Janeiro feminist movement) lobbied for inclusion of a clause that would allow women to be beneficiaries of the reform and to receive land titles directly. Because they did not have the endorsement of the rural labor organizations, their efforts failed, and women were not named beneficiaries of the reform. The rural labor organizations justified withholding endorsement on the grounds that this was not the right moment to pressure the government on the issue. The commission only succeeded in having four lines referring to women written into the agrarian reform law: "Accordingly, the difficulties particular to rural women and the important functions they fulfill will be taken into account so that their autonomy is recognized and they are granted freedom and equality."[9]

Reflections Based on a Case Study

Rural women wage workers show the greatest potential among rural women for political mobilization because they are in contact with other workers and, through the process of socialization, are more likely to develop class consciousness. When a woman goes into the fields to cut cane or pick oranges as a wage worker, her participation is extracted from the private domain and is publicly exposed, becoming the subject of comment, praise, criticism, and, above all, measurement.

In late 1985, the boias frias went on strike in Guariba, São Paulo state, demanding that the law requiring equal pay for men and women be enforced and asking for wage increases and better working conditions. The women demanded that they be guaranteed de facto (as opposed to de jure) equality; this approach suggests a grassroots movement in the process of becoming class and gender conscious. Significantly, government repesentatives and employers negotiated and approved this demand, which in effect aknowledged discrimination against rural women.

Is this attempt to mitigate the discrimination faced by women evidence of a new political maturity among the participating agents and institutions? Or is the "visibility" that women's work has acquired as a result of being "raised" to the category of wage work the key element in this process? Studies carried out in India during the 1970s showed that there was a correlation between rural women's political mobilization, through which they demanded their rights as workers, and the degree to which their work was "visible" (Ahmad 1984).

Women's active participation in the São Paulo strikes and their demands can perhaps be understood as the culmination of a process of building self-confidence and empowerment which, in turn, was the result of the market value that women's work had acquired. Also important here is the fact that when rural women perform the same tasks as men in temporary agricultural work their obvious strength, skill, ability, and productivity invalidate the arguments of female "fragility" and "incompetence" that have heretofore justified and sustained women's subordination and discrimination.[10] For example, during the planting and harvest seasons, wages are calculated on the basis of productivity (as piecework) and women's wages not only equal those of men but in some cases even exceed them.

One of the main arguments sustaining differential male and female wage levels is that they carry out jobs of differential worth: Male tasks are defined as more difficult or heavier (Hirata and Humphrey 1983). This argument has justified keeping wages for boia fria women 25 to 30 percent lower than those for men (in some regions the difference is greater). This practice was successfully challenged by the striking women workers of Guariba.

A fundamental challenge is to consolidate this movement in order to achieve long-term political gains. Although the Guariba strike won women equal pay, it had very few positive repercussions for other aspects of their work or daily life. For example, although the demand for women workers is high during the harvest period, it declines in the postharvest period, sometimes by 50 percent. The payment of equal wages would probably precipitate an increase in seasonal female unemployment.

Why do employers prefer to contract male labor when they themselves acknowledge that women are more skilled and competent and show higher productivity than men do? Part of the answer rests in women's responsibility for biological and daily reproduction. Women are usually dismissed when they become pregnant. As women are now able to litigate this issue and are likely to receive favorable judgments, their year-round employment can be problematic for managers. Moreover, female boia frias who are married and have small children cannot always work for their employers on Saturdays because they must use the weekends for the domestic work that has accumulated during the week. Although a worker loses the right to a paid Sunday if absent for one day during the week, management has little interest in employing workers with predictably high rates of absenteeism.

Housework and child care interfere with women's integration into the labor market in other areas as well. It discourages women from demanding employment contracts and from being listed on the payroll. It is generally believed that workers who are not listed on the payroll have more freedom. Although Saffiotti (1984) concludes that management may encourage this belief, other factors must be taken into consideration. If women do not have one paid day of rest during the week and presumably have other absences deducted from their wages, being included on the payroll has little benefit for them. This is also the case if their husbands' and sons' employment benefits or union affiliations already include medical care. Such facts indicate how a socially imposed limitation can transform a first-class working woman into a second-class wage earner.

Moreover, particularly at harvest time married women commonly work in the same field as their husbands. When asked about this, some women responded evasively, saying that this arrangement was their personal preference; others, that it was their husbands' preference. A union leader (a former boia fria) interpreted this preference as follows: "If they don't work in the same *roca*, and the truck is delayed, or the woman's workplace is farther away than her husband's, she might return home later than he does. Husbands don't like to wait for their dinner or to have to pick up the children at the neighbor's." Thus, even when the unit of production is both structurally and geographically separate from the unit of household reproduction and even when a woman's participation has acquired "value," the man determines where and when she will work.

The way women dress to work in the fields—a skirt over tight slacks—also reflects some of the specific problems of working women. According to the women, the tight slacks give them more freedom of movement, allowing them to climb with ease into the trucks that transport them to the fields each day, and protect them from the scratches of plants and bushes in the fields. They protect themselves from the sun by wearing tight-sleeved blouses, broad brimmed hats, and scarves. The women wear skirts to identify themselves as "sensible, modest girls." In their words, "you have to wear a skirt or men will stare at you and then people will talk and say that so-and-so is your lover or whatever." Skirts also have a practical function. They afford women protection from the stares of men when they are forced to respond to the "call of nature" in the fields.

Thus, women are subject to social control as a gender even when they can cut—skillfully and fast—as many tons of cane as men or pick as many boxes or sacks of fruit or grain or bring home the same amount of money. There are other, much less superficial, forms of domination and control than the informal dress code that are probably much more difficult to endure.

In their discourse, however, women do not reveal that they perceive these situations as limiting their freedom or subjecting them to men. Women say that they like to go to the fields, that they like working, especially in a group, and, although the work is hard and dangerous, they prefer it to domestic work. "It's more fun to work in the roca," "time goes by faster," "you can see the work you've done," "it's more enjoyable to be part of a group," were among the women's comments. Even though the women say they like to work, they always note that they work to "help" their husbands or the family—the main reason men say they "let" the women work.

The fact that women do not like to do domestic work because "you never see it" or because "it's irritating" is never given as a reason for wanting to liberate themselves from domestic work. Social dictates make it clear that "a woman's place is in the home." As one union leader said: "Women work outside the home because they must contribute when money is short. They are also expected to take good care of the children and the house, though." The underlying logic of this statement is that women's participation in wage work is temporary and it must be endured until "things get back to normal." That is why the way women are treated has not changed. Thus women's labor market participation does not alter their traditional subordination to men in the home. As a result, the hypothesis—that "the fact that women wage workers are exploited by capital improves the possibilities for the struggle against oppression and discrimination within the family, since women's economic dependence shifts from the man to capital, dismantling one of the foundations of domination"—is not supported by fact.[11]

In terms of the gender division of labor with respect to reproduction, nothing seems to have changed greatly. Women—wives, mothers, and daughters—are still exclusively responsible for domestic labor. The burden of overwork brought about by the combination of women's productive and reproductive responsibilities takes more than just a physical toll. Research on the psychological strain would be useful and might shed some light on how heavy, dirty, and dangerous work such as cane cutting, performed under highly exploitative and discriminatory conditions, could be coveted and considered desirable by women.

The political struggles and victories in Guariba have failed to ignite a consistent and dynamic movement. Union officials have difficulty motivating their coworkers to attend meetings and assemblies, and although the rate of union membership has increased, the ratio of those attending meetings remains small and is much the same as it was before the strike. A variety of tactics, such as the fairly successful, recent one of hiring a show with local artists as bait, have been employed to attract boias frias to the meetings.

Women's participation in union activities is marginal. Their explanation for this—which is generally valid—is that they simply do not have the time. Women tend to use the union as a service center, particularly for medical attention. The union, however, has not made any specific overtures to the women or attempted to accommodate them.

Despite their poor attendance at union meetings, women are generally held to be more interested and concerned than men about workers' rights whenever these are challenged or the subject is raised. Women sometimes go to union meetings without their husbands' knowledge to find out about their rights if they feel that a situation of exploitation exists. Because they are quicker to understand the discussions, they are regarded by some union leaders as more intelligent than men.

Women have the potential to participate more actively in union activities if social conditions were more favorable. Women are socially limited, not apathetic, apolitical, or alienated. They are newcomers to the process, like the unions that represent them, and perhaps should be considered apprentices.

Documenting the injustices, publicizing the social "conspiracy" that makes women's participation invisible, and challenging the fallacy that the gender division of labor is natural are only the first steps. Although we are on the right track, we clearly must go beyond these moves and create the material, political, and ideological conditions that will allow women to challenge the model of reality presented to them as the ideal.

Acknowledgments

This chapter was translated by Katherine Pettus.

Notes

1. The introduction of free, as opposed to slave, labor into the coffee economy of Brazil took place during the colonial period through the system known as *colonato*, which was based on the migration of families from Europe—particularly from Italy. The colonists (*colonos*) were contracted by plantations to farm coffee. They were paid wages and given a subsistence plot. The basic selection criterium was that the colonist have a family, that is, that the husband have a young wife and children, at least one of whom was of working age.

2. Migration figures for Brazil show that, during the 1960s, 12.9 million people migrated from the rural areas. In the 1970s the volume of rural immigrants rose to 15.6 million. In 1970, 45 percent of the population lived in rural areas, whereas in 1980 only 30 percent did so.

3. The agricultural sector was also called upon to help reduce petroleum imports after the crisis of the 1970s. Under the energy substitution program, alcohol-based fuels derived from sugar cane and corn were to increasingly replace petroleum. The main objective of this program was to prevent a crisis in the automobile industry, thus guaranteeing a stable internal market.

4. For example, in 1980 inflation was on the order of 110 percent, whereas interest rates averaged 20 percent (Martine 1983).

5. Although two minimum wage laws for rural workers had been passed in 1940 and 1953, these had not been translated into concrete regulations and remained "dead letters" until 1963.

6. "PRO-Rural" is the Brazilian Rural Social Welfare System legislated in 1963.

7. Article 310 of Draft Law No. 5778C, 1985.

8. See "Relatorio de Congresso de CONTAG," CNT, 1985.

9. Item 2, Basic Principles of Agrarian Policy, point no. 9 of the Organization of Beneficiaries, final paragraph.

10. Countless stories adducing that the women "set the pace" of the field work confirm this hypothesis. The *machista* tradition demands that the husband and other males then intensify their pace of work. The president of the rural workers' union of Santa Rosa de Viterbo reported another piece of evidence that clearly illustrates women's "ability." In 1984, the only boia fria in the region who had to pay income taxes was a woman. Only those who receive, on average, more than two minimum salaries per month, pay income taxes.

11. This hypothesis was proposed by Paulo Sandroni and debated in the seminar on "Women, Agriculture and Modernization in Latin America," held in September 1983 in São Paulo, Brazil. See Spindel (1985) for a fuller discussion.

References

Ahmad, Zubeida, "Las mujeres en el medio rural y su trabajo: como favorecer su independencia," *Revista internacional del trabajo* 103, no. 1, 1984.

Brito, Sebastiana Rodrigues, ed., "O trabalho volante na agricultura brasileira," IBGE, Geography Department, Rio de Janeiro, 1984.

Gallano, Ana Maria, "Sindicalismo e reforma agrária no Brasil," in *Questão e reforma agrária nos anos 80, Tempo brasileiro* (Rio de Janeiro), no. 77, April/ June 1984.

Hirata, Helena, and John Humphrey, "Processo de trabalho, divisão sexual do trabalho e reinvindicações femininas," paper presented at the 7th Annual Meeting of the National Association of Social Science Graduate Study and Research, São Paulo, October 1983.

Kageyama, Angela and Silva, José Graziano, "Diferenciação camponesa e Mudança Technológica: O caso dos Produtores de Feijão en São Paulo," UNICAMP/ IICA, Campinas, 1983.

Martine, George, "As transformações na estrutura de produção agrícola paulista: determinantes, consequências e perspectivas," Social Impact of Development Project, ILO/UNDP (International Labour Office/UN Development Program), Brasilia, 1983, mimeo.

Noronha, Olinda Maria, "De camponesa a 'madame': Trabalho feminino e relações de saber do meio rural," doctoral thesis, Catholic University of São Paulo, 1984.

Quedes Pinto, Luiz Carlos, "Notas sobre a política de credito rural no Brasil," paper presented at the Legislative Assembly of the State of São Paulo (Special Commission of Inquiry on the Situation of Temporary Workers—Boia-Frias) August 1981, mimeo.

Saffiotti, Heliethe, "Política agrícola no Brasil contemporâneo e suas consequências para a força de trabalho femenina," São Paulo, 1984, mimeo.

————, "Mulheres em movimento na zona rural paulista, São Paulo," 1985, mimeo.

Silva, José Graziano, ed., "Tecnologia e campesinato. O caso brasileiro," Universidade Estadual de Campinas, UNICAMP, Instituto Interamericano de Investigação sobre Tecnologia Agropecuaria, Campinas, 1982.

Sorj, Bernardo, and John Wilkinson, "Processos sociais e formas de produção na agricultura brasileira," in *Sociedade e política no Brasil pós-64* (São Paulo: Ed. Brasiliense, 1983).

Spindel, Cheywa R., "Capitál, familia y mujer en la evolucion de la producción rural de base familiar—un caso en Brasil," in M. León, ed., *Las trabajadoras del agro* (Bogotá: ACEP, 1982).

————, "Temporary Work in Brazilian Agriculture: 'Boias Frias,' a Category under Investigation," in Guy Standing, ed., *Labour Circulation and the Labour Process* (London: Croom Helm, 1985).

4

Mexican Agricultural Development Policy and Its Impact on Rural Women

Lourdes Arizpe and Carlota Botey

Over the past decade, an increasing number of studies have focused on rural women's participation in production and reproduction. Few of these studies, however, have explored the relationship between women's participation and state agrarian policy. Nevertheless, women's participation is directly affected by changes in the productive structure induced by agrarian policy. Moreover, the gender division of labor within the peasant household itself generates differential effects on agrarian processes. The topic is complex, and before assessing the impact of agrarian policy on rural women, we will attempt to organize the available data and then propose some hypotheses.

The Mexican Agrarian Reform created the conditions for development of the peasant economy by establishing the ejido and the Indian community as the basic units of social property. These divisions were conceived of not simply as units of agricultural production but also as social and cultural entities encompassing all sectors of the population—men, women, children, youth, and the elderly—all of which had defined places and specific functions and employment within the productive community. However, the workings of the market economy, together with demographic growth and the urban bias in public policy, have brought about the breakdown of the internal social organization of the ejidos and Indian communities in recent decades. This breakdown has resulted in unemployment, migration, and cultural disruption.

The peasant sector in particular has been affected by changes in women's economic and social participation. Women play a fundamental role in maintaining family and community cohesion and in transmitting basic cultural norms and social mores. In addition, they perform both primary and secondary tasks in agricultural production. In spite of the central role women play in rural community life, agrarian planners have failed to consider the various ways that women participate in farm and agro-industrial production, their access to income, and their role in social organization. The agrarian reform benefited only male heads of households and ignored the question of how economic change would affect the access of other family members to productive inputs and to income-generating activities.

Mexican Agrarian Policies

The Agrarian Reform

Mexican agrarian policy, whose centerpiece is the agrarian reform—defined as the set of legally enacted economic, social, and political policies that gave land rights to the peasantry—reflects the historic struggle between collective and private forms of landholdings (Reyes Osorio 1972). The 1915 Agrarian Reform legislation in Mexico, promulgated after the 1910 revolution, was the first of its kind in Latin America. The reform replaced the Roman legal principle of unrestricted private property with one that recognized, first and foremost, that land and water rights must serve a social function. Over six decades, the obsolete *latifundia* system that had dominated the Mexican countryside for more than four centuries was dismantled. Gradually, a more democratic land tenancy system, which encompassed both smallholder private property and the social property of the ejido and Indian community structures, was consolidated.

This social property combined indigenous, Spanish, and English forms of land tenancy: It reestablished the pre-Columbian communal form of property enriched by European colonial influence as well as the principles of the North-American homesteading movement which, in the Mexican Civil Code, has its counterpart in the family holding.

As forms of landholding, the Mexican ejido and Indian community system are based on the following principles:

1. Land, water, and forests returned or given to an ejido or recognized as belonging to a community are the property of each village or agrarian unit granted legal status by presidential resolution; land is not nationalized.
2. Under the Mexican Civil Code, ejido and community lands have the same legal characteristics as family holdings, being inalienable private property.

3. Within each agrarian unit, the members included in an official census have individual rights and obligations with regard to the personal usufruct of the ejido's resources, rights that can be inherited by economic dependents in accordance with the relevant law.

Land redistribution began in 1915 but did not gather momentum until 1934 when President Lazaro Cardenas' administration foresaw the development implications of collectively held property and community organization. Between 1915 and 1983, approximately 103 million hectares were redistributed to 25,589 ejidos and 1,486 Indian communities, benefiting 2.8 million heads of household.

Although almost half of the land in Mexico is now collectively owned, its development potential is limited because only 11.8 percent of this total area is suitable for cultivation and only an additional 2.2 percent has access to irrigation. The bulk is largely grazing land of varying quality; although some is wooded, much of the area is either unsuitable for commercial agriculture or livestock or is useless. Nevertheless, the successful growth (more than 5 percent annually in the 1930s and 1940s) of agricultural production on agrarian reform lands provided the cheap food, labor power, and resources Mexico needed to industrialize in the 1950s.

The agrarian reform, besides establishing ejidos and titling community-held land, consolidated a sector of individual private property through the subdivision of the latifundia and the titling of national lands. There were fewer than 50,000 smallholders in 1910; they now number over one million.

Although rural living standards are clearly higher than they were seventy years ago, peasant income levels are still quite low, particularly relative to those of other social groups. Land redistribution must be recognized as only a precondition for a more extensive program of rural development. However, the economic and social efficiency of the peasant sector and of social property was greatly undermined in the 1950s and 1960s when state investments favored capitalist private property.

The new agrarian problem centers on the uneasy balance between the two main agricultural sectors, one based on social property and the other on capitalist private property. To this problem is added that of the large mass of landless agricultural laborers who compete with smallholders for seasonal wage work in the countryside. Once rural population growth exceeded the physical capacity of the distribution program, the problem of insufficient employment generation in manufacturing could no longer be resolved through the periodic redistribution of land. Yet no viable alternatives for the landless have been proposed.

The contemporary agrarian problem demands long-range planning of new productive activities and the requisite training programs.

Women's Rights in the Mexican Agrarian System

The first agrarian law to be promulgated after the Mexican Revolution (January 6, 1915) made no specific reference either to individual land rights or to the size of landholdings beneficiaries were to receive: Land was either given or returned, with legal title, to communities. The land rights clauses in the 1917 constitution also made no reference to gender.

The 1920 Ejido Law—the first piece of legislation to establish that land should be distributed equitably among heads of households—made no mention of women. Article 9 of the By-Laws, ratified in 1922, stated that "wherever land is granted to ejidos, the heads of households or individuals over the age of eighteen shall receive from three to five hectares of irrigated or rainfed lands." The 1927 law is the first statute to refer to women: Article 97 establishes that ejido members shall be "Mexican nationals, males over the age of eighteen, or single women or widows supporting a family." It is interesting that the "supporting a family" qualification refers only to women.

Legal equality between men and women is not explicitly established until 1971—nearly fifty years later—in Article 200 of the Federal Law of Agrarian Reform. To receive land beneficiaries had to be "Mexican by birth, male or female over sixteen years of age, or of any age if with dependents." Female ejido members (*ejidatarias*) were to have the same rights as males (*ejidatarios*). To stress this point, Article 45 stipulates that "women shall enjoy all the rights pertaining to ejido members, shall have voice and vote in the General Assemblies, and shall be eligible for all positions in the Committees and Vigilance Counsels." Articles 76 and 78 were also designed to favor ejidatarias:

Land rights conferred in the foregoing Article may not be the subject of sharecropping, leasing, or third party contracts, nor may land be farmed by wage workers, unless the beneficiary is a female head of household prevented by domestic obligations and the care of young and dependent children from farming the land herself, and the beneficiary resides in the community.

Individuals may not accumulate land units. . . . If an ejidatario marries or becomes the common law spouse of an ejidataria having land rights, each shall retain their separate holding. Under agrarian law, it shall be considered that the marriage was celebrated under the rule of separation of properties.

The Women's Agro-Industrial Units

A novel feature of the 1971 law was its provision for the creation of agro-industrial units for Women (Unidad Agrícola Industrial de la Mujer—UAIM) in the ejidos. All women over the age of sixteen who were not ejidatarias in their own right were given access to a collectively held plot of land for special agricultural or agro-industrial projects. The UAIM is, to date, the main state initiative with respect to rural women.

In the fourteen years since the program's inception, 8,000 UAIMs were provided with legal status. Fewer than one-fourth (1,224) of this original number actually began operations, however, and credit was extended to only 1,112 units. In some cases, particularly in ejidos with insufficient land for the men, the latter denied women their right to a collective plot of land. In many cases, once they received it, women simply used their land to cultivate maize or other agricultural products. The majority of projects that received credit were maize-grinding or tortilla shops, poultry and pig farms, sewing and embroidery collectives, or food canning and preserving operations. They function as production cooperatives in which the women's remuneration is determined according to the income from sales.

UAIMs all over Mexico face the same problem: Despite the women's dedication, these small enterprises are not commercially viable. Part of the problem arises from the monopoly and oligopoly control of distribution outlets; as a consequence the UAIMs often cannot find a market for their products. But the quality of their products, especially garments, is also a problem. Rarely are the UAIMs competitive with the large national or transnational manufacturers because their products are more expensive than their more technically sophisticated counterparts (Barbieri et al. 1981).

On the other hand, the UAIMs have succeeded in spreading awareness of the need to expand employment opportunities for rural women, particularly young women who prefer to stay in their rural communities rather than migrate to the cities as did their elder female relatives. The UAIMs give visibility to the potential of these young women workers. In addition, the UAIMs provide the legal context to make women's participation in ejido and community activities politically and socially acceptable.

Despite the provisions of the 1971 law, cultural conditioning and discriminatory patriarchal practices continue to limit women's access to land. Female ejido or community members accounted for 15 percent of the total in 1984; the majority were elderly widows who inherited their husbands' land plots. Few participate directly in the productive process, and the control of the parcel is usually in the hands of a son or brother.

The Rural Women's Program

Although the UAIM provided an institutional base for women to participate in rural production, the first large-scale program to target rural women, the "Women's Program for Rural Development" (Programa de la Mujer para la Consecusion del Desarrollo Rural—PROMUDER)[1] at the Ministry for Agrarian Reform, was not initiated until 1983. The program was based on the assumption that rural women's participation varied at the generational level and that women of different age groups required different sets of income-generating activities.

Accordingly, PROMUDER proposed the following projects: (1) The UAIMs were to target young women living in the ejido or community; (2) horticultural projects would be developed for more senior women and mothers, who had difficulty working outside their household compound; (3) women farmers would receive training in agricultural production, new technologies, and food storage and preservation; (4) younger women engaged in agro-industrial or assembly line work would receive training in manufacturing technical skills and in labor legislation; (5) poor rural women and young women working in domestic service in the cities would receive training and legal counseling in family and land rights issues; (6) all rural women were targeted for a literacy program.

The program supplied only broad guidelines, the idea being that the women themselves, in the different regions and communities, would define the details and implement the projects. Community representatives, local and state officials, and extension workers in charge of the program worked together to accomplish these objectives.

Perhaps the most striking feature of the program, as projects got under way, was the enthusiastic response it received from rural women. Although initially wary, the women were soon demanding more and more projects for their communities. The desperate need for cash income, combined with the lack of employment opportunities for women in the communities and their new-found awareness that they could participate fully in economic activities, provided a strong incentive to experiment with the various projects.

Inevitably, however, problems arose. In some communities, the men were either uninterested in helping to set up the women's projects or openly hostile to them. Having little experience in working as a team, the women had difficulty in getting organized, as well as in carrying out accounting, quality control, and marketing operations. This lack of organization and training sometimes resulted in the extension worker's becoming the dominant figure in the project, and the women's participation and opportunity to learn new skills were curtailed. Nevertheless, the very fact that such projects were proposed at the upper policy-making echelons and that they were initiated throughout the country with a ripple effect meant that rural women found new avenues for participation open to them.[2]

The Agrarian Crisis

Mexican industrialization began in the 1940s, stimulated by the U.S. wartime demand for manufactured goods, and continued as an import substitution program under a policy of "stabilizing development" until the end of the 1960s. Under this economic development model, the concentration of property and income in the agricultural, industrial, banking, and service sectors intensified; profits from industry were not reinvested with the result that industries failed to expand and productivity fell. Most important, this model was inherently pro-urban, and it severely undermined the peasant sector. Government investment in agriculture declined, and the few investments made were directed toward the establishment of irrigation systems for large-scale capitalist agriculture. The terms of trade also worked against the agricultural sector, and farm incomes lagged well behind urban incomes. Yet another way the peasant communities subsidized the expansion of the Mexican urban economy was through migration of young women and men to the cities. Industrial growth slowed down, and "by the end of the 1960's, income distribution became increasingly skewed, the current account of the balance of payments went into deficit, and public finance became unbalanced. Growth with price stability turned into its opposite, stagnation with inflation, in the 1970's" (Blanco 1981:297).

The "Mexican Miracle" was over. The rural crisis was first evident in agricultural production where the annual growth rate fell from 4.2 percent in 1955–1965 to 1.2 percent between 1967 and 1970 and 0.2 percent during the 1970–1974 period. Thus the average annual growth rate between 1965 and 1974 was less than 0.8 percent, and it continued to decline in subsequent years (Luiselli and Mariscal 1981:440).

During the second half of the 1970s,

the crisis in agricultural production which began in 1965 and, fueled by low relative prices continues today, hit the national economy in two particularly sensitive areas: it increased inflationary pressures, brought on by the unprecedented rise in food prices and raw materials from the rural sector, where supply could not satisfy national demand and, as the economy became food importing, as opposed to food exporting, the already serious deficit in the trade balance—i.e. of foreign exchange needed for economic growth—worsened. (Luiselli and Mariscal 1981)

These were only the immediately observable effects of the crisis; it also brought about a shift in cultivation patterns. Mexico was no longer self-sufficient in food production—in growing the corn, beans, and wheat that are the dietary staples of low-income groups and are therefore socially important. An indicator of the agricultural crisis is that between 1970 and 1975 the area cultivated in corn decreased by more than two million hectares (Montes 1981:59). This shift restructured the sector in favor of export-oriented agriculture such as beef production and horticulture at the expense of basic grains (Rodriguez 1980:65).

The cause of the agricultural crisis that began in 1965 can be found in this restructuring of rural production, which is directly related to the position of the Mexican agricultural sector in the international division of labor. In other words, changes in the world economy affected the Mexican economy as a whole and the agricultural sector in particular, reorienting it to the production of cash crops for export. This shift has had important economic and social effects on small farmers and, therefore, on rural women.

Rural Women and the Agricultural Crisis

The agrarian transformation of recent decades, in which capitalist agriculture displaced the traditional food crops cultivated in the peasant economy, has also changed the way low-income rural women participate in production and social reproduction.

Recent history has shown that highly centralized industrialization policies—which create a surplus labor force in peasant economies—first affect women. The rural exodus in much of Latin America, and especially in Mexico, is primarily female: Women from rural communities migrate to the urban areas in search of work in the informal and service sectors. Rural women have thus played a central role in shaping the three basic characteristics of recent Mexican development: the rural exodus, the expansion of the urban service sector, and the growth of the informal sector of the economy. The imbalances created in rural areas by capitalist development have altered the social reproduction of the peasant economy and, more recently, have led to the expansion of a rural female proletariat. However, the heterogeneity of women's roles—the fact that they are members of peasant families, workers, *and* women—has hindered analysis of the differential effects of this process on them.

As members of peasant families, women must contend with the sharp decline in farm incomes that result from low world prices for agricultural products and from national policies that drain the surplus from the rural sector to finance urban industrialization. This situation is made more acute by the present financial crisis; the peasantry is expected to help repay the foreign debt by increasing production of export crops, which means that families must buy their food in the open market. For women, this expectation has meant heavier work loads while family health and nutrition deteriorate. Women have also had to compensate for this unequal exchange, either by intensifying their unpaid labor on the family plot, entering the wage labor force, or reducing their own personal food consumption.

As wage workers in agriculture or agro-industry, young rural women face unfavorable conditions. Because they lack legal and union protection, are discriminated against in the labor market, and are conditioned to behave in a docile manner, young women are more vulnerable than men to exploitation. Moreover, they face a fluctuating labor market controlled by middlemen and agents who often demand sexual favors in exchange for work.

As women, peasant women are still responsible for feeding, socializing, and protecting their children and families under very precarious economic conditions and often without the support of their husbands or partners, who have migrated. Women, moreover, are exposed to sexual violence both within the home and outside. Their gender subordination in social and political life makes it even more difficult for peasant women to improve their situation.

These problems are all interrelated: They do not affect women as isolated individuals nor are they derived from subjective issues. The fundamental problem is the larger process of subordination and exploitation of the peasantry, which is superimposed on women's gender subordination. Thus, the situation of rural women cannot be analyzed exclusively in terms of gender—the fact that they are women—nor can they be treated only in terms of their socioeconomic role—the fact that they are peasants.

Agrarian Structures, Women's Work, and Capitalist Development

The position of rural women in Mexico cannot be understood without taking into account the heterogeneity of their situation. Failure to do so can lead to abstract stereotyping of "peasant women" and to programs whose superficial priorities do nothing to mitigate the fundamental problems brought about by changes in agricultural production patterns.

In the division of labor by gender, peasant women are in charge of all the unpaid labor of reproduction, which in agrarian societies is much heavier and more strenuous than that performed by urban women. Also, although all rural women participate either directly or indirectly in agricultural production, how and to what degree they do so is determined by the type of productive unit to which they belong. In Mexico, there are currently three types of productive units, each of which corresponds to a stage of the process of agrarian capitalist development.

For analytical purposes, the three types of family production units—subsistence, semiproletarianized and proletarianized households—can be differentiated according to the extent to which each is dependent upon the market to satisfy its needs. The gender division of labor provides the focal point for the following description of the kind of changes these units have undergone.

Since the 1930s, land distribution under the Agrarian Reform has provided for the reconstitution of subsistence peasant economies in the majority of the Indian communities and ejidos. The gender division of labor tends to be rigid, based on traditional cultural norms, and the role of women is oriented primarily toward the production of use values for family consumption. Women are exclusively responsible for the work of reproduction—all the activities that contribute to the reproduction and maintenance of the family labor force. These activities include storing, preserving, processing, and preparing food; socializing and educating children, providing medical and psychological care; and performing domestic chores. Women are also responsible for reproducing social networks—a very important activity that maintains solidarity and communication in subsistence communities. These activities range from visits and exchanges with family and extended kin in urban neighborhoods to performance of community ceremonies and collective rites.

Whether women participate in farming activities depends on the internal composition of the family labor force. Some tasks, such as carrying food to the men working in the fields, planting and harvesting (especially corn), and caring for the smaller livestock (chicken and pigs), are considered exclusively women's work. Women's participation in other activities, such as plowing, weeding, irrigation, and transportation, depends on the availability of male family members or community labor exchanges with relatives. The extent to which women are responsible for feeding and caring for cows or horses also depends on whether there are male relatives to perform these tasks.

Hewitt (1979) has suggested that the position of women in Indian communities tends to be better than that of the *mestizo* women in peasant communities. This suggestion does not imply, however, that women and men have equal positions in the subsistence peasant economy. The gender division of labor throughout rural communities is asymmetrical.

This division means that when there is extra work in areas considered "men's work"—when productivity has to be increased to compete with capitalist farms or when a husband or son has migrated to another area—women are naturally expected to fill the gap. But when there is an overload of "women's work"—when children are at school or daughters migrate and there is no one at home to help with the domestic chores—men only rarely try to help with household chores. As the economic crisis deepens, an invisible overload of work for rural women develops that demands that they expend greater physical effort and work longer hours than men.

A very important theoretical point emerges from this situation. The proposition that capitalist development, by subordinating workers to the interests of capital, is responsible for women's subordination is untenable. Gender subordination exists in traditional peasant economies even though women in indigenous cultures tend to have a higher social standing than their counterparts in mestizo society.

Women and Demographic Growth

In the 1930s and 1940s, the success of the agrarian reform was reflected in higher farm incomes and better levels of health, nutrition, and education among peasant families. Mortality, especially infant mortality, decreased significantly. Because fertility did not decline at an equivalent rate, population growth rates increased. New lands were opened for cultivation, and farming was intensified on land already in production. Although larger family size meant a heavier domestic workload, the more children in a family the more help women had with household and farm chores. In addition, higher incomes enabled families and peasant communities to support widows, divorcées, and single mothers. Since labor was needed to produce food, to build cities, and to create industries, all children and hands were welcome.

The tide began to turn in the 1950s, and the situation worsened in the 1960s when capitalist development intensified in the countryside. As the peasant economy became monetized, rural families had to purchase the labor, services, and goods that they had previously obtained through reciprocal exchange (Young 1978). As relations of reciprocity broke down, some families began to acquire economic advantages over others. More advantages accrued to those with more children as long as agricultural expansion and demand for cottage industry products and handicrafts—almost always the responsibility of women—were sustained. This fact clearly acted as an incentive to large family size, so that despite the decrease in mortality rates, peasant families did not take steps to reduce their high fertility rates.

When the public investments supporting ejido and Indian community farming began to diminish and family incomes fell, young women were sent out to work in the cities so they could send back remittances. Migration thus became a strategy for peasant families to obtain cash income as the rural economy became increasingly monetized and the demand for rural labor remained stagnant.

Young women were the first to migrate. Discrimination against women in agricultural, commercial, and service activities in rural areas meant that male children had better local employment opportunities than female children. Furthermore, the growth of the cities, and especially of the urban middle and upper classes, created a large demand for domestic servants—a secure and stable occupation for female migrants to the city.

The Proletarianization of Peasant Smallholders

Migration of some family members provided a survival strategy for core peasant families because it allowed them to subsist in the countryside, even as living conditions continued to worsen. At first, the strategy served to complement household farm and handicraft income, and daughters were the main members to migrate. By the beginning of the 1960s, however, migration became a sine qua non for rural social reproduction, and sons also began to migrate but most frequently to other rural areas where agricultural work was available or to the United States. A pattern of relay migration was thus established (Arizpe 1985). Because mothers and older women were left with a minimum of assistance, either female or male, their workload increased to intolerable levels: Women were now responsible for agricultural and livestock chores in addition to the work of reproduction.

One of the main problems confronting women small farmers is getting the state to provide them with the credit and technical assistance to which they are legally entitled. Often a woman's brother, cousin, or nephew uses this as a pretext to take control of her allotted land. In any event, deprived of access to credit, technology, and other inputs, women are prevented from substantially improving the productivity of their land.

Older women who have no access to land as protection are often driven out by their families because of their low household incomes. This situation has led to a new and most cruel form of rural female migration—that of women over the age of fifty.

Semiproletarianized peasant households show a very clear pattern of female migration by age (Arizpe 1978). After the stage of greatest female migration—of single women between the ages of fifteen and twenty-two—there is a slowdown in the rate of female migration, particularly of married women up to the age of fifty. After this age, migration of both married women with their husbands and widows increases slightly. These older women end up either begging for a living or "imposing upon" a relative in the city.

As a result of this pattern, there is an important intergenerational differentiation in women's work. The workload of mothers in reproductive and productive activities tends to increase over their life-cycle because their daughters are now integrated into the labor market. Any agrarian policy or development program directed toward women in semiproletarian households—now the majority in the Mexican countryside—must take these generational differences into account.

This semiproletarianization process of rural families fosters greater heterogeneity in women's productive participation, ranging from increased unremunerated family labor on the land to full integration into the wage labor market. This observation concurs with the findings for the Andean region where Deere and León (1982) have shown that no unilineal or determinant relationship exists between the process of capitalist development and the gender division of labor in production. In their study Deere and León showed that women's participation in production varies according to the specific tasks that need to be performed, forms of labor recruitment, and the class position of the family. Further studies of semiproletarianized households in Mexico are needed to specify the changes in women's participation.

The Proletarianization of Rural Women

The single most important process affecting rural women in Mexico since the 1960s has been their entry into the rural labor market. The percentage of women in the rural wage labor force rose from 2.8 percent in 1970 to 5.6 percent in 1975. Although most women wage workers belong to peasant households, the pattern is changing, and many now come from landless proletarian households.

Mexican women become proletarianized in one of four ways. In one form, the household remains in the community, and all family members seek wage work in the immediate area. Mothers and daughters work either in agriculture or in sporadic jobs almost always related to domestic service. The second form also involves the family members' remaining in the community and doing wage labor at home in a variant of the putting-out system. This type of wage labor, which involves mostly sewing and assembly of consumer goods, is shifting from urban to rural households. Work is subcontracted to rural women by middlemen who come from the cities. This new kind of home work provides an alternative to migration.

The third option involves seasonal migration toward the regions of commercial agriculture. An important feature of this migration is that the women usually travel with their families. These people, whether married or single, live under the worst conditions, receive the lowest wages, and suffer from constant physical exhaustion, poor food, and broken family lives (Díaz and Muñoz 1978; Roldan 1982). Their children cannot attend school, and there is a high incidence of alcoholism and desertion by spouses. No legislation has been passed to protect these agricultural laborers; they are not unionized, and no government programs address either their needs or those of their children. Because they are often subjected to abuse and sexual harassment, young women prefer not to work as migrant agricultural workers.

Migrant women employed in agribusiness—located mostly in the northwest zone of the country—work under similar conditions (Roldan 1982). Young peasant women employed in agro-industry in their own region work under slightly better conditions. They live in their own homes (rather than in barracks), and although their wages are low and they receive practically no benefits, at least going out to work opens up a whole new world for them (Arizpe and Aranda 1981). This research has shown, however, that even when women are wage earners in their own right, they are not necessarily guaranteed more autonomy or authority within the family.

The massive entry of rural women into wage labor makes it imperative that legislation be enacted that takes into account their economic and social conditions and that programs be set up to provide them with technical and educational training. Of particular concern is the fact that the majority of jobs now available to rural women, including home-based work, are quite precarious. Employers take advantage of the fact that women get married or become pregnant to dismiss them; often as a result young women who have already left their families or communities become drifters with little hope of finding permanent work. One consequence, common all along the U.S. border, is that the women end up in prostitution.

These trends suggest, especially as the financial crisis deepens, that the proletarianization of rural women and their families will continue to increase. The priority given to export agriculture, together with greater control by multinationals, will drive more women into the wage labor force. What is alarming is that the proletarianization of rural women still remains "invisible" both to the state, responsible for agrarian policy, and to the social institutions in a position to offer rural women assistance.

Conclusions

Some important conclusions emerge from the foregoing analysis of the impact of agrarian policies on the situation of rural women. First, a given policy will affect rural women differently, depending on whether it is conceived of as an "agrarian" or an "agricultural" policy. As explained in the first part of the chapter, the Mexican agrarian reform established the ejido as an integrated social organization: By redistributing land, it strengthened the peasant economy as a way of life, not just as a specific productive activity. Although women were not designated as beneficiaries of specific programs—because the policy supported the family and the community as basic social units—the gender division of labor was subject to the equilibrium inherent in the peasant economy.

Thus, although women were still exclusively responsible for the tasks of social reproduction, they had some advantages in terms of social position. For example, they engaged in income-generating activities such as cottage industries, handicrafts, and petty trade. The labor exchange network—a mechanism that maintained labor force equilibrium among households in the community—enabled them to avoid an overload of work. Likewise, the community sheltered and protected widows, divorcées, and single mothers.

The process of proletarianization ushered in a new era in the gender division of labor, which became markedly differentiated. The incursion of manufactured goods and large-scale trade into rural communities deprived women of many of their income-generating, home-based activities, and, with the reduction in peasant income levels, the need to obtain cash income became a priority, precipitating the migration of young women to the cities. The workloads of senior female household members increased, and young women faced a discriminatory and exploitative rural labor market.

Given this situation, an agricultural policy focusing exclusively on productive activity not only does not support women but actually makes them economically and socially more vulnerable. An agricultural policy that gives priority to production of export crops might create female employment, but by being defined narrowly as an "agricultural" policy it does not take responsibility for the deplorable working conditions prevalent in the majority of the jobs it generates. Its aim, as a policy, is only to sustain economic growth or to service the debt of an urban and industrially oriented development model. By the terms of this model, the fact that rural women have suffered rapid proletarianization is only incidental to agricultural policy.

The aim of an agrarian policy based on land distribution is, on the other hand, to develop peasant society and enable it to supply the rest of the country with the necessary food and raw materials. This type of policy must provide rural women with the resources they need to be subjects of rural development and agents of their own social transformation rather than objects—disposable labor—of a growing economy benefiting only urban elites.

An agrarian policy, therefore, must support the productive activities of rural families and generate new productive activities for young women while providing them with the necessary technical and professional training. Ejidatarias and female smallholders must, in turn, be assured of access to credit, inputs, technology, and extension services.

In sum, to the extent that a peasant economy is still viable, the impact of agrarian policies upon rural women will largely depend upon the internal equilibrium of households and communities. However, since rapid proletarianization is well under way, a policy that fails to include programs specifically targeting women will only put them at a further disadvantage in the rural labor market.

When these policies are narrowly conceived as agricultural rather than agrarian, their negative impact is increased. The result of ignoring the serious social consequences of promoting commercial—and above all export—agriculture is the illegal and deplorable conditions under which proletarianized rural women currently must work.

Until there is an agrarian conception of rural development that explicitly includes rural women, and until the labor legislation and technical and social support they need is forthcoming, the peasant social base in the countryside will continue to erode. As long as this erosion continues, the future confronting rural women will be one of increasing exploitation, alienation, and economic insecurity.

Acknowledgments

This chapter was translated by Katherine Pettus.

Notes

1. L. Arizpe helped develop this program, which was set up by former Undersecretary for Agrarian Organization Beatriz Paredes; it was coordinated by Margarita Velazquez.

2. The program ran into budgetary and other restrictions, and most of the people involved in setting it up had left the ministry by 1985. It still continues, largely in conjunction with the National Population Council (CONAPO), which, in the Mexican government, is the main policy-making body in charge of women's programs.

References

Aranda, Ximena, and José Blanco, "El Desarrollo de la crisis 1970–76," in R. Cordera, ed., *Desarrollo y crisis de la Economia Mexicana* (Mexico: Fondo de Cultura Económica (FCE), 1981).

Arizpe, Lourdes, "Las mujeres migrantes y economía campesina: Analysis de una corriente migratoria a la ciudad de Mexico 1940–70," *América Indígena* 38, no. 2 (April–June 1978):303–326.

_____, "Relay Migration and the Survival of the Peasant Household," in Gorge Balán, ed., *Why People Move* (Paris: UNESCO, 1983).

_____, and Josefina Aranda, "The 'Comparative Advantage' of Women's Disadvantages: Women Workers in the Strawberry Export Agribusiness in Mexico," *Signs* 7, no. 2 (1981):453–473.

Barbieri, Teresita, et al., "Un estudio de dos UAIM," Mexico, ILO, 1981, mimeo.

Blanco, Jose, "El Desarrollo de la crisis 1970–76," in R. Cordera, ed., *Desarrollo y crisis de la Economia Mexicana* (Mexico: FCE, 1981).

Chavez, Martha, *El Derecho Agrario en Mexico* (Mexico: Porrua).

Deere, Carmen, and Magdalena León, "Producción Campesina, proletarización y division sexual del trabajo en la zona andina," in M. León, ed., *Las trabajadores del Agro* (Bogotá: ACEP, 1982).

Díaz Ronner, Lucia, and Ma. Elena Muñoz Castellanos, "La mujer asalariada en el sector agrícola," *América Indígena* 38, no. 2 (April–June 1978):327–334.

Fabila, Manuel, *Cinco siglos de Legislación Agraria* (Mexico: Centro de Estudios Históricos del Agrarismo en Mexico (CEHAM), 1982).

Guttelman, Michel, *Capitalismo y Reforma Agraria* (Mexico: Editorial ERA, 1974).

Hewitt de Alcantara, Cynthia, *La Modernizacion de la Agricultura Mexicana* (Mexico: Edicion Siglo XXI, 1979).

Luiselli, Cassio, and Jaime Mariscal, "La crisis agrícola a partir de 1965," in R. Cordera, ed., *Desarrollo y crisis de la Economía Mexicana* (Mexico: FCE, 1981).

Macias, Ruth, et al., *El Desarrollo agrario en Mexico y su marco jurídico* (Mexico: Centro Nacional de Investigaciones Agrarias (CENIA), 1982).

Montes de Oca, Rosa Elena, "La cuestión agraria y el movimiento campesino," in R. Cordera, ed., *Desarrollo y crisis de la Economía Mexicana* (Mexico: FCE, 1981).

Naciones Unidas, "Examen de las Políticas y Estratégias de Reforma Agraria en Mexico," Report No. 1, Rome, 1983.

Paré, Luisa, *El proletariado Agricola en Mexico* (Mexico: Siglo XXI, 1977).

Reyes Osorio, Sergio, *Estructura Agraria y Desarrollo Agrícola en Mexico* (Mexico: FCE, 1972).

Rodriguez, Gonzalo, "Tendencia de la producción agropecuaria en las dos ultimas decadas," *Economía Mexicana* (Mexico: CIDE), no. 2, 1980.

Roldan, Martha, "Subordinación Genérica y Proletarización Rural: Un estudio de caso en el Noroeste Mexicano," in M. León, ed., *Las trabajadores del Agro* (Bogota: ACEP, 1982).

Secretaría de la Reforma Agraria, *Ley Federal de Reforma Agraria* (Mexico: SRA, 1985).

Young, Kate, "Modes of Appropriation and the Sexual Division of Labor: A Case from Oaxaca, Mexico," in A. Kuhn and A. Wolpe, eds., *Feminism and Materialism* (London: Routledge and Kegan Paul, 1978).

5

Colombian Agricultural Policies and the Debate on Policies Toward Rural Women

Magdalena León

In 1984, the National Council on Political Economy approved the first explicit policy toward rural women in the history of Colombian agrarian policy.[1] The current concern with peasant women and the potential scope and viability of the new policy, which is embodied in a document entitled "Policies on the Role of Peasant Women in Agricultural Development," can only be evaluated in terms of the agrarian policies designed, ratified, and implemented in Colombia during recent decades. The 1961 Agrarian Reform Law, which sought to redistribute land, and the Integrated Rural Development Program (DRI), which aimed at stabilizing the peasant economy, constitute the cornerstones of Colombian agrarian policy. Neither approach was able to transform the peasant sector.

The Agrarian Reform Program

During the 1950s, Colombian industrialization was guided by a policy of import substitution.[2] The agricultural sector, however—the *latifundia-minifundia* system that had developed with high indices of property concentration—was marked by unequal distribution of wealth and income and was locked into a land tenancy structure that was unable to support the rapid development of commercial agriculture. According to the 1960 Agrarian Census, more than one million peasants (86 percent of the landholders) held only 15 percent of the total land area and farmed parcels that measured less than 20 hectares. Only 8,000 landowners (0.7 percent of the total) held 41 percent of the land, owning estates larger than 500 hectares. Large numbers of peasants had been evicted from their lands and were employed in unstable conditions under productive systems that generated backward and conflictual social relations.

The goal of the 1961 Agrarian Reform Law was to modernize agriculture by strengthening the small peasant landowning class. Motivated both by fear of the example of the Cuban Revolution and by the desire to bypass the problem of urban unemployment by keeping the rural population in the countryside, the law's approach was reformist, derived from the tenets of the Alliance for Progress, rather than constituting part of a broader development strategy.

The reform's authors saw the nascent industrialization process endangered by the narrow internal market for manufactured goods, a direct reflection of low peasant incomes. They hoped that land redistribution would result in income redistribution, which would broaden the market for manufactured goods. According to one analyst, the agrarian reform's ultimate goal was to promote capitalist development in the countryside and resolve certain economic and social contradictions (Machado 1984:56).

The practical failure of the agrarian reform demonstrated that Colombian agriculture, continuing the trend of the 1950s toward land concentration, was irrevocably on the path of consolidation of large capitalist properties. The 1970 Agrarian Census showed that the land consolidation process had in fact intensified during the 1960–1970 agrarian reform decade. The agrarian reform had only affected 18,300 hectares and had directly benefited a mere 12,570 families. For the peasant economy, property concentration and development of commercial agriculture accelerated the process of proletarianization and increased rural-urban migration. Pressure on the rural sector was channeled into the development of a peasant movement that initially took the form of administrative participation in the agrarian reform itself; it later entered a period of internal conflicts that weakened its ability to effectively challenge agrarian policy during the 1970s.

The conception of the agrarian problem that had inspired the 1960's agrarian reform underwent rapid transformation at the beginning of the following decade. The reform moved to a secondary place in agrarian policy, and an attempt was made to dismantle it in order to provide greater security for private ownership and thus to create the conditions for rural capitalism to develop.

The Chicoral Accord of 1973 became the legal instrument of the new policy. Law 4a, by exempting land that met the minimum productivity and yield criteria from the reform, made expropriation almost impossible and determined the standard of capitalist development to govern the countryside. Law 5a established mechanisms for capitalization of the farm sector, restructuring credit to favor capitalist production and opening the way for modernization. The policy's emphasis on the need to mechanize in order to raise productivity dealt yet another blow to the already deteriorating peasant economy.

Despite this reversal, the peasant economy retained its presence in the agrarian panorama, and its dynamic of reproduction brought it into the purview of subsequent agrarian policies. Throughout this period, the peasant sector continued to be an important producer of foodstuffs, particularly labor intensive crops.

The Program of
Integrated Rural Development

The Integrated Rural Development (DRI) program was designed as a government-sponsored alternative to the agrarian reform, which had all but halted. The activities of INCORA (Instituto Colombiano de Reforma Agraria), the institute charged with its implementation, had been drastically cut back, and national discussion of the reform had receded. Land policies, whether implicit or explicit, have been absent from development programs of subsequent administrations. The DRI, which as one analyst remarked was "a substitute for a real agrarian reform" (Fajardo 1983:135), functions in a conceptual framework that considers the development of capitalist agriculture and the modernization of peasant agriculture to be both compatible and viable.

The DRI was designed as the production component within PAN, the National Food and Nutrition Plan, formulated as a response to the critical level of malnutrition afflicting the labor force. Because malnutrition—in addition to contributing to high health costs for a considerable sector of the population—was having direct negative effects on production and on the possibilities for training and educating the labor force, the DRI was a multisector strategy, emphasizing food production and distribution as well as health, hygiene, and nutrition education. As the production component of this policy to resolve the food problem, the DRI tried essentially to convert peasants potentially able to increase their efficiency and income into small entrepreneurs. To help the peasant economy generate certain levels of productive employment and absorb the new technology, the government developed a series of credit, technical assistance, infrastructure, and social service programs for the DRI's target population.

Primarily because its focus on the middle-upper stratum of the peasantry precipitated further social differentiation, and second because its coverage was so limited, the DRI failed to stabilize the peasant economy. Potential beneficiaries of the DRI program were farmers owning parcels between 1 and 20 hectares in size (in noncoffee producing areas). The DRI program reached an estimated 20 percent of the potential beneficiaries at most and systematically excluded smallholders, the poorest peasants (Garcia 1983:32).

A 1983 evaluation of the DRI program made it clear, just as had prior evaluations of the Green Revolution and the Plan Puebla project in Mexico (de Janvry 1981), that the success of such programs is contingent upon the access to land (Fajardo 1983:125). The extent to which new technologies alone can help peasants to increase food production is limited if they do not have sufficient access to land. In the zone where the peasantry had the best lands and a good location with access to markets—conditions not applicable to the majority of peasants in Colombia—the DRI program results were, not surprisingly, positive.[3]

The present government has announced its intention of modifying certain aspects of the DRI program, reaffirming the underlying food supply problem by pointing out that, since commercial agriculture is fundamentally committed to producing raw materials for industry and export crops, the peasant sector (which declined from 61.4 percent of the total population in 1950 to 36.4 percent in 1980) must meet the expanding urban economy's demand for food. It is estimated that the peasant economy produces 40 percent of all nonprocessed foods for direct human consumption and almost 20 percent of all agricultural raw materials for industry (Machado 1985:15).

Through a series of subprograms focusing on production, commercialization, infrastructure, and community and social development, the new DRI program aims to raise the incomes and living standards of peasant producers. Other objectives are to raise production and rationalize the market, thereby creating productive employment for family members and perhaps even wage employment in the peasant sector. It is hoped the program will promote and strengthen peasant organization.

This new dynamic, which is part of a plan to reactivate domestic demand, seeks to increase agricultural productivity, favoring food production for the internal market. It has suffered, however, from the 1984/85 IMF stabilization program, which has caused the peasant economy to deteriorate still further, polarized the commercial agriculture-peasant economy relation and increased tensions in the countryside and urban areas (Machado 1985:36–37). The DRI proposal "to design and promote measures to qualitatively improve the situation of rural women" as part of the project to raise family living standards (Departmento Nacional de Planeacion 1984b:59) was presented just as this economic crisis—which is expected to seriously affect government social policies—was getting under way.

Policies for Peasant Women

The "Policy on the Role of Peasant Women in Agricultural Development" noted at the beginning of this chapter, and the announcement by the DRI (which in its coordinating function has assumed responsibility for executing the policy) were indications that, for the first time in Colombian agrarian policy, the existence and presence of rural women had been acknowledged.[4]

Two factors can account for this acknowledgment—the growing body of research on Colombian rural women and the current international focus on women as food producers. Social science research of peasant economies has provided convincing evidence that these economies are based on the family labor force. The analysis of the sexual division of labor within peasant households has highlighted the important role of rural women.[5] In addition, it has been demonstrated that the development of commercial agriculture often relied upon female wage workers, especially in the Sabana de Bogotá floral industry.[6]

From these studies some general conclusions have emerged regarding rural women's participation in production and their social subordination:

1. Rural women's participation in peasant production and in the agricultural labor market has been statistically underestimated in recent censuses.[7]

2. The sexual division of labor in productive work varies widely according to region, specific agricultural tasks performed, modes of labor contracting, and the class position of the household.

3. Rural women by themselves do not constitute a homogeneous category, and analysis of their position must take into account the social differentiation of the peasantry. Women from the poorest stratum of the peasantry show a greater tendency to participate in agricultural production. The higher presence of women in food production is, therefore, an expression of rural poverty or pauperization of the peasantry.

4. When an agricultural labor market develops, men are the first to become proletarianized whereas women assume responsibility for subsistence agricultural production, almost as an extension of their domestic work. The labor market also offers different opportunities for men and women. Women are found in the lower paying jobs—the tedious, repetitive, labor intensive activities that appear to be extensions of their domestic tasks.

5. The development of the floral agro-industry has created employment for women, the majority of whom are recruited from the peasant sector. Their participation in wage labor means a double workday; the rhythms and organization of domestic work are subordinate to the demands of the capitalist workplace.

6. The sexual division of labor and the subordination of women are the products of interrelated economic, political, and ideological factors.

7. The gender division of labor in agricultural production must be considered a concrete manifestation of the subordinate position of women rather than the root of women's subordination.

Faced with the growing world food crisis, international development agencies have emphasized the importance of peasant women—who are disproportionately represented in the rural population—in food production. For example, in the resolutions of the World Conference of the UN Decade for Women (Copenhagen 1980), which signified a step forward with respect to recognition of the problems faced by rural women,

> the importance of women in food production was recognized, and the need to increase food production at the level of the family unit was insisted upon. To do this, it was requested that women be given access to the necessary resources to increase their productivity, thus assuring the food supply both for the family and the community. (CEPAL 1984:3)

The International Fund for Agricultural Development (IFAD), which seeks to increase food production and raise income and nutritional levels in the poorer sectors, pointed out in its evaluation of the Decade for Women that

> the failure to recognize that rural women need assistance in their own right hinders production, skews income distribution, and detrimentally affects nutrition. Support of rural women may prove to be the best means to substantially reduce poverty . . . in Latin America. Women's contribution to production and marketing is significant. . . . Women who are small, marginal landowners have the most responsibility for food production. (IFAD 1985:2-3)

Proposals such as these are presented at international seminars and considered at a national level by interested governments.[8]

The broader goal of the present Colombian administration's policy toward peasant women is to extract the agricultural sector from its current crisis, expressed in the reduced supply of food for domestic consumption and of raw materials for industry: "Questions of social justice aside, women are starting to play an important national economic role because they are increasingly assuming responsibility for production on the minifundio—the primary supplier of foodstuffs" (Lopez and Campillo n.d.:14).[9] As in the DRI-PAN program, the food problem, which is seen as urgent, is inspiring a new policy. In the past decade,

Colombian food imports tripled: from 400,000 tons in 1970 to 1,300,000 tons of corn, beans, lentils, and vegetables—products previously produced by small farmers—in 1983. The aim of the new policy is "to modify the present conditions of rural women's social and economic participation, enabling them to improve their productivity, increase the food supply, and raise family living standards" (Lopez and Campillo n.d.:19). In Table 5.1 Lopez and Campillo (n.d.) show the specific aims, strategies, components, and operating mechanisms that compose the general framework of the policy.

The new guidelines reflect an earlier analysis of women's participation in agricultural production and the sociodemographic changes that have taken place in rural areas.[10] Among the central points are the following:

1. Significant female participation in rural production is now being registered officially, although this participation is most common in the occupational categories of unpaid family workers and own-account workers.
2. Rural women's fertility has declined in the 1970s, especially among those over thirty, the group simultaneously showing greatest participation in production.
3. Younger women show greater migratory mobility, whereas adult women, mothers and producers, remain in the countryside.

Although the study indicates that women are increasingly working the family parcels and assuming more agricultural responsibilities as unremunerated family laborers, this phenomenon is stimulated by "the conditions underlying rural poverty" rather than by the stabilization and modernization of the peasant economy (León and Deere 1982:125).

The study concludes that priority should be given to raising women's productivity, focusing on women as direct agents of development rather than just as beneficiaries of social welfare initiatives. Traditionally, a paternalistic focus considering women as beneficiaries of services offered for their welfare marked both public and private projects to "integrate women into development." Such services include instruction in child care, nutrition, health, and food preservation; training in sewing and handicrafts (such as embroidery, postcard and doll production) for cottage industry, and improvements in housing and water purification procedures. According to the classic rural extensionism model, the purpose of rural extension work is "first, to persuade and assist farmers to increase agricultural production through adoption of improved practices and techniques, and second, to improve family living conditions by teaching women home economics and by training modern young farmers in youth clubs" (Coombs and Manzur 1974:27).

TABLE 5.1
Policy on the Role of Peasant Women in Agricultural Development, Colombia

General Purpose: To change present conditions of peasant women's economic and social participation to raise efficiency in their productive work, increase the food supply, and improve living standards for peasant families.

Specific Objectives	Strategies	Elements	Operative Mechanism
1. Guarantee access to the instruments of productive work, land, credit, technical assistance, and training.	1. Bring current instruments of agrarian policy into line with growing female employment in rural areas.	-Land -Credit -Technical assistance -Marketing -Training -Education and research -Housing -Peasant organiza- tion -Nutrition	To concretize administration of this policy at the local level and ensure that reorientation of development instruments really benefit peasant women, the Rural Development Program (DRI), the Colombian Agrarian Reform Institute (INCORA), and the National Federa- tion of Coffee Growers are deve- loping a set of production pro- jects with women agricultural workers.
2. Ensure participation in income-generating projects.			
3. Stimulate participation in community organizations.	2. Intensify social actions allowing women to develop productive and domestic functions in a more favorable context.		
4. Improve the conditions for domestic labor.			
5. Increase educational levels.			

Source: Cecilia Lopez and Fabiola Campillo, "Problemas Teóricos y operativos de la ejecución de una política para la mujer n.d., p. 21, mimeo.

The sharp divisions produced by this model are reflected both in the extension workers operationalizing the policy—with men, the extension officers and agronomists, and women, the home economists, social workers, and health promoters—and in the types of concrete actions targeted at rural men and women. On one hand, this model ignores the important role of women in production, and on the other, the potential importance of men in the social aspects of the domestic unit and of the community.[11]

The new Colombian policy toward rural women aims to dismantle the traditional extensionist model in the following terms:

> The first strategy is to increase women's productivity by adapting the mechanisms of current agrarian policies to the specific needs of the women who work on the minifundio and to involve them in community and national decision-making processes. Explicit directives are considered necessary to assure women's access to credit, land, technical assistance, and agrarian research, etc.
>
> The second strategy includes social actions to improve women's overall wellbeing, but in the context where women play an important economic role. Some of the programs, like rural housing and technological training, will be implemented by the Ministry of Agriculture, while others, the health, nutrition, and formal education policies, will continue under the auspices of the social policy agencies. The main focus, however, will be on the family, rather than just on women.
>
> The most important actions are those related to land, technical assistance and credit. Legal reform will seek to increase women's access to land, guaranteeing them not only the right to participate in agrarian reform programs as direct beneficiaries, but also converting them into natural heirs of the parcel in the case of abandonment or death of the partner. Institutional changes must be made to increase available credit resources and adjust collateral requirements to working conditions and the producer's ability to repay loans. Reorientation of technical assistance is more complex and ranges from hiring female personnel and overcoming cultural barriers in some zones, to development of technological packets for products dependent upon predominantly female labor, in others. These and other activities such as those projected to increase literacy, improve the instruments of domestic work and the foster women's organizations, must be an integral part of a national campaign to raise consciousness regarding the significance of women's work in the countryside. (Lopez and Campillo n.d:19–22)

The program's short-term accomplishments, although limited primarily to projecting the policy at an institutional level, have been important. The executive agencies "have started adapting their programs and personnel to better reorient their traditional work with peasant women" (DRI-PAN 1985:1). A DRI credit line has been established at the Agrarian Bank and a Rural Women's Credit Union has been incorporated so that women can apply for loans independently and have collateral requirements adjusted to reflect working conditions. Development of an organizational and training structure for peasant women has also begun.[12]

The drive to organize rural women culminated in the first Congress of Peasant Women, held in Bogotá at the end of 1984. The Ministry of Agriculture–UNICEF project, which seeks to organize and train rural women, is attempting to consolidate a National Committee and initiate local and regional organizations.[13]

Limitations of the New Policy

Although any thorough evaluation of the rural women's policy would be premature at this point, discussion of some of its inherent limitations could prove useful. Although significant as a project to integrate women into development, the policy has serious structural limitations in terms of Colombian agrarian policy as a whole. Deeply rooted patriarchal social structures, moreover, constitute a further set of limitations not confronted directly by the policy.

Agrarian Policy as a Limitation

By not identifying the agrarian problem as one of access to land and by attributing the current crisis only to one of its direct consequences— the insufficient food supply—the framers of the policy lose sight of the basic prerequisite for real social change in the Colombian countryside. The agrarian reform, instead of redistributing land,[14] consolidated existing holdings still further, and the DRI program, though showing some gains, affected only that sector of the peasantry having sufficient access to land. Ten years from now, when the rural women policy can be evaluated from the perspective of time, this same structure barrier will be seen as limiting the policy's ability to serve as a partial strategy for reactivation of the agrarian system. Conferring the necessary gender specificity on an agrarian policy targeting the peasant sector is insufficient to even partially reverse more complex macro phenomena such as the deterioration of the agricultural sector and of the peasant economy in particular. To attempt to alleviate the immediate economic needs of peasant women without changing the structures producing the entrenched pattern of social differentiation implies a welfare bias in the policy. The sectors controlling the governmental structure have allowed the rural women's policy to be approved precisely because it does not alter the prevailing agrarian structure. Nor is the policy's implementation expected to have political repercussions that challenge this structure.

The insufficiency of the food supply cannot be attributed solely to low productivity in the peasant economy and to an inadequately trained female labor force lacking credit and technical assistance to improve yields. Rather, rising production costs have decreased profitability, forcing peasant producers to decapitalize and lower their productivity (Blanco n.d.:83).[15] Similarly, because it must purchase a portion of its basic consumption goods from the manufacturing sector, the peasant household has to earn a portion of its income in monetary form. The most common strategy is for family members to become either fully or partially proletarianized. This serves as a disincentive to food production on the family parcel. The price difference between peasant products and manufactured goods and farm inputs discourages food production and aggravates the food crisis. Although agricultural policy as a whole must be reformulated to correspond to the structural nature of the crisis afflicting the farm sector, reactivation of peasant production depends upon revising the terms of trade and establishing the necessary mechanisms to support farm prices (stocks, adequate marketing facilities, and so on).

Since women's participation and status in the peasant economy are not homogeneous, any agricultural development program must take into account the sector's social differentiation and identify the various groupings (some improving their status, others stable, and others in a state of decline). In the Andes, women's participation in farm work is most significant within peasant households in a process of decline or decomposition (where proletarianization or semiproletarianization is significant).[16] Female food producers are found in the poorest stratum of the peasantry, a crucial distinction that the rural women's policy—in referring to the peasant economy in a more or less indiscriminate manner—fails to make. As a result, the coverage of the proposed actions will probably be insufficient because of institutional inability to reach the women farmers whom the policy aims to make more efficient.

The coverage suffers from the same restrictions as the DRI program, which reached only 20 percent of the potential beneficiaries. In 1984-1985, 10,500 women received assistance primarily for income generation projects, and 3,500 additional women per year are scheduled to receive assistance through 1987 under the DRI-INCORA agreement.[17] The agreements with INCORA represent an effort to increase coverage and accelerate the process of institutional projection of the policy. INCORA itself gave technical assistance and credit to 1,316 women in 1984-1985; the target is to provide service for 1,500 women per year through 1987.[18]

Information on the qualitative impact of the program and the extent to which its goals have been achieved is not yet available. Since other program evaluations have demonstrated that coverage is an insufficient indicator of substantive achievements, it is crucial to establish a permanent evaluation system (Caro 1982).

Given the meager resources usually made available to social development projects and the current Colombian fiscal crisis and resulting public spending cuts, it is doubtful that the program will be able to meet its proposed coverage goals. The February 1985 DRI report pointed out that the women's project faced a severe budgetary shortfall since sufficient external funding had not been forthcoming and the project could not count on regular basic funding for FY 1985 (DRI-PAN 1985:4–5).

For high coverage to be achieved in the short run, skilled human and budgetary resources must be available. In this area the program faces a choice between high numerical coverage and a more reduced, but qualitatively more significant, coverage. The argument supporting a broad coverage is based on the magnitude of the problem diagnosed and the desire to distribute existing resources equitably. A qualitative approach would concentrate resources in a few given locations but at the expense of the wider visibility of the program. Although this question is fundamentally political, budgetary and human resources are constraints.

Because their traditional work styles will require basic reorientation, considerable attention must be paid to the teams that will carry out the projects in women's programs. Work with women touches very closely on ideological constructions of gender and personal self-awareness and presupposes changes in consciousness and in the human agents themselves rather than simply presentation of the policy to participating extension workers in technical terms or programming of actions as a series of goals, as is normally the case with extension agencies. Although clearly "negotiation" of the policy on peasant women in terms of poverty, living conditions, and economic development facilitated approval of a concrete policy addressing peasant women's issues, extension workers— those having direct contact with peasant women and their families—in order to be effective, must confront aspects of their own gender identity and consciousness.

The "women and development" focus is based on recognition of women's role in production and the need to raise their productivity in order to contribute to the solution of rural poverty.[19] This has been the focus of the Colombian policy on peasant women and clearly represents progress in the right direction relative to the "rural extensionism" or paternalistic focus that identifies women as beneficiaries of social policies. However, without "transforming the transformers," the qualitative effects of the policy are jeopardized. It is necessary to go one step further and focus policy explicitly on *equity*, which rather than simply trying to alleviate the poverty of rural women promotes gender equality. The focus on equality takes into account who decides, plans, designs and implements development actions, as well as who benefits from them.

Patriarchal Ideology as a Limitation

A major obstacle to the implementation of the women's policy is the deeply rooted nature of patriarchal social structures, reflected in the assumptions governing male-female relations both within the domestic unit and in society as a whole. Reproductive work, housework, and the care and socialization of children are perceived as women's natural role and, consequently, her fundamental responsibility. The very definition of a woman as a person is tied to her compliance with the obligations derived at the domestic-private level. In contrast, participation in the productive sphere defines men socially, and women's presence in production is viewed as "support" or "help" and justified primarily when it represents an extension of their domestic role. This ideological schematic buttresses differential power hierarchies for men and women in the domestic sphere and society in general.

Patriarchal ideological constructions are expressed through gender. This category is distinguished from the variable, sex, in that the latter is basically a demographic variable whereas the notion of gender is a socioeconomic and political construct encompassing sexual roles, the sexual division of labor, ideological constructions of masculinity and femininity, and self-perceptions. Gender ideology affects both men and women, and although gender is a function of the different biologies of the sexes, it is not determined biologically but socially and culturally.

The patriarchal schematic has been internalized by men and women alike to the extent that it generally remains unchallenged by either sex. Although women's increasing incorporation into social production has been unable by itself to break down patriarchy or to give women greater personal autonomy, neither has it given rise simply to new forms of subordination. Concrete conditions define the direction of change; it does not occur mechanically. Women's participation in social production is, therefore, a necessary but not sufficient condition for women's emancipation. Thus the high rate of women's participation in agricultural production in the role of unpaid family labor has not been accompanied by changes in the sexual division of domestic labor, which continues to be women's responsibility. If women continue to be solely responsible for domestic labor once their productive conditions have been improved— through training, credit, technical assistance—the result will be simply to increase the already burdensome double day and maintain previous hierarchies. The change from unpaid family labor to income generation, which is the goal of the women's policy, is no guarantee by itself that the subordination of peasant women will be overcome.

Since the specific forms and meanings of subordination vary according to social class—so that women will perceive their own subordination differently—the training programs focused on peasant women must make the ideology, meaning, and perception of gender and subordination explicit to ensure that the various forms of gender hierarchies are understood and that women themselves develop strategies to overcome them.[20] If the programs articulate women's social self-perception according to patriarchal ideology, together with the policy being offered them to change their situation, they will be able to mount an effective challenge to subordination and develop a sense of their self-identity and autonomy (empowerment). An awareness of subordination is necessary to develop ways to overcome it. Only in this way will a policy that incorporates women as actors in development also be an emancipatory project from their subordinate social position.

It will be important to see to what extent the new policy, upon facilitating women's productive work, opens up new possibilities for autonomy while imposing new restrictions. The training programs must be designed from this perspective; change can also spawn contradictions. In Third World women's programs, the policy could develop a serious paternalistic bias and exhibit contradictions between intentions and implementation if the financial and coverage difficulties discussed are not resolved in the median term (Buvinic 1984). The program's success is to a great extent a function of the pressure that organized rural women's groups can apply to ensure their access to resources. Identity autonomy, consciousness, and organization from the standpoint of gender will serve to overcome the economic, technical, and political obstacles facing the policy and provide the impetus to pressure for its application if the institutional and political context for its implementation changes, as may be the case given the financial restrictions of the stabilization program and the upcoming change of government.

It is not yet clear what kind of ideological project will result from the peasant women's organization currently being formed. If the organizational dynamic focuses simply on the technical-economic defense of the policy, it will be difficult for it to succeed or to confront patriarchal ideology, and it may easily become co-opted by other stronger organizations or by male repesentatives of the rural community.[21]

Finally, it is important to note that the policy has been formulated at a politically opportune time. Its authors say that the "political will" exists to deal with women's issues at the highest levels of government, which explains why the policy was approved in the first place. Nevertheless, they also identify a "slow response in the governmental agencies of the agricultural sector directly responsible for administering the policy," where the idea that rural women play important economic roles has not yet been totally assimilated (Lopez and Campillo n.d.:24). The presence and power of the patriarchal ideology, more commonly known in Latin America as *machismo*, are thus structural barriers at the ideological-cultural level.

A limited perspective reflecting the assimilated gender culture is characteristically held by high- or middle-level officials (male or female) who fail to perceive the economic role of rural women. To confine a policy like the one under discussion to technical aims such as solving the food crisis and improving the quality of life, when the issue is patriarchal ideology, is to court failure. The strategies and concrete actions defined in the policy, i.e., technical consciousness of women's economic role, must be accompanied by methodologies that confront the identity autonomy of gender roles among the functionaries and extension workers themselves. A more comprehensive way to approach a women's program would be to combine the issues: women's struggle to be agents of development and a process that fosters the elements strengthening identity and autonomy.

Local or regional supervisory agencies are projecting their own ideological resistance when they reject or obstruct application of the new independent credit regulations for women or claim to have cultural problems in applying the policy because they are running counter to the family unit. Also, female functionaries responsible for social assistance programs are indulging in ideological mythification deriving from their own cultural conditioning when they refuse to recognize the multifaceted roles and activities of rural women that often go beyond the traditional gender-defined categories of work.[22]

Without a doubt, the program's effort to improve economic opportunities for rural women implies changes in the political and social relations between male and female beneficiaries of the programs. These changes demand that society's cultural values be restructured. But development agencies are unprepared to modify cultural variables, and extension workers are often reluctant to implement programs of this kind. This phenomenon is reinforced when the change not only directly affects the gender roles of the beneficiaries but also challenges the roles of the extension workers. A place on the agenda for this type of discussion must be found in the regional and local seminars for extension workers to ensure that the policy becomes a personal project as well as a technical goal. The gap between intentions and implementation will be diminished to a certain extent when pressure from rural women can be combined with ideological preparation of the policy's executors.

Final Notes

The policy for peasant women represents progress in several dimensions. It involves recognition that the findings related to the economic participation of women have political implications. These political implications have translated into a development strategy that includes an explicit policy toward women, and the policy has resulted in concrete programs such as those reviewed here. Nevertheless, the policy for peasant women has been conceptualized from a reformist angle, and the following aspects must be kept clearly in mind:

1. The problem of access to land. As a structural prerequisite for the success of agrarian policies, land redistribution must respond to gender-specific needs while bringing about fundamental changes in the agrarian structure.
2. The current process of disintegration of the peasantry. The policy must be oriented to those sectors of the peasantry where women's agricultural work is indeed significant, and the necessary institutional coverage must be guaranteed.
3. The vigorous patriarchal ideology structuring society and the state. It must be attacked with methods that include both discussions of autonomy identity and technical arguments. Demystification of gender ideology must extend to the beneficiaries, so that the organizations promoted by the policy can—through the women's identity-autonomy process—generate sufficient power to struggle for women's control over their own lives and thereby to change society.

If these problems are not taken into account, the policy runs the risk of being no more than an interesting, timely project, or an advanced academic work, while disintegration of the peasant economy continues, the agricultural crisis worsens in the absence of any positive response to the problem of food production, and hundreds of thousands of rural women remain locked in a situation of chronic poverty and gender subordination.[23]

Acknowledgments

This chapter was translated by Katherine Pettus. The author wishes to thank Patricia Prieto, Fabiola Camillo, Francisco Leal, Angela Melendro, and Diana Medrano, for their comments on a preliminary version of this chapter.

Notes

1. National Planning Department, Document DNP 23109, "Política sobre el papel de la Mujer Campesina en el Desarrollo Agropecuario" Bogotá, March 17, 1984. This policy was approved by CONPES (National Council on Political Economy) on May 18, 1984.

2. The subsequent analysis is based on the following works: Fajardo (1983); Machado (1984 and 1985); Zamosc (1978); Kalmanovitz (1978); Garcia (1983); and Blanco (n.d.).

3. The reference is to the *Oriente Antioqueño*. However, this zone has received previous governmental attention through the ICA; this attention provided a material base that facilitated implementation of the DRI program. See Garcia (1983:30).

4. See the Ministry for Agriculture Program DRI-PAN "Development Project with Peasant Women," DRI-PAN-INCORA Agreement, Bogotá, March 1985, p. 3, mimeo.

5. See León (1980). In this project a team of researchers analyzed the sexual division of labor in four regions of Colombia, each exhibiting a different degree of capitalist development. Women's productive and reproductive work in the colonization zones has been analyzed by Towsend and De Acosta (1983) and Mazo and Alvarez (1983).

6. See Silva (1982) and Medrano (1982) on the floral industry and Cuales (n.d.) on agroindustry.

7. The ACEP study shows that between 44 percent and 56 percent of women thirteen years and older participate in peasant agricultural production or in the rural labor market (León 1980:285).

8. The Round Table on "Strategies for Survival in Peasant Economies: The Role of Women," organized by the Regional FAO for Latin America and the Caribbean and held in Bogotá on November 22–25, 1983, provided a strong boost for reflections on the subject. Colombia acted as host country, and after accepting this responsibility, its concern for the development of a rural women's policy at the governmental level increased.

9. The principal documents consulted were National Planning Department Document DNP-2109 UEA (1984a); Lopez and Campillo (n.d.); Campillo (1983); Ministry of Agriculture (n.d.a and n.d.b); DRI-PAN (1985); and Ministry of Agriculture—UNICEF (1984).

10. The analysis draws upon Campillo and Garcia (1984); Florez et al. (1983); Ordoñez (1983); León (1980); Deere and León (1982b).

11. An analysis of this model and its consequences is found in the evaluation of the Outreach Program of the National Federation of Coffee Growers, an organization that has had programs specifically targeting women since the 1960s. See Caro and León (1981).

12. This development is established in the Agrarian Bank Gazette No. 120, December 7, 1984.

13. These activities have been carried out through use of didactic materials designed specifically for outreach activities, such as the film *Mujer Rural*, from the Cine Mujer collective, and the "Guias de trabajo para la realizacion de Talleres Regionales de Mujeres Lideres Campesinas" (May 1985).

14. Alvaro Garcia (1983:32) concludes his analysis of the DRI program by pointing out that: "It is clear from the above that the Agrarian Reform constitutes a prerequisite for the promotion of agricultural development permitting both increased production and equitable distribution of the fruits of the process.

Without such a reform, the entire stratum of subsistence parcels and the enormous quantity of producers who are not landowners, will continue to be excluded in one form or another from the benefits of this or any other similar program."

15. The rise in production costs is the result of the use of a modern technological package. The prices of farm inputs have been rising dramatically. See Balcazar Vanegas (1982).

16. Based on a comparative analysis of Peru and Colombia. See Deere and León (1982a, 1982b).

17. Interview with Patricia Prieto, DRI official.

18. Interview with Fabiola Campillo, Ministry of Agriculture.

19. A discussion of the women and development and equity focus can be found in Buvinic (1983, 1984). The author contends that the focus on women and development has been indispensable to break down the communication barriers between those who study economic development theories and those who study the problems of women in the framework of development. I agree with this approach at the level of political strategy but consider a focus on equity also indispensable. See Kate Young (1984) for an analysis of the differences and consequences in the long run between the welfare and equity focuses.

20. The number of studies is still insufficient, particularly on this latter issue, to provide the basis for new training methodologies. Besides, training must be inscribed in the values of regional and local groups covered by the policy. Training methodologies along the lines of action-oriented research will be indispensable; the training scenario itself allows for discovery of expressions and forms taken by ideology.

21. In many documented cases, women's projects, after gaining some success, have been undermined by men, including close relatives of the beneficiaries.

22. These obstacles have already been identified in the implementation of the policy, according to interviews with Patricia Prieto, a DRI official, April 25, 1985. On the other hand, expressions like "a more concentrated focus on the family than on women" (Lopez and Campillo n.d.:22) have reinforced, at the level of the administrators, the notion that the family is an egalitarian and unquestionable unit.

23. For example, Absalon Machado (1985:38–47) provides guidelines for an alternative program for nutritional security.

References

Balcazar Vanegas, Alvaro, "El proceso tecnológico y la crisis de la agricultura en Colombia," in *Estudios Rurales Latinoamericanos* 5, no. 2 (May–August 1982).

Bejarano, Jesus Antonio, "Industrialización y Política Económica 1950–1976," in *Colombia Hoy* (Bogotá: Siglo XXI, 1978).

Blanco, Armando, "Producción campesina y capitalismo Colombiano," n.d., mimeo; forthcoming in *Estudios Rurales Latinoamericanos*.

Buvinic, Mayra, "Women's Issues in Third World Poverty: a Policy Analysis," in M. Buvinic et al., eds., *Women and Poverty in the Third World* (Baltimore: Johns Hopkins University Press, 1983).

_____ , "Projects for Women in the Third World: Explaining their Misbehaviour," International Center for Research on Women, April 1984.

Caja de Credito Agrario Industrial y Minero, *Cicular Reglamentaria No. 120*, December 7, 1984.

Campillo, Fabiola, "Situación y perspectivas de la mujer campesina en Colombia. Propuesta de una política para su incorporación al desarrollo rural," Bogotá, Ministerio de Agricultura, November 1983, mimeo.

_____ , and Carlos Garcia, *Situación social de la población rural Colombiana, 1970–1983* (Bogotá: Ministerio de Agricultura, 1984).

Caro, Elvia, "Programa de Desarrollo y participación de la mujer en Colombia," in Magdalena León, ed., *Debate sobre la mujer en America Latina y el Caribe*, vol. 1, *La Realidad Colombiana* (Bogotá: ACEP, 1982).

_____ , and Magdalena León, "Mujer rural y capacitación," Bogotá, ACEP, June 1981, mimeo.

CEPAL, *La mujer rural de America Latina: un actor social del ultimo decenio (1975–1984)*, October 1984.

Coombs, Philip, and Manzur, Ahmed, *Attacking Rural Poverty* (Washington, D.C.: World Bank, 1974).

Cuales, Sonia, "Accumulation and Gender Relations in the Flower Industry in Colombia," n.d., mimeo.

Deere, Carmen Diana, and Magdalena León, "Producción campesina, proletarización, y division sexual del trabajo en la zona Andina," in M. León, ed., *Debate sobre la mujer en America Latina y el Caribe*, vol. 2, *Las Trabajadores del Agro* (Bogotá: ACEP, 1982a).

_____ , *Women in Andean Agriculture* (Geneva: ILO, 1982b).

de Janvry, Alain, *The Agrarian Question and Reformism in Latin America* (Baltimore: Johns Hopkins University Press, 1981).

Departamento Nacional de Planeacion, Documento 2109-UEA, "Políticas sobre el papel de la mujer campesina en el desarrollo agropecuario," Bogotá, March 17, 1984a.

_____ , "El programa DRI-PAN en el plan de Desarrollo con Equidad," in *Revista Nacional de Agricultura*, No. 863, June 1984b.

DRI-PAN, "Informe sobre la situación del proyecto mujer para el desarrollo integral de la familia campesina, coordinado por el programa DRI-PAN," February 19, 1985, mimeo.

Fajardo, Dario, *Haciendas, Campesinos, y politicas agrarias en Colombia, 1920–1980* (Bogotá: Naumann Foundation, 1983).

FAO, *Estrategias de sobrevivencia en economias campesinas: el rol de la mujer*, Santiago, November 1983, DERU-G REV-1.

Florez, Carmen Elisa et al., "El Papel de la Mujer Campesina en el Desarrollo Rural" (Bogotá: CEDE [Centro de Estudios del Desarollo Económico], Universidad de los Andes, 1983), mimeo.

Garcia, Alvaro, "Un Intento de Planificación Alimentaria Integral: El Programa DRI-PAN de Colombia," OIT-PREALC, Monograph on Employment no. 35, September 1983.

International Fund for Agricultural Development, "IFAD Experience Relating to Rural Women," revised version, March 8, 1985, mimeo.

Kalmanovitz, Salomon, *Desarrollo de la Agricultura en Colombia* (Bogota: Editorial La Carreta, 1978).

León, Magdalena, *Mujer y Capitalismo Agrario* (Bogotá: ACEP, 1980).

————, and Carmen Diana Deere, "La proletarización y el trabajo agrícola en la economia parcelaria: La división del trabajo por sexo," in M. León, ed., *Debate sobre la mujer en America Latina y El Caribe*, vol. 1, *La Realidad Colombiana* (Bogotá: ACEP, 1982).

Lopez, Cecilia, and Fabiola Campillo, "Problemas teóricos y operativos de la ejecución de una política para la mujer campesina," n.d., mimeo.

Machado, Absalon, "Reforma Agraria: Una mirada retrospectiva," *Economia Colombiana*, nos. 160–161, August–September 1984.

————, "El Sistema alimentario en Colombia," paper presented at the Latin American Seminar on Agricultural Food Systems, sponsored by CEPAL-FAO, Lima, June 1985.

Mazo, Clara Ines, and Marta Alvarez, "Informe final: La mujer como agente de desarrollo en la unidad famliar y en las comunidades agricolas campesinas de la Primavera, Tierra Dentro, y la Eugenia, Bajira, Urabá," Corpurabá-Convenio Colombo-Holandés, Programa de Ayuda Agrícola Integral (PAAI), Medellin, November 20, 1983, mimeo.

Medrano, Diana, "Desarrollo y explotación de la mujer: Efectos de la proletarización feminina en la agroindustria de las flores en la Sabana de Bogotá," in Magdalena León, ed., *Debate Sobre la Mujer en America Latina y el Caribe*, vol. 1, *La Realidad Colombiana* (Bogotá: ACEP, 1982).

Ministerio de Agricultura, "El credito y los estudios de factibilidad en el programa de desarrollo de la mujer campesina del DRI," n.d.a, mimeo.

————, Caja de Credito Agrario Industrial y Minero, "Credito Rural feminino," n.d.b, mimeo.

Ministerio de Agricultura and UNICEF, "Plan de operaciones para el Proyecto: Organizacion y capacitacion de mujeres campesinas," November 28, 1984, mimeo.

Ministerio de Agricultura—Programa DRI-PAN, "Proyecto Desarrollo con la mujer campesina, convenio DRI-PAN-INCORA," Bogotá, March 1985, mimeo.

Ordoñez, Myriam, "Análisis de la situación de la mujer campesina: Características socio-demográficas de la población rural," FEI (Facultad de Estudios Interdisciplinarios), Universidad Javeriana, Bogotá, 1983, mimeo.

Silva, Alicia Eugenia, "De mujer campesina a obrera florista," in Magdalena León, ed., *Debate sobre la mujer en America Latina y el Caribe*, vol. 1, *La Realidad Colombiana* (Bogotá: ACEP, 1982).

Towsend, Janet, and Sally De Acosta Wilson, "Gender Roles in Colonization of Rainforest: A Colombian Case Study," 1983, mimeo.

Young, Kate, "Bienestar y Equidad: Alcances de esta diferencia a largo plazo," paper presented at the seminar "Participación Económico-social de la mujer en el desarrollo," Centro Flora Tristán, Lima, August 1984, mimeo.

Zamosc, León, *Los Usuarios Campesinos y las Luchas por la Tierra en los Años 70* (Bogotá: CINEP [Centro de Investigacion de Educacion Popular], 1978).

6

Women, Development, and the State in Rural Ecuador

Lynne Phillips

Changes in the Ecuadorian countryside over the past twenty years have had a dramatic effect on the lives of rural women. Yet, until very recently, neither the academic community nor Ecuadorian policymakers have shown much interest in exploring gender issues in Ecuador. In this chapter, I examine the changing experiences of rural women specifically within the context of the country's agrarian reform program implemented during the 1960s and 1970s.

Not surprisingly, the general lack of interest in Ecuadorian gender issues is reflected by the paucity of reliable material on the subject. The Ecuadorian state itself has shown little regard for the problem of gender inequalities in the countryside. For example, none of the country's agrarian reform programs has been concerned specifically with the integration of rural women. Women have been included in these programs only insofar as they are members of "families," and therefore no data exist that differentiate beneficiaries and agricultural cooperative members on the basis of gender. The typical perspective of the state on women's issues, at least until the late 1970s, is summarized in the response from the Ministry of Labour and Social Welfare to the questionnaire approved by the world conference of International Women's Year (1975): "In Ecuador those questions with special reference to women are considered inseparable from the problems of the society as a whole. For that reason, it has not been deemed necessary to initiate or stimulate within the state apparatus special agencies differentiated on the basis of sex" (Martinez 1977:9, cited in Salamea and Likes, n.d.).

When the formal "redemocratization" of Ecuador's political system began with the election of Jaime Roldos in 1978, the government appears to have taken a greater interest in integrating women in particular into national development. In 1980, an *Oficina Nacional de la Mujer* (ONM) was created, apparently thanks to Roldos' wife, Martha Bucuram.[1] The mission of the ONM was to carry out a five-year plan for women that was inserted into the five-year Development Plan (1980–1985) for the country as a whole (Buvinic 1980). A key objective of the plan was to "better the conditions of health, employment, education and work of Ecuadorian women, and particularly those of the marginal sectors of the city and countryside" (Placencia 1984:90).

However, with the death of Roldos in 1981 and subsequent changes in government, any development objectives of the ONM have been completely undercut. Under the present neo-liberal regime of Leon Febres Cordero, ONM's "outreach" to the countryside seems to be limited to organizing beauty courses for peasant women. It should also be noted that none of the Secretariat for Integral Rural Development's (SEDRI) twenty-nine rural development projects focuses specifically on the problems of rural women.[2]

Today, the only national-level data available on rural women in Ecuador are highly suspect. For example, the latest census (1982) shows that a mere 7.5 percent of the people economically active in agriculture are female and that only 7 percent of rural women are economically active. Such statistics help us little in our understanding of the situation of rural women; they indicate, more than anything, the strong gender biases inherent in categories such as "economically active."[3]

Because of the inadequacy of statistical or other national-level data on rural women in the country, researchers are obliged to rely on the few case studies available that do deal explicitly with gender issues. Existing studies on rural women in Ecuador can be divided into two basic types: (1) those that focus on the problem of the "exclusion" of rural women from national development, or what might be called the Boserup approach (see Buvinić 1980; Luzuriaga 1980), and (2) those that focus on the various roles of women within the peasant household, or what might be broadly labeled a Chayanov approach (see Balarezo et al. 1984). The latter studies, all undertaken in the sierra, emphasize the importance of women's labor to the reproduction of the peasant household, given the recent changes in the agrarian economy. The Chayanov approach implicitly rejects the first approach by focusing on the articulation of rural women's activities to capitalist development in the countryside rather than on their exclusion (Prieto 1985).

The perspective taken in this chapter differs somewhat from both these approaches. First, though the importance of the household as a unit of analysis in the study of the peasantry is undeniable, far too often the Chayanov approach limits our understanding of women's activities to self-exploitation and the need for the peasant household to reproduce itself. Obviously the indisputable inequalities between women and men within such households in Ecuador demand that we go beyond an analysis of the common interests of household members (e.g., that of household reproduction) to understand the forms of oppression and exploitation within the household, particularly those of age and gender. An approach that may help us in this respect is to view the sexual division of labor within the household as a medium and expression of the kinds of struggles taking place rather than as an outcome of the needs of such households.

Second, in evaluating the impact of Ecuador's agrarian policy on rural women, a researcher can find elements of both integration and exclusion. This finding has as much to do with class differences in the countryside as with the strong regional differences within the country itself. With regard to the latter, Ecuador's three principal regions (the coast, the sierra, and the *oriente*, or eastern Amazon) have in may ways been reinforced by differential state policies for the countryside. For example, the Agrarian Reform of 1964 was concerned primarily to eliminate the *huasipungo* system (a system in which laborers were tied to agricultural estates) in the sierra and to promote the colonization of underpopulated areas, particularly the oriente, whereas the reforms of the 1970s were directed principally at the *precarismo* system (a system of precarious tenancy within large haciendas) of production in coastal agriculture. Also, over and above differences in agricultural production, one finds considerable variations in gender ideologies (activities considered appropriate for men and women) between the country's three regions as well as within them.

In this chapter, I will focus on two of the country's regions—the sierra and the coast—since the oriente has become significant on a national level relatively recently, and no studies are available on the effects of colonization on oriente women. Also, variations within these two regions will not be emphasized so as to draw out more clearly how the relationship between gender and forms of agricultural production differs by region. In the first section, I analyze the historical differences between coastal and highland Ecuador in terms of agricultural production and the sexual division of labor. The second section focuses on the nature of the agrarian reform programs implemented by the state during the 1960s and 1970s. This section is followed by a discussion of the effects of these reforms on agriculture in the two regions. In the final section I analyze the specific situation of rural women within the context of these agrarian transformations.

Historical Background
to Sierran Agriculture

Although the causes of the differences in the forms of production on the coast and on the sierra may be traced to the Inca period,[4] the period of sierran history most important to us is the years just before passage of the 1964 Agrarian Reform Law.

Until the 1960s, the sierran agriculture system was based on the traditional hacienda (Barahona 1965) as the dominant unit of production. Land was highly concentrated within large holdings, and the relations of production were based on the extraction of rent (in kind and labor) from a largely immobile labor force. For its production of potatoes, barley, wheat, corn, and milk, the hacienda relied upon a complex set of labor arrangements: The *huasipungueros* worked four to six days a week for the *hacendado* in exchange for a small plot of land and access to pasture land; the *yanapas*, often from the nearby Indian communities, worked a couple of days a week (or paid the hacendado) for access to hacienda resources such as wood, roads, water, and pasture; the *partidarios* were sharecroppers and the *arrendatorios* cash renters; and the *peones libres* or free peons worked for wages and were either from the Indian communities or linked to the hacienda through kin ties with *huasipunguera* families (Barsky 1984; Guerrero 1975).

Although a number of different agricultural situations exist in the sierra today—developing in part from the varied social relations within the hacienda during this period—I concentrate herein principally on the huasipungo system because this was the system that the 1964 reform sought to abolish. The most significant point for our purposes is the importance of the extended huasipungo family within the hacienda context (Guerrero 1975). The extended family appears to have been a specific response to the increasing extraction of surplus labor by hacendados, on the one hand, and the decreasing ability of the nuclear huasipunguera family to reproduce itself on the other (Ferrin 1982). Thus, over and above the specified male labor of the huasipunguero (who apparently assumed this position as household head), other members of the family were expected to undertake specific tasks within the hacienda.

It is important to note that personal services within the house of the hacienda (called *huasicamía*) were expected to be undertaken by the women of the huasipunguera family. Women were also expected to do various jobs in exchange for hacienda resources, and they fulfilled any extra obligations that might be imposed as punishment on the family by the hacendado. None of these activities was remunerated, although women were paid a minimal amount (always less than the male laborers of the hacienda[5]) for their work as milkmaids. Salamea and Likes (n.d.:26) also mention the use of *pongas*. By this practice the labor of the younger women in the family was transferred from the hacienda to the convents of local priests. In exchange these women "received the indoctrination of the church without which they could not be married by the priest." This practice existed until about 1959.

A key characteristic of the extended huasipungo family was the substitution of labor categories within the family such that if one family member could not fulfill particular labor obligations to the hacienda, another would, irrespective of gender or age. Such flexibility clearly was important within the sierran family long before this period. For example, Ackerman (1977) mentions that in the early 1800s it was not uncommon to draft sierran rural women for the *trabajo subsidario*, labor that financed public works in the country.

Thus, the predominance of noncapitalist forms of labor exchanges within the sierran hacienda, the importance of women's labor to the huasipungo system, and the influence of the church and state (e.g., for road building) on rural labor and on women in particular are the factors we should keep in mind in our consideration of the coastal situation, where agricultural production differed considerably.

Historical Background
to Coastal Agriculture

Up until the 1920s, one product dominated agricultural production in coastal Ecuador: cacao.[6] The large landholding (hacienda) was also the dominant unit of production in this region, but it differed from that in the sierra in a number of important ways.

First, the Indian community was not an important form of social organization in most areas of the coast, and smallholders quickly disappeared with the rapid expansion of the cacao haciendas in the nineteenth century. Second, unlike in the sierra, the Catholic church owned very little land on the coast and had a minimal impact on the coastal laboring population. Third, the hacienda was specialized in one product that was produced by renters (*sembradores*) who were paid in cash by the hacendado. Vast areas of virgin land could be exploited on the coast, and once the cacao trees had matured (in five to seven years) the sembrador simply moved on to clear another plot, often in another hacienda. Day laborers (*jornaleros*), sometimes the sons of sembradores, then took over the care and harvesting of the matured trees. Yet in both cases, family labor was essential to the production process; sembradores were not hired unless they were "married and with a family" (Chiriboga 1980:199).[7]

Cacao production itself had a tremendous impact on the national economy—Ecuador cornered the world market by the late 1800s—and cacao hacendados had a great deal of control over the political situation in the country, often holding key political positions. Thus, hacendados were able to ensure that coastal laborers (most often in short supply) were exempt from fulfilling labor obligations for the state (e.g., military service, public works) because such labor was seen to "distract them from their specific functions" (Chiriboga 1980:35). Also, to lure sierran laborers to coastal haciendas, labor conditions were relatively better (e.g., higher wages were earned).

These points suggest that even by this early period the laboring family in the sierra had been shaped by quite different processes than such families on the coast. Although coastal agricultural production was dramatically altered after the 1920s, the lack of church and state control over the production process and the relative mobility of coastal labourers are important factors to consider in our evaluation of social relations in the countryside today.

However, with the collapse of the cacao market in the 1920s and the subsequent spread of plant diseases to cacao haciendas, cacao production was all but abandoned. This crisis period in the economy marked the first exodus of agricultural laborers to the coastal city of Guayaquil, as well as the emergence of smallholders and renters (*finqueros*) in the countryside.[8] Also during this time, a system of precarismo (precarious tenancy) for the production of short-cycle crops, especially rice, emerged as the dominant form of labor exchange within the ex-cacao hacienda.

In his literary work on the coastal peasantry during this period, De La Cuadra emphasized that rice production, both within and outside of the hacienda, was undertaken on a family basis. He noted that the roles of men and women in agricultural production were entirely interchangeable "from milking a cow to sowing rice with a digging stick" (1937:41). He also stated: "In the concerns of proper campesino tasks, the woman, with logical exclusions, is as capable and as expert as the male *montuvio*" (1937:41).[9] Of course, we do not know to which "logical" exclusions De La Cuadra is referring, but it appears that at least for the period just after the cacao crisis, family labor (and here we are noting in particular women's labor) continued to be important in agricultural production.[10]

By the late 1940s another dramatic shift had taken place in agricultural production on the coast, resulting primarily from the influx of sugar and banana interests. The large-scale production of these crops for export encourged changes in the relationship between labor and capital and, apparently, in the role of women in agricultural production. A study by Leonard (1947) indicates the emergence of a number of important features in the area that contrast with those of earlier periods: (1) medium and small, not large, landholdings are the norm, (2) mostly day laborers are being hired, (3) there is a high rate of intraprovincial migration (only one-fourth of the population of the hacienda he studied had lived there for more than ten years), and (4) women are not involved in agricultural production; "their duties are largely limited to domestic tasks" (1947:8).[11]

These economic transformations were reinforced considerably by the consolidation and expansion of the Ecuadorian state in the late 1940s. Not unrelated to this expansion was the strong U.S. presence in the country by this time. Contrary to the historical policy of rural development in the country, the Ecuadorian state was now expected to intervene in and control agricultural production; U.S. loans were made available on this condition. Thus, under the presidency of Galo Plaza (1948–1952), the United Fruit Company was welcomed to such an extent that Ecuador quickly became the world's largest exporter of bananas (Larrera 1982). Also during Plaza's presidency, much capital was invested in renovating rice and cacao production, and absentee landowners began to return to their haciendas to expel their renters and replace them with wage labor. Although this policy clearly met resistance from tenants (see, for example, Uggen 1975), as much as 52 percent of the rural labor force on the coast were independent day laborers by 1954, whereas only 2 percent of agricultural workers could be categorized as such in the sierra (Hurtado 1980).

By the early 1960s there was a strange mixture of agricultural production relations in the country. In the sierra, though the nonsalaried character of labor on many haciendas persisted, a significant number of landowners were beginning to invest in agricultural technology and to hire labor on a daily basis only. Some landowners, anticipating the coming of an agrarian reform law, voluntarily delivered land (generally poor) to resident huasipungueros to avoid the expropriation of more fertile land (Barsky 1984; Murmis 1980).[12] On the coast, though wage laborers were used on banana and sugar plantations, peasant production of rice and cacao was still important; however, it clearly was threatened by the increasing commoditization of the countryside. Not surprisingly, during this period the peasantry emerged as an important political entity in the country as a whole,[13] but at the same time the state made an unprecedented attempt to politically manipulate that entity, particularly through its agrarian reform programs.

Ecuador's Agrarian Reform

By 1964 a provisional military junta had introduced the country's first agrarian reform law. Ecuador's plans for agrarian reform were not devised independently but were closely aligned to the development ideas of the

Alliance for Progress. As is commonly pointed out, the Alliance for Progress was a U.S. vehicle for the promotion of capitalist development in Latin America, a strategy seen by the United States as essential for the prevention of another Cuban revolution.

The 1964 Agrarian Reform Law in Ecuador was developed to promote change in the specific areas of agriculture that restricted the accumulation of capital (e.g., feudal relations of production). Because the coast was regarded as more advanced in this respect, the reform law focused primarily on sierran agriculture (Verduga 1978), specifically on the huasipungo system. Thus, any huasipunguero who occupied the same plot for ten or more years automatically became its owner. Moreover, sierran haciendas could be expropriated by the state if they exceeded 800 hectares, but an additional 1,000 hectares of *paramo* (pasture) was permissible.[14]

On the other hand, when the huasipunguero did receive land it was generally the poorest in the hacienda and insufficient for the reproduction of the huasipunguera family. Furthermore, to avoid political confrontations with sierran landowners, a greater emphasis was placed on the expropriation of publicly owned lands and the colonization of new areas than on the expropriation of privately owned lands (Cosse 1984).[15] Changes in land distribution in the sierra from 1954 to 1974 reduced the share of land held by large landholdings (over 1,000 hectares) from 41 percent to 25 percent of the total to the benefit of farms in the 10 to 100 hectare size range (Censo Agropecuario 1954 and 1974).[16] Nevertheless, the concentration of land in the hands of a few persisted.

One important consequence of the 1964 reform for the country as a whole was the formation of IERAC, the Ecuadorian Institute of Agrarian Reform and Colonization. As the mediating institute between landlord and peasant, IERAC not only promoted the idea of monetary compensation to landlords in cases of land expropriation but implicitly excluded peasant women as beneficiaries by adjudicating land to the ex-huasipunguero household head only. Stolen (forthcoming) argues that in the Valle de Machachi this practice had serious repercussions on gender relations because before this time land was always bought in the name of both spouses.

Not until 1970 was a government decree (Decreto 1001) introduced that had a more radical impact on the coastal agrarian situation. With this decree, rice precarismo became illegal and ex-precaristas were to be organized into production cooperatives. These cooperatives were to be owned communally, and, in principle (although seldom in practice), at least some of its land was to be worked cooperatively.

However, little in the way of coastal reform took place until 1973, when Ecuador's second Agrarian Reform Law was passed, once again by a military junta.[17] In many ways the state's vision of agricultural progress in the country was clearest in this reform—to develop capitalist agriculture. For example, no ceilings were placed on the size of land-holdings (that the farm unit was economically efficient was considered more important; Cosse 1984), and agricultural credit was greatly expanded because of the new oil riches of the country. Land distribution figures during this period confirm that despite its rhetoric concerning land distribution, the agrarian reform had influenced the concentration of landholdings very little (Redclift 1978).

Furthermore, any transference of land that did take place primarily involved male beneficiaries; the Ley de Cooperativas implicitly discrim-inated against women by stipulating that legally both spouses could not be *socios* (members) of the same cooperative and that women needed to have authorization from their husbands to become cooperative *socias* (Titulo III, Art.17b; Art.19). Also, since the precarista contract normally involved the male household head, it is not surprising that the over-whelming majority of cooperative socios are male.

In a study of the Guayas River Basin CEDEGE (1978:17) investigators found that of the 3,147 beneficiaries polled, only 5.7 percent were women. My own research in the Vinces-Baba area (located within the basin) indicates a somewhat higher percentage: Of forty-six cooperatives in the area, 8.8 percent of the members are women. However, this average reflects the unusually large numbers of women in four or five cooperatives; 37 percent of the cooperatives have no women at all. Also, many of the female cooperative members are widows with (male) children too young to take over the role of socio.

In sum, although the country's agrarian reforms are said to have been formulated "for the campesino" (according to the laws themselves), the primary aim of the various forms of state intervention clearly was to eliminate remaining obstacles to the accumulation of capital in the countryside.[18] In the sierra, such development meant mechanizing ag-ricultural production and animal husbandry within the hacienda and promoting a process of proletarianization for industrial expansion. On the coast, it meant no intervention in banana and sugar production (already considered efficient) and the reorganization of rice production and marketing in order to feed an ever-increasing number of urban consumers. In the final section of this chapter the effects of these transformations on the specific situation of rural women are examined.

Gender Relations
and Postreform Agricultural Production

Most peasants in the sierra were freed from the hacienda only to find themselves with access to insufficient land and other resources to reproduce themselves. In our focus on the huasipunguero we must differentiate two emerging forms of organization: (1) the smallholder/ minifundista and (2) the *comunero* or *cooperativista*. In the former, though land was not delivered specifically to women through the agrarian reform, women are largely responsible for the production of such parcels. Men, on the other hand, migrate to the coast or sierran cities in search of a wage (in banana or sugar production and construction work) to supplement household income. For example, Buvinić (1980) notes that because of male out-migration, 80 percent of subsistence farms in Salcedo (Cotopaxi) are operated by women (see also Chiriboga 1984). At the same time, women in this area earn half the agricultural wages of men (MAG/IICA 1978, cited in Luzuriaga and Zuvekas 1983:116).

In the case of communal or cooperative organizations, most socios appear to be male, whereas women provide meals to the men in the fields and work on the land during peak labor periods (e.g., harvesting) (see, for example, Ferrin 1982). If the organization has cattle, the wives of the socios are responsible for milking (see, for example, Furche 1980).

In addition to women's labor on the parcels in the provision of food and in the care of domestic animals, rural women in the sierra are responsible for a wide variety of tasks, most of them undertaken in conjunction with work commonly defined as domestic. Thus, women hire themselves out as milkmaids within the capital intensive haciendas, although still for lower wages than men receive as day laborers (Barsky et al. 1984). They are also involved in various types of artisan work, such as the making of straw hats for the international market (Balarezo 1984), knitting (Gladhart and Gladhart 1980; Meier 1982), and spinning (Rosero 1982). In fact, Stolen (forthcoming) argues that sierran women in the area where she studied can undertake almost any task (with the possible exception of ploughing).

However, even though women's labor is indispensable to the survival of the peasant family—and women's activities in particular clearly preserve the "peasantness" of sierran agriculture—their labor seems to be consistently undervalued vis-à-vis that of men. This low valuation can be seen not only in the lower wages paid but in ideologies concerning the value of certain kinds of labor relative to others.

Balarezo's (1984) study of women hat weavers (producers of the so-called Panama hat) indicates that although income earned from such work exceeds that of other family members (including the male household head's income through migration), it is considered less valuable because it is spent on food rather than on durables such as clothes and shoes. Furthermore, both case studies in Balarezo et al. (1984) show that though men spend most of their time outside of the area because of migration, women still do not make decisions regarding when/what to plant on the subsistence parcel; men return home to make such decisions.[19]

Another ideological constraint placed on rural women in the sierra is the emphasis on sexual control. Stolen (forthcoming) argues that ideas about the importance of the *apellido* (family name), male sexual conquest, and female purity are important mechanisms for subordinating rural sierran women. The historical influence of the church may be key to these types of ideologies since ideologies concerning sexual control differ considerably on the coast.

In contrast to the sierran situation, women on the coast tend not to have the responsibility for the family plot, peasant production is more oriented toward the market, and new technologies, which in some cases have actually displaced the labor of women (e.g., corn grinding machines, insecticides), are controlled by men. Also, coastal women are much more restricted in their productive activities, most often referring to themselves as *domésticas no más* (only housewives). In fact, a woman working consistently in the fields may be labeled *machona*, indicating that her gender may be in question.

These points should be considered in our understanding of why women were excluded as cooperative members on the coast. The problem was not only one of the state's discriminatory policies against women within the agrarian reform program. As one male cooperative member from the Vinces-Baba area told me: "I remember we were all in agreement—'The cooperatives are only for the men,' we said. We rejected the idea of having women as members because the women '*no valen*' (are of no value)." However, he also noted that "things have changed"; more recently formed cooperatives often have more women members. A man from a cooperative formed in 1982 explained the presence of twelve women members: "We were 'collecting' members to form a cooperative and the women had nothing to do so they became members too."

Nevertheless, few women who are cooperative members work the land themselves; their mates, brothers, or sons are usually responsible for such production. Also cooperatives hire male laborers during peak labor periods rather than employing female family labor.[20] However, this is not to say that women who are attached to cooperatives through their mates or as members do not work, as is often claimed. Under the broad category of domestic tasks, such women supervise the preparation of cacao and rice for the market (these crops are dried in the sun before they are sold), degrain corn for family consumption, collect and chop wood for cooking, raise chickens and pigs for the market, sew, and attend small stores set up within their homes, as well as perform the usual tasks of cooking, caring for the children, washing clothes, cleaning the house, and sweeping the *solar* (house plot). Poorer women undertake small-scale *negocios* such as selling candies and cigarettes, wash clothes for a wage, or scavenge food from other properties, although the latter two activities are not commonly admitted. Among the poorer women in particular we can clearly identify a daily struggle with the contradictions between gender ideologies that restrict what women can do and the need to undertake certain tasks to survive.

On the other hand, though coastal women are more limited in the tasks they can do compared to sierran women, there is much more flexibility in the question of the sexual control of women. Although plural unions are common on the coast and only men are (publicly) permitted more than one mate, the unimportance of marriage and the relative unimportance of virginity in the region help to give women more flexibility in their relationships with men. For example, visiting unions and female-headed households—two arrangements that give women considerable independence from their mates—are far from unusual.[21]

Another important point in our evaluation of rural women on the coast is that, though men generally control land, waged employment, and household income (men, not women, purchase the food for the household), women generally control the network of family and friends essential to the reproduction of the household. Similar to the sierran situation, household reproduction for the coastal peasantry is precarious because most cooperatives have access to insufficient land to reproduce the family. Through such networks women can borrow foods and money and gain information about jobs for their mates/sons, resources that have become an important part of household survival. Although the literature on the sierran situation does not emphasize this point, I suspect that, given the importance of the extended family and the migration of men, rural women in the sierra have a great deal of control over such networks as well and that from such control they derive a certain amount of power within the household.

Among the networks in the countryside in which coastal women have been active are the distribution committees (organized during the disastrous floods of 1983) that still exist today. These consumer-oriented organizations buy food and other household items by bulk for distribution among cooperative members and their friends and family. This system was essential for survival during the floods, but it is just as important today given the economic squeeze that most rural households are experiencing. A brief survey of forty-three committees associated with the Union of Cooperatives in the Vinces-Baba area shows that women constitute 24 percent of the committee members, a considerably higher percentage than that for the cooperatives themselves.

Conclusions

This chapter has highlighted the importance of viewing the effects of agrarian reforms in very broad terms. Focusing only on the amount of land women received through such reforms, for example, would give us very little idea of the actual situation of rural women in the country since in most cases women were formally excluded from access to this resource. Yet the various forms of state intervention have clearly had a profound effect on women's lives.

We have been concerned here primarily with the interrelationship between the specific transformations in agriculture in the sierra and the coast and the ideologies that shape gender relations in the two regions. From this perspective the contradictions in rural women's lives become evident. For example, a review of the literature does not allow us to conclude that capitalist development in the countryside excludes or domesticates women in Ecuador. The fact that some aspects of state intervention have proletarianized the peasant household while others have reinforced its peasant character, as well as the fact that different gender ideologies are linked to these contradictory processes, indicates the extent to which such labels oversimplify the situation of rural women.

Also, because of the historical approach in this chapter, we are able to make some interesting observations regarding the relationship between gender relations and the formation/transformation of the coastal and sierran regions. Most important, we can pinpoint more precisely why there is so much more variety in the laboring activities of sierran women compared to those of rural women on the coast. For example, we have seen that as members of the huasipunguera family, sierran women were expected to fulfill obligations—within the context of a variety of power relations (with the hacendado, the church, and the state)—outside of agricultural production itself. Also, perhaps tied historically to the reproduction of the relatively independent Indian community, sierran women were (and are) important in artisan activities. Yet not only was the indigenous community not encouraged in many coastal areas, but there is some evidence that, along with smallholders, coastal artisans quickly vanished under the impact of the cacao era (Chiriboga 1980:101). Though coastal women often did domestic work within the home of the hacendado or *mayordomo*, such work was not part of the renter's or day laborer's contract with the hacendado. Thus, with the nonexistence of pongas and the exemption of coastal labor in general from obligatory labor for the state, women's productive labor on the coast was dedicated almost entirely to agriculture proper.

It is probably also significant that, given the greater access to land, higher wages, and mobility of the labor force on the coast, the reproduction of the rural coastal family did not demand such a high rate of exploitation of women's productive labor as it did in the sierra. On the other hand, perhaps because of the historically unhealthy living conditions on the coast (yellow fever and malaria have been constant problems), coastal women's labor seems to have been expanded in reproductive activities (ensuring the reproduction and indeed the expansion of a scarce labor force). Even today rural coastal women tend to bear more children than rural women in the sierra (Scrimshaw 1981).[22]

Given these historical differences, capitalist penetration in the countryside in the 1940s and 1950s and the Agrarian Reforms of the 1960s and 1970s clearly have had differential effects on the two regions and on women in particular. In the sierra, women's productive labor has been extended to an even greater degree. The lower wages paid for their labor suggests that these women generally provide a cheap labor force for the sierra, whereas the multidimensional character of their activities helps to buffer the peasant household from complete proletarianization. On the coast, capitalist production for export undercut the need for family labor, and new technology in agriculture tended to replace the few agricultural activities that rural women did undertake by the 1970s. Placing redistributed land in the hands of men only reinforced women's unequal access to resources in the countryside.

Despite the more rigid sexual division of labor on the coast and the coastal women's clear dependence on the monetary resources of men, the sexual division of labor appears to be the reason that women have been able to maintain control over noncapitalist relations (e.g., kin), which have become essential for day-to-day survival during the current economic squeeze. On the one hand, this situation suggests that changes on the coast have increased women's labor in reproduction (both in terms of the reproduction of noncapitalist relations and of the higher birth rate of coastal women) and, on the other hand, it indicates that although the sexual division of labor on the coast has constituted the basis for the exclusion of women from the direct benefits of the agrarian reform, it has also been the means through which coastal women have gained a certain degree of power over their daily lives (e.g., in consumer organizations). This latter point indicates that although the sexual division of labor may be the basis of women's oppression in Ecuador, it may also be the medium through which these women struggle with that oppression. Such an argument, however, awaits further research.

Notes

1. A decree passed in 1970 legally introduced such an office, but the ONM did not exist in fact until 1980 (*Nueva Mujer* 1982:30).

2. Thanks to Susana Balarezo for this point. SEDRI is the Secretariat for Integral Rural Development.

3. However, for those interested in more discussion of the census data and women's salaried work see Farrell (1983), Finn and Jusenius (1976), and Luzuriags (1980).

4. The Incas were never nearly as successful at integrating the coastal population of Ecuador into a system of tribute as they were with the sierrans. This factor greatly influenced the ability of the Spanish to control the coastal population at the time of the conquest because the coast clearly lacked social systems of centralized production (e.g., Indian communities) onto which the Spanish could graft their demands.

5. The CIDA (Comité Interamericano de Desarrollo Agrícola) report (1965) cites the example of one hacienda in Pichincha where the eight permanent workers "were paid S./6 per day, the same rate paid to twenty-five additional workers at harvest time. Wives and other family members serving as milkmaids received S./4 per day" (cited in Luzuriaga and Zuvekas 1983:109).

6. The analysis of coastal Ecuador is limited to material from the Guayas River Basin.

7. Male *jornaleros* were paid three pesetas (about one sucre) a day, the women, two pesetas and children from eight to fourteen years, one (Weiner, cited in Guerrero 1980:30).

8. Finqueros cultivated long-cycle crops such as bananas and cacao.

9. The montuvio (the coastal rural laborer whether he or she is technically a peasant or a wage hand) is often characterized as independent, melancholy, oversexed, and violent—a stereotype that differs considerably from the docile, subserviant "Indian" characteristics attributed to the sierran rural laborer (Middleton 1979).

10. On the other hand, one should note that the Labour Code for the country during this period (1938) stipulates differential wage rates for men and women: "The minimum salary of women will be equal to 1/3 of that earned by a day labourer or agricultural worker over 18 years old" (cited in Salamea and Likes n.d.:27).

11. This is the earliest statement that I found referring to the fact that coastal women did not work in the fields. At least three explanatory factors should be considered in understanding how and why this was the case: the rapid expansion of Guayaquil, which involved an increased demand for domestic service, the more extensive use of wage labor (sugar and banana production were based clearly on the use of male wage labor), and the (by then) abundant supply of laborers on the coast.

12. Through what has been called landlord initiative, 15 percent of huasipungo plots were handed over to huasipunguera families before the 1964 Reform Law (Cosse 1984:32).

13. For the sierra, see Guerrero (1984), Velasco (1979); for the coast, see Redclift (1979), Uggen (1975). Guerrero mentions that one of the peasant demands in the sierra during this period was the abolition of women's domestic service obligations to the hacienda.

14. Coastal landowners could own 2,500 hectares of land plus 1,000 hectares of pasture without fear of expropriation.

15. Cosse (1984:32) points out that land holdings offered through colonization was considerably larger in size than those redistributed within the hacienda. He suggests that this policy tended to promote a "farmer" road of agricultural development in previously unoccupied areas of the country and at the same time encourge capitalist investment/proletarianization within existing haciendas.

16. This is not to argue that the agrarian reform was the sole cause of such changes. Here it is important to note a debate in the country that centers on whether the changes in the Ecuadorian agrarian structure were a result of independent technological innovations within a modernizing agriculture, the response of landlords to the increasing resistance and political organization of the peasantry, or state intervention (see especially Barsky 1984 and Guerrero 1984).

17. Between the two reform laws, Ecuador returned to civilian rule, although direct efforts toward agrarian reform seemed to be limited during this time.

18. This process was reinforced further by the *Ley de Fomento y Desarrollo Agropecuario* passed in 1979. Its main purpose was to "increase production and productivity of the agricultural sector in an accelerated and continual way, to satisfy the food requirements of the Ecuadorian population, to produce exportable surpluses and to provide raw material for national industry" (Titulo I, Art. 1b).

19. This situation may in fact be reinforced by the state. A SEDRI engineer told me that it was difficult to organize project meetings in Salcedo because the area is *pura mujeres* (only populated by women); he thus waits until the weekends when the men return.

20. On the other hand, in the coastal province of Manabí, located outside the Guayas River Basin, coffee is harvested almost entirely by women. However, the history of Manabí is quite distinct from that of the basin proper (see PUCE-CIID 1983).

21. In a survey of 107 households in the Vinces area, 23 percent were female headed (Phillips 1985). Women prefer *compromisos* (consensual unions) over legal marriages.

22. Scrimshaw found that coastal village women have approximately two living children more than sierran village women (1981:283). Although there are references to the practice of infanticide in the sierra (Luzuriaga and Zuvekas 1983:102, 118), I have found no historical evidence of this practice on the coast. McKee (1980) suggests that indirect female infanticide still exists in the sierran countryside because male children are breastfed up to a year longer than female children. In contrast, on the coast it is often considered inappropriate to breastfeed male children for too long because they may become too *bravo* (ill-tempered) or *amoroso* (amorous—a trait often considered the cause for men's involvement in plural unions) once they become adults.

References

Ackerman, S., *The Trabajo Subsidario: Compulsory Labour and Taxation in Nineteenth Century Ecuador*, Ph.D. thesis, New York University, 1977.

Balarezo, S., "Tejedoras de Paja Toquilla y Reproducción Campesina en Cañar," in S. Balarezo et al., eds., *Mujer y Transformaciones Agrarias* (Quito: CEPLAES [Center of Planning and Social Studies], 1984).

_____, O. Barsky, L. Carrion, P. De La Torre, R. Rosero, and L. Salamea, *Mujer y Transformaciones Agrarias* (Quito: CEPLAES, 1984).

Barahona, R., "Una tipología de haciendas en la sierra ecuatoriana," in O. Delgado, ed., *Reforma Agraria en América Latina* (Mexico: Fondo de Cultura Económica, 1965).

Barsky, O., *La Reforma Agraria Ecuatoriana* (Quito: FLACSO [Latin American Faculty of Social Sciences], 1984).

_____, L. Carrion, P. De La Torre, and L. Salamea, "Modernización Hacendal y Nuevos Roles de la Mujer Campesina," in S. Balarezo, et al., eds., *Mujer y Transformaciones Agrarias* (Quito: CEPLAES, 1984).

Buvinić, M., "Una Estrategia para la Mujer en el Ecuador," Centro Internacional de Investigaciones sobre la Mujer, 1980, manuscript.

CEDEGE (Comisión de Estudios para el Desarrollo de la Cuenca de Guayas), "Primer Censo a las Organizaciones Campesinas de la Llanura del Daule," Guayaquil, 1978, manuscript.

Chiriboga, M., *Jornaleros, y Gran Propietarios en 135 años de Exportación Cacaotera (1790–1925)* (Quito: Consejo Provincial de Pichincha, 1980).

_____, "Campesinado andino y estrategias de empleo: El caso Salcedo," in M. Chiriboga, G. Ramon, J. Sanchez-Parga, A. Guerrero, J. Durston, and A. Crivelli, eds., *Estrategias de Supervivencia en la Comunidad Andina* (Quito: CAAP [Center of Artists for Popular Action], 1984).

Cosse, G., *Estado y Agro en el Ecuador* (Quito: FLACSO, 1984).

De La Cuadra, J., *El Montuvio Ecuatoriano*, Instituto de Investigaciones Económicas de la Universidad Central del Ecuador, 1937.

Farrell, G., "Participación de la mujer en el sector moderno de la economía," *Revista Economía y Desarrollo* (Quito: IIE-PUCE, 1983).

Ferrin, R., "De la forma huasipungo de trabajo a la economía comunitaria: Un caso de transformación de las relaciones sociales de producción," in C. Sepulveda et al., eds., *Estructuras Agrarias y Reproducción Campesina* (Quito: IIE-PUCE, 1982).

Finn, M., and C. Jusenius, "La posición de la mujer en la fuera laboral de Ecuador," *Estudios Andinos*, ano 5, vol. 5 (1976):99–116.

Furche, C., "Lógica de funcionamiento interno y racionalidad económica en empresas campesinas: El caso de las cooperativas en el Canton Cayambe," in O. Barsky et al., eds., *Ecuador: Cambios en el Agro Serrano* (Quito: FLACSO/CEPLAES, 1980).

Gladhart, P., and E. Gladhart, "The Sweater Industry of Mira, An Account of a Regional Cottage Industry Developed by Rural Women" (Quito: AID [Agency for International Development], 1980).

Guerrero, A., *La Hacienda Precapitalista y la Clase Terrateniente en America Latina y su Inserción en el Modo de Producción Capitalista: el Caso Ecuatoriano* (Quito: Universidad Central, 1975).

_____, *Los Oligarcas del Cacao* (Quito: El Conejo, 1980).

————— , *Haciendas, Capital y Lucha de Clases Andina,* 2nd ed. (Quito: El Conejo, 1984).

Hurtado, O., *Political Power in Ecuador* (Albuquerque: University of New Mexico Press, 1980).

Larrera, C., "Transnational Companies and Banana Exports from Ecuador, 1948–72," *North South* 7, no. 14 (1982):3–42.

Leonard, O., "Pichilingue, A Study of Rural Life in Coastal Ecuador," U.S. Office of Foreign Agricultural Relations, Report No. 17, 1947.

Luzuriaga, C., *Situación de la Mujer en el Ecuador* (Quito: Graficas San Pablo, 1980).

————— , and C. Zuvekas, *Income Distribution and Poverty in Rural Ecuador, 1950–1979* (Tempe, Ariz.: Arizona State University, 1983).

Martinez, G., "Repuesto al Cuestionario sobre la Aplicación del Plan de Acción Mundial Aprobado por la Conferencia Mundial del Año Internacional de la Mujer," Informe del Ministerio de Trabajo y Bienestar Social, Quito, 1977.

McKee, L., *Ideals and Actualities: The Socialization of Gender-Appropriate Behaviour in an Ecuadorian Village,* Ph.D. thesis, Cornell University, 1980.

Meier, P., "Artesanía campesina e integración al mercado: Algunos ejemplos de Otavalo," in C. Sepulveda et al., eds., *Estructuras Agrarias y Reproducción Campesina* (Quito: IIE-PUCE, 1982).

Middleton, D., "Migration and urbanization in Ecuador: A view from the coast," *Urban Anthropology* 8, nos. 3 and 4 (1979):313–332.

Murmis, M., "El agro serrano y la vía prusiana de desarrollo capitalista," in O. Barsky et al., eds., *Ecuador: Cambios en el Agro Serrano* (Quito: FLACSO/CEPLAES, 1980).

Nueva Mujer, "Entrevista con María Mercedes Placencia y Rocío Rosero," no. 4 (March 1982):30–33.

Phillips, L., *Gender, Class and Cultural Politics: A Case Study of Rural Vinces, Ecuador,* Ph.D. thesis, University of Toronto, 1985.

Placencia, M. M., "Integración de la Mujer a los Procesos de Desarrollo," in Oficina Nacional de la Mujer, eds., *Seminario sobre la Participación de la Mujer en la Vida Nacional* (Quito: productora de Publicaciones, 1984).

Prieto, M., "Notas sobre el Movimiento de Mujeres en el Ecuador," prepared for the conference Movimientos Sociales Frente a la Crisis, Universidad de Naciones Unidas, programa para America Latina/CLACSO, 1985.

PUCE-CIID (Catholic University of Ecuador–International Development Research Center [Canada]), *Economias Campesinas, Estructura Agraria y Formas de Accumulación: El Caso de Manabí a Partir de la Revolución Liberal* (Avance de investigación), Quito, 1983.

Redclift, M., *Agrarian Reform and Peasant Organization on the Ecuadorian Coast* (London: Athlone, 1978).

————— , "The influence of the Agency of International Development (AID) on Ecuador's agrarian development policy," *Journal of Latin American Studies* 2, pt. 1 (1979):185–201.

Rosero, F., "El proceso de transformación-conservación de la comunidad andina, el caso de las comunas de San Pablo del Lago," in C. Sepulveda et al., eds., *Estructuras Agrarias y Reproducción Campesina* (Quito: IIE-PUCE, 1982).

Salamea, L., and M. F. Likes, "The Changing Role of Rural Women in Ecuador," Quito, n.d., manuscript.

Scrimshaw, S., "Adaptation and family size from rural Ecuador to Guayaquil," in N. Whitten, ed., *Cultural Transformations and Ethnicity in Modern Ecuador* (Urbana: University of Illinois, 1981).

Stolen, K. A., *Mujer Doméstica y Domesticada: Realidad Económica y Machismo en la Sierra Ecuatoriana* (Quito: CEPLAES, forthcoming).

Uggen, J., *Peasant Mobilization in Ecuador: A Case Study of Guayas Province,* Ph.D. thesis, University of Miami, 1975.

Velasco, F., *Reforma Agraria y Movimiento Campesino Indigena de la Sierra* (Quito: El Consejo, 1979).

Verduga, C., "Algunos rasgos de un caso particular de intervención estatal en el desarrollo del capitalismo en el agro," *Revista Ciencias Sociales* 2, no. 7–8 (1978):286–300.

7

Impact of the Sandinista Agrarian Reform on Rural Women's Subordination

Martha Luz Padilla,
Clara Murguialday,
and Ana Criquillon

The day women win their right to be equal will come; on that day, men too will be freer and society will have won its most beautiful battle. We must ensure the coming of that day, not only for the sake of women but for the people as a whole.
—Commander Tomás Borge, 1982

When the Sandinista Popular Revolution came to power in 1979, its leaders inaugurated a process of agrarian reform in an effort to transform the inherited agrarian structure. In seven years of revolution, the agrarian reform has changed the structure of Nicaraguan land tenancy and access to bank credit and has encouraged peasants and rural workers to participate in cooperatives and trade unions.

The FSLN (Sandinista National Liberation Front) inherited a dependent, backward economy and an agrarian structure characterized by unequal development both within and between productive sectors. The expansion of capitalist production had impoverished and proletarianized the peasantry, forcing many to migrate from better quality Pacific coast lands to inferior lands in the central and frontier agricultural zones.

The development of the agro-export economy had also proletarianized rural women. In 1977 women constituted at least 15 percent of the economically active agricultural population; the majority were seasonal agricultural workers (CIERA 1984a). Women also engaged in their socially assigned work of reproducing the family labor force and participated in many of the tasks of subsistence agricultural production.

Nicaragua's dependence upon agriculture (which contributed over two-thirds of export earnings in the late 1970s) left the country particularly vulnerable to the world economic crisis. Prices of manufactured goods and imported raw materials have continued to rise, whereas export prices have fallen. Partly as a result of this deterioration in the terms of trade, the external debt has grown to US$4 billion.

Systematic military attacks, directed and financed by the United States, have compounded the economic crisis. The attacks have affected both productivity and living standards and have hindered the process of agrarian transformation. Counterrevolutionaries have attacked agricultural cooperatives and destroyed grain storage silos, transport facilities, and fuel depots. The damage has amounted to more than US$3 billion, and thousands of human lives have been lost. As a result, the defense budget has been increased and the human resources necessary for production have been redirected to defend the country.

In this chapter, we will describe the principal features of the agrarian reform and evaluate its impact on women's access to land and employment and on working conditions. In our conclusion, we will analyze the revolution's prospects for raising gender awareness and organizing Nicaraguan rural women.

The Sandinista Agrarian Reform

The agrarian reform encompasses three basic sectors: state farms, the cooperative sector, and independent producers who have received individual land titles.

The expropriation, immediately after the Triumph, of the properties owned by Somoza and his allies gave the state control of more than 50 percent of the modern agricultural sector, although this land constituted only 20 percent of the total cultivated area (CIERA 1985a:4). The immediate objectives were to reactivate production, to develop new forms of economic management, and to improve the working conditions and living standards of agricultural workers.

The country's most important worker management experiences have taken place on the state farms. The creation of the Area of People's Property (APP) opened the door to the democratization of farm management. Worker participation has been institutionalized in the production and management councils at the farm and enterprise levels, respectively (ATC 1984a:4). Despite their current limitations, the councils provide the mechanism for workers to participate in the decisions regarding working conditions, production targets, and the delivery of social services. The Association of Rural Workers (ATC), the most important organization of agricultural workers, consistently promotes both participatory management and better working and living conditions for the rural working class.

The Law of Agrarian Reform and the Cooperative Law were passed in 1981, two years after the start of the revolution. Although the focus of the Agrarian Reform Law is the transfer of idle or underutilized land to poor and landless peasants, the Cooperative Law has stimulated a vigorous cooperative movement characterized by a variety of organizational forms. Small producers, the majority owners of their means of production, or farmers who rent lands or have acquired land through the agrarian reform have organized into credit and service cooperatives (CCS), which constitute 45 percent of the total number of cooperatives. Farmers join these cooperatives in order to apply for credit, receive agricultural extension services, and, in some cases, collectively utilize machinery. Sandinista agricultural cooperatives (CAS) or production cooperatives represent 20 percent of the total; in these, both the means of production and the work processes are socialized (CIERA 1984a: Table 6). The remaining cooperatives are mixtures of these two forms.

In 1978 only twenty-two cooperatives were operative in the country; by the end of 1982, according to the First National Cooperative Census, there were 2,849 cooperatives, with a total of 68,434 members. The membership included an estimated 45 percent of all small producers in the country (CIERA 1984a:23). By 1985, 3,213 cooperatives, with a total of 82,000 members, were in existence.[1] The cooperative movement has encouraged and strengthened the organization of peasants and farmers. Forty percent of the Nicaraguan peasantry belong to the National Union of Farmers and Cattle Ranchers (UNAG), the strongest organization of agricultural producers in the country (CIERA 1984b:50).

During its first two years, the agrarian reform focused on the distribution of lands to cooperatives and on the consolidation of the state farms. This focus changed during 1983; the process of land transfer to poor peasants was judged to have been very slow, and the development of collective forms of production was proving difficult, particularly in sparsely populated regions. Consequently, the agrarian reform was reoriented to favor the transfer of land to individual farmers. By December 1984, 35,000 peasant families had received title to some 1,250,000 manzanas of land (Wheelock 1984:26).[2]

In sum, the agrarian reform has transformed Nicaraguan land tenancy. By the end of 1984, the APP controlled 19 percent of the cultivated land, and the production cooperatives, 7 percent; thus the collective sector constituted 26 percent of the total area. Estates larger than 500 manzanas accounted for more than 36 percent of all property in 1977; this figure has now been reduced to 13 percent. Of the 61 percent of

TABLE 7.1
Evolution of the Structure of Land Tenancy by Property Sector, Nicaragua
(percentages)

	1978	1983	1984
Individual Farms	100	65	64
Greater than 500 mz[1]	36	14	13
200 to 500 mz	16	13	13
50 to 200 mz	30	30	30
10 to 50 mz	16	7	7
Less than 10 mz	2	1	1
Reformed Sector	--	35	36
CCS[2]	--	10	10
CAS[3]	--	5	7
APP[4]	--	20	19
TOTAL	100	100	100

Source: "The General Direction of Agrarian Reform (DGRA)." Ministry of
Agricultural and Agrarian Reform, Managua.

1. Mz is the abbreviation for manzana, a land measure equivalent to
   0.71 hectares.
2. CCS refers to credit and service cooperatives.
3. CAS refers to Sandinista agricultural cooperatives.
4. APP refers to Area of People's Property.

the land remaining in the hands of small and medium-sized private producers, 10 percent is held by members of credit and services cooperatives (see Table 7.1).

In the five years between the Triumph and 1984, the agrarian reform delivered land and titles to more than 60,000 peasant families (Wheelock 1984:27). The reform also supplied peasants with the credit, technical assistance, inputs, and marketing facilities necessary for production and provided training in such areas as basic accounting and pest control to cooperative members of both sexes.[3]

The Sandinista agrarian reform is more than an act of land redistribution: It is an instrument in the hands of the working class and peasantry to dismantle the Somocista agrarian structure. It is the legal framework for the destruction of old social relations of production and the construction of new ones based on the principles of participation, collectivism, cooperation, and mutual assistance (ATC 1984a:4). Creation of the APP, transfer of lands to poor peasants, and the development of cooperatives are the foundations for dramatic changes in the organization of work—the introduction of economic planning, the elimination of anarchy in production, the eradication of backward concepts, styles, and methods of management—as well as better conditions for rural workers.

Incorporation of Rural Women
into the Sandinista Agrarian Reform

Gender equality is essential to a process of revolutionary social transformation in the service of the popular classes, such as that now under way in Nicaragua. The legal expression of this equality is provided by the Statute of Rights and Guarantees of the Nicaraguan People (1979), the Agrarian Reform Law (1981), and the Law of Cooperatives (1981). These statutes grant women, for the first time, equal rights to land, cooperative membership, and equal pay for equal work.

The Law of Cooperatives explicitly states that women shall be fully integrated into the work of production cooperatives and incorporated as members under the same conditions as men; this statute ensures that all cooperative members, male and female, have the same rights and duties. The law does not require that women's participation in the agrarian reform depend on their being a household head or having adult male children; wives and daughters of male household heads may be beneficiaries of the agrarian reform in their own right. The Sandinista Agrarian Reform Law is in fact the first statute in Latin America to allow women, regardless of their family position, to be direct beneficiaries of agrarian policies. Thus the social position of rural women has been legally redefined, and the preconditions for their incorporation into new social relations of production have been established.

The process of integrating women into the cooperatives has had a limited scope, however. According to the First National Census of Cooperatives, though 44 percent of the cooperatives have at least one woman member, only 6 percent of the total number of cooperative members are women (CIERA 1984a:25–26). In addition, women constitute 8 percent of the beneficiaries of individual land titlings.[4]

For the first time, women who were landless agricultural wage workers now have access to good, productive lands, machinery, inputs, credit with preferential interest rates, and guaranteed prices as members of production cooperatives. As owners of collective means of production, they now work in all phases of the productive cycle and have guaranteed employment for the better part of the year. These women have also been able to improve their standard of living through the cooperatives' cultivation of staples for family consumption.

Another positive aspect of cooperative membership is the self-affirmation women gain through this new form of work and their participation in decision-making about work organization, cultivation methods, use of credit, and other cooperative concerns. Women also value the knowledge they receive from technical and organizational training in the cooperatives; it helps them raise their productivity and take greater responsibility for the smooth functioning of the cooperative. Since family members who are not themselves members of cooperatives have no access to this training, only women who join the cooperatives in their own right can upgrade themselves on a par with men.[5]

Female farmers join credit and service cooperatives (CCS) primarily to raise productivity on their parcels. The high proportion of female household heads in the small landowner sector explains why 60 percent of the CCS have women members whereas only 20 percent of the CAS do so. The majority of women in the CCS cooperatives, who have benefited along with men in technical and organizational training courses, manage their own farms and work directly in production, although they often seek assistance from family members or hire wage labor.

Although women cooperative members have benefited considerably from the agrarian reform, the fact that total female membership nationally is low indicates that rural women wishing to incorporate themselves into the new forms of agricultural production and organization still face significant obstacles. Some rural women, rather than taking on the responsibility of working in a production cooperative throughout the year, have opted to remain as seasonal wage laborers.

The dominant ideology—that females are subordinate, that productive work should be restricted to men, and that women belong in the home—continues to be a major impediment to rural women's incorporation. Men tend to undervalue women's productive work and then use this low evaluation to justify denying their right to participate in the cooperatives. A further assumption is that women are incapable of making agricultural decisions. Ideological values such as these are reinforced by state functionaries responsible for supporting and promoting the cooperatives and often are voiced by rural women themselves.

Occasionally, to justify not including women, cooperative members use economic excuses such as land scarcity or a shortage of full time employment. More common arguments are that women are not as productive or as experienced in farming or that men must be given priority because they are the heads of families. Often invitations to the organizational meetings for a cooperative have not been extended to women under the pretext that they are not interested. In some cases women have been allowed to join the production cooperatives only if they own land that they are willing to pool; the requests for admission of landless women have been denied.

Absence of infrastructure support to reduce the burden of women's socially assigned tasks—housework and child care—also effectively prevents women from joining the cooperatives. Because of the double day, taking on the obligations of full time productive work implies accepting an average fifteen-hour workday.

Within the Area of People's Property, farm workers have gained greater employment stability. However, women wage workers continue to be employed primarily on a seasonal basis. Their participation within the seasonal labor force has in fact increased considerably. Seventy percent of coffee cutters in the 1984-1985 harvest were women, compared with 42 percent in the 1983-1984 harvest; more than 70 percent of the workers in the tobacco harvest and 60 percent of the manual pickers in the cotton harvest were women and children, considerably higher percentages than in the past (ATC 1984b:8).

This increase in the relative number of seasonal female workers can be attributed to the shortage of seasonal male workers resulting from their more frequent permanent employment on state farms, the growth of the cooperative movement, and male participation in defense (CIERA et al. 1985). Many women have been compelled to enter the agricultural labor force to earn the household's income because the males are absent on war duty.

Only in the tobacco industry and in the contingency plan for cotton and corn is there a notable increase in the number of women working in stable form for the greater part of the year. Although they work for more than six months of the year, women continue to be hired as temporary laborers because the work is sporadic. This is also the case in coffee planting, an area in which women are increasingly employed because of the war.

The increases in female employment have taken place disproportionately within the state sector. Private employers are less concerned that agricultural tasks be carefully executed, and many, when faced with a shortage of male labor, prefer to let a task go undone than to hire a woman. Moreover, the private sector has not experienced the male labor shortage to the same degree as the state sector because the number of men joining the voluntary defense batallions is lower than in the APP.

Finally, few women occupy mechanized or technical positions in either private or state sectors. With the exception of a few women tractor drivers in the northern tobacco-producing zone, women workers are not encouraged to train for mechanized work. This limitation is particularly worrisome in cotton production, which each year is becoming more mechanized. Women workers are being relegated to the heavier and lower paid manual tasks, whereas men have monopolized the mechanized and more skilled jobs. In addition, mechanization of the cotton harvest has decreased, in absolute terms, the volume of female employment.

To sum up, although the new laws were given relatively wide publicity when they were enacted, few rural women are aware of their legal rights. Their ignorance is often shared by local state farm managers and cooperative support personnel, since the necessary guidelines are still not included in training curricula for state technicians and cooperative promoters. Furthermore, the absence of sanctions to enforce compliance has meant that the laws have often been reduced to a mere declaration of intent. Formal legal changes alone are insufficient to ensure true equality of opportunity.

The usefulness of the new legal framework is limited by its failure to consider certain gender-specific problems that require resolution if women are to become equal beneficiaries of the agrarian reform. To be an effective instrument of women's struggle, the law must take into account those elements that structure women's subordination: the gender division of labor and the role assigned women in reproduction. Although the legal framework of the agrarian reform is indispensable, it alone is insufficient to guarantee the incorporation of rural women and real equality between the sexes.

Changes in Organization
and Working and Living Conditions

In the production cooperatives, women members participate in almost all phases of the productive process. The main ones in which they do not participate are mechanized tasks, such as soil preparation, grading, and planting, and heavy tasks, such as fence repairing, which they carry out only with male assistance. The organization of work by gender generally takes one of three forms: mixed brigades, separate male and female brigades, and auxiliary projects carried out only by the women. In the first two forms, women are totally integrated to the productive process; in the last, women carry out secondary activities such as poultry or beekeeping projects. Although women may appear marginalized, this last form of production can be considered a first step toward women's integration into collective work (CIERA 1984a).

The sexual division of labor has not changed much in the state farm sector except in tobacco and coffee production in the northern zone. In that region, which is most affected by the war, the male labor shortage has reduced the number of strictly defined male tasks. As more women are employed during the preharvest period and gain more technical knowledge of cultivation, they begin to break taboos (e.g., that driving a tractor causes sterility) and cause the revision of the protective and discriminatory arguments often used against them. New forms of work organization have also been introduced, and in some cases women are supervising all-women work brigades.

With respect to income levels, members of the production cooperatives allocate themselves a small, daily remuneration (equal for men and women) and at the end of the harvest divide the profits according to the days worked by each member. Social benefits are tied directly to the cooperative's profitability. Only a few have been sufficiently profitable to provide maternity subsidies to women members.

Within the state sector, nominal salaries have risen considerably to keep them in line with the high rate of inflation afflicting the Nicaraguan economy and damaging rural workers' purchasing power. Most important, however, is that the social salary (health, education, transportation, housing, water, electricity) has increased considerably, and real purchasing power is maintained through basic grain subsidies and the assured supply of staples at official prices at work centers.

"Equal pay for equal work" was transformed several years ago from slogan to reality on the state farms. The National System for Organization of Work and Wages, which was applied for the first time during the 1984-1985 cycle is designed to regulate salaries and offer production incentives to improve the quantity and quality of work. The application of the system to manual work has caused sharp debate on differences in productivity by sex for certain tasks (CIERA et al. 1985).

The standards, based on the traditional productivity of male workers, could operate as disincentives for women wishing to take on traditionally male tasks. To counteract this danger, it has been proposed that the basic standard be reformulated to adapt it to the reality that women will increasingly perform these tasks. An alternative proposal is that different standards be established for each sex for the same task. This last option, however, is regarded as both paternalistic and discriminatory. Although the first option is problematic because it raises labor costs across the board, it does take into account the current feminization of the agricultural labor force.

Our concern however, is that the country runs the risk of closing the debate by selecting one option or the other without analyzing in depth the circumstances (not always contingent upon physical strength) that lower women's productivity. For example, women's lack of training and experience in nontraditional tasks often accounts for differential productivity, as does pressure to leave work as early as possible to do housework, tiredness caused by the double day, and fatigue and physical wear and tear resulting from multiple pregnancies, births, and nursing.

As a direct result of new government regulations and worker-management agreements, wage workers have benefited from greatly improved working conditions such as occupational health and safety, improved diet, vacation and sickness leave, social security, shorter hours, and a trend toward permanent contracts and daily wages rather than piecework. Female wage workers, however, have not had equal access to these gains because they are employed mostly as temporary workers whereas male workers occupy most permanent jobs in agriculture. Many of the benefits (such as paid leaves and social security) accrue only to permanent workers. Another factor contributing to gender differentiation of benefits is that women are still not signed up as coffee pickers in their own names, even though registration is mandatory for all workers over age fourteen. A significant number of female coffee harvest workers—wives, mothers, unmarried daughters—work as "helpers" to their husband or father, who then collects the salary earned by the woman. This practice has repercussions not only for the class consciousness of the worker (who does not consider herself a worker at all) but also for labor force statistics and calculations of productivity and thus for wage policy at the macroeconomic level.

In the areas of organization and working conditions, the Revolution has responded positively to the class interests, whether explicit or not, of both female and male cooperative members and wage workers, but the steps taken so far have not had equal results for rural women and men. The mechanisms that maintain and reproduce women's subordination do not simply disappear because women participate more actively in social production (in more tasks and for more months in the year) and because their working conditions are improved. As long as women work a double day and the work of reproduction is not shared by both sexes to the same extent as productive work, the gender division of labor will continue to reproduce relations of power and subordination among working-class men and women. Such relations will prevent not only the liberation of women but also the emancipation of the working class as a whole.

Transformations in the Reproductive Sphere

The Revolution has responded to immediate, gender-specific needs of rural women by establishing thirty-four rural day-care centers, all on the state farms, and children's dining rooms; these facilities will provide improved attention for workers' children and socialize their care thereby facilitating women's incorporation into work, unions, and political activities. The maternal-infant health program for protection of pregnant women and newborns has been brought to the countryside. Permanent women workers consider the extension of maternity subsidies in the agricultural sector one of women's greatest achievements in recent years. Vaccination campaigns (in which women actively participate), eradication of diarrhea as a primary cause of infant mortality, and the total elimination of poliomyelitis have alleviated much of the suffering that rural women experience in their role as the persons primarily responsible for child care and health. Remote areas that lacked electricity, clean water, and plumbing now have these services, thereby reducing rural women's domestic workload. Similarly, distribution networks for food and household staples via assured channels and at official prices eliminate the need for female wage workers and peasant women to walk many kilometers to buy food at the city market.

On other counts, despite the obvious hazards caused by multiple pregnancies (many terminating in abortions, stillbirths, or infants who die in their first year), Nicaragua has no national family planning policy. Rural women do not have access to the information and mechanisms necessary to freely control their fertility. In the great majority of the country's hospitals voluntary sterilization is conditional upon age, number of children borne (not less than four or five), and, in many cases, the approval of the husband or partner.

New legislation, strategies, and ideological campaigns have been initiated to eliminate irresponsible paternity, physical abuse, rape, and all types of sexual aggression toward women. The use of women as sex objects in the media or advertising has been prohibited. Nevertheless, little effort has been directed toward confronting and challenging the mechanisms that sustain and reproduce women's subordination in the family. Although housework is valued as socially necessary and it is generally believed that all members of the family should participate in it, the practical steps (ideological struggle, massive education) to make this division of labor a reality have not yet been taken.

Participatory Democracy: New Social Relations of Production in Agriculture

Female participation in cooperative management is relatively limited. In general, women only serve on the executive councils when the majority of cooperative members are women.[6] Female participation in production and financial decisions is closely linked to the degree of decentralization and organizational structure of the cooperative. Women members have more opportunity to participate meaningfully when decisions are made in decentralized committees (production, finance, education) and then ratified in meetings of the cooperative as a whole (CIERA 1984a:60).

Women CCS members have more potential to participate actively in decision-making because as owners of their own farms they prepare their own production plan. Delegation of decision-making to an adult male son is not uncommon, however. In both the CAS and the CCS, nonmember women are totally excluded from the cooperative management and decision-making processes even when they participate in production as nonsalaried family workers and/or as wage workers during the harvest period.

Attendance at cooperative meetings provides women members with an organizational and technical education as well as with a political one. The level of revolutionary consciousness displayed by women members in most cooperatives is noteworthy, especially when compared with that of women who are relatives of members and do not attend cooperative meetings (CIERA 1984a:62).

Because as a social group women are differentiated by gender subordination, they are denied the right to participate equally with men in cooperative management and decision-making. When they join the cooperatives, they bear the social devaluation both of their productive labor and of their work in the domestic sphere plus the paralyzing effects of an ideology that maintains that women are incapable of exercising leadership.

Attention to the specific problems of rural women is only guaranteed when women participate in the cooperative executive councils. In those exceptional cases where women form a majority of the executive council, they have tackled gender-specific problems and provided a powerful incentive for other women to join the cooperative.

The issue is what participatory democracy means for women. Women will only be able to participate effectively in cooperative decision-making if they are given equal access to technical education and training and if the dominant ideology that attributes leadership qualifications only to males is challenged. Furthermore, women can only accept more responsibility within the cooperatives if household domestic chores are shared by all family members.

Participatory Worker Management

Female agricultural workers are largely absent from the participatory management structure of the APP. Their participation in the union base committees is also limited by the obstacles they face in even participating in union activities. The fourteen to sixteen hour double day of domestic and wage work leaves women little time to participate in organizational activities or even to rest. Multiple pregnancies also drain women's strength and oblige them to dedicate large amounts of time and energy to nursing and child care.

Women's position as seasonal wage laborers, because it reduces them either to the status of dependent wives or to employment in the informal sector for the rest of the year, objectively limits the development of their class consciousness. Female workers do not attend union meetings, not only because of the hour at which meetings are called (when women are making dinner or looking after children) but also because they do not understand why the goals of the technical or economic plan or the problems of a particular crop (whose cultivation practice they may know nothing about) are relevant to their lives.

Various ideological factors reinforce this negative motivation. On one hand, according to the prevailing social norm it is "not a woman's place" to attend meetings (especially those held outside the farm unit), much less to speak at them or to discuss problems of crop yields with the administrator. On the other hand, women are less experienced in organizational situations than are men; their cultural level is lower, and they have yet to overcome their personal insecurity. Their fear of speaking in public increases when the issues raised are gender specific rather than "class issues" collectively recognized as legitimate. Clearly, then, women workers are not the direct subjects of worker management primarily because they are only marginally incorporated into the union activity that sustains worker participation.

This does not mean, however, that women are indifferent to worker participation in management. They benefit as workers from the progress made by the rural working class, thanks to the Revolution, through union organization and participatory management. Progress has been made in meeting both the general and specific needs of women workers, such as better working conditions and enhanced social services (housing, electricity, water, cooked food, health, education).

As noted, the war has accelerated women's incorporation into production. A qualitative leap forward has taken place in terms of women's employment in many traditionally male jobs. However, that leap is only embryonic in regard to women's access to mechanized and more technically skilled jobs. And women's increased participation in production has not led to their greater involvement in the rural unions. The union boards have been losing male members to the military service; yet women have not been promoted to leadership positions—a move that could help minimize the disruptive costs of the war on the unions.

Once again, the dominant ideology that posits that women are ill equipped for the task of leadership and the material obstacles that women face in assuming more responsibilities have blocked women's access to union leadership and worker management during a period when the presence of women workers not only would enrich the functioning of these institutions but also would ensure their very survival.

An exceptional situation prevails in the northern, tobacco-growing region where large numbers of women and children traditionally have worked in almost all phases of tobacco production. The effects of the counterrevolutionary attacks were first felt in this region in 1982, and the war, with all its atrocities, has stimulated the organization and militancy of women tobacco workers. These actions were also the direct result of the FSLN and ATC initiatives to include female workers in all union and management structures. The women are now using their positions of responsibility to promote both class and gender issues, at least to a much greater extent than are cotton workers (on the Pacific Coast, in the rearguard zone) and coffee workers (who have felt the effects of the war more recently).

In short, rural women's progress is directly related to their levels of class and gender consciousness and organization. For Nicaraguan rural women, significant progress has taken place in the last few years in terms of class consciousness, but their gender awareness lags behind.

A patriarchal framework of male-female relations continues to define women's participation in agricultural production and political-organizational structures. Even when they work outside the home and participate in mass organizations, women are regarded primarily as "wife-mothers," whereas men are perceived formally as heads of household, workers, and heroic soldiers.

The decision not to challenge gender relations for fear of precipitating divisions and conflict among the working class during imperialist aggression has had unfortunate consequences. Many problems specific to women have been relegated to the back burner, especially those whose solutions require attacking male privilege within the family, in production, and in political life. This strategy, in turn, has a negative effect on the development of women's class consciousness. The limited direct access to land for peasant women and to worker management for wage workers, combined with their relatively lower participation in the rural mass organizations compared with men, affords rural women fewer opportunities to identify with the class to which they belong. Rural women's expectations of the Revolution continue to be mediated through family members; they value the benefits that the revolutionary process has brought to their children, husbands, brothers, and relatives and to the people as a whole.

Future Perspectives

The new and mammoth tasks faced by the revolutionary government include developing the country's productive structure during a decade of economic crisis while facing economic blockade and the intensifying military threat from the United States. In this context, and given the general scarcity of resources, the prioritization of economic development, though urgent and necessary, makes the attainment of other revolutionary goals—among them gender equality—contingent upon the success of the development strategy (Molyneaux 1985).

This focus could lead to a certain productionist bias in state policies while indefinitely postponing the moment when energies are directed to meeting the Revolution's full program for women's emancipation. Nevertheless, the political will of the Sandinista Front and the revolutionary government regarding democratizing society and encouraging popular participation at all levels is undeniable. The revolutionary project will succeed only with the massive, organized support of the people.

Women are increasingly the most available labor force, but their traditional social role has limited their contribution to economic development and has inhibited both the transformation of political and economic structures and national defense. The urgency of economic development and the need to strengthen the mass organizations have come into conflict with the roots of womens' subordination, creating favorable conditions for the development of class and gender consciousness. Coming to terms with this contradiction, the revolutionary government and the mass organizations have taken some steps to alter the traditional patriarchal order.

In the light of other revolutionary experiences, we know that to the extent that the state takes into account the need to transform both the material and ideological bases of capitalism and the roots of women's subordination women can play a very important revolutionary role. The state can create many of the necessary preconditions to ensure higher levels of female participation in the revolutionary process, but the laws must be effectively enforced.

Among the tasks ahead are the definition and application of employment policies and technical training policies that take women specifically into account; the promotion of information campaigns about family planning with contraceptives made available to rural women, and the extension of the existing social services (rural day-care, children's dining rooms, popular cafeterias) to reduce domestic work to a minimum. The mass media and the educational and training system must be utilized to eradicate the stereotypes, myths, and ideologies that determine gender roles both in the countryside and in society at large. And the development of an autonomous women's organization to promote both class and gender consciousness is essential for rural women's participation to improve both qualitatively and quantitatively.

The need to attend to the specific problems of rural women has been felt within the rural union movement. Coinciding with the fifth anniversary of the creation of the ATC, the First National Congress of Women Agricultural Workers was held in April 1983, cosponsored by the Association of Nicaraguan Women "Luisa Amanda Espinoza" (AMNLAE). More than 100 women workers participated, who were affiliated with the rank and file in the various state and private coffee, cotton, rice, and cattle farms.

Discussion centered on the problems of the delegates and proposals relating to legislative changes, work organization, female unemployment, occupational health and safety, lack of technical training for women, child-care problems, difficulties of food supply and, finally, women's low union participation. The dialectical relation between women's socially assigned role in the family and society and the conditions under which women participate in productive work and union activities was evident.

As a result of the congress, the ATC decided to undertake an in-depth analysis of the specific problems of women agricultural workers. The analysis presented in this chapter is part of the initial study, which began in January 1984 (in coordination with the Center for Study and Research of the Agrarian Reform [CIERA-MIDINDRA] and the Center for the Study of Work [CETRA-MITRAB]), as the first phase of an integrated and continuous process of research, training, union activity, and reflection to be carried out by women workers themselves. The objective is to create new forms of union organizing that will incorporate women workers into a process of transformation of their own lives, both as wage workers and as women.

Integrating a research process into union work is a new experience in Nicaragua. It is both an academic and political-organizational challenge for the ATC to carry out a participatory study on a national, rather than just a community, scale. Since its subject is rural working women, it will illuminate the intersection between class consciousness, gender consciousness, and women's organization. The objective is to ensure that the specific situation of women is considered and attended to in every political-organizational structure of the Revolution. This is also the aim of the women's association (AMNLAE) in defining itself as a political-ideological movement. As women, we must try to organize ourselves at every level, defending our gender interests while offering support to each other. We must also raise consciousness in our respective organizations so that these groups include women's demands in their programs of action and assume women's issues as their own.

In other words, we are convinced that the contradictions between production and reproduction, and class struggle and the struggle for women's liberation, must and can be resolved. Capitalism is patriarchal, the life of a woman is an integrated whole, and women's struggle for emancipation is an irreducible part of all peoples' struggle for their right to self-determination, democracy, and peace.

Acknowledgments

During 1984 and 1985, the authors collaborated on a national-level study of rural women wage workers (CIERA et al. 1985). They would like to thank the other team members, particularly Paola Perez, for their collaboration in the preparation of this article. This chapter was translated by Katherine Pettus.

Notes

1. CIERA 1985 estimates are based on data from the National Development Bank and the DGRA (the General Direction of Agrarian Reform, Ministry of Agriculture and Agrarian Reform), December 1984.

2. One manzana is equal to 0.71 hectares.

3. Under Somocismo, only 16,000 producers received bank credit; in 1980, 81,000 received credit for the first time (CIERA 1984a:26).

4. Prepared by the CIERA Rural Women's Research Group, based on data provided by DGRA, December 1984. It was impossible to calculate how many of these new female landowners have now joined credit and service cooperatives. It may be assumed, however, that the proportion of female members has increased substantially since the 1982 Cooperative Census.

5. Women who are not cooperative members work as wage workers in the production cooperatives particularly during the harvest season when demand for labor is highest. They receive the same wage as members but do not participate in the cooperative decision-making process or in the training courses.

6. According to the 1982 Cooperative Census, women accounted for over one-half of the total membership in forty-five of the cooperatives of the country (CIERA 1984a: Table 6).

References

ATC, "Los Trabajadores del Campo y el Impacto de la Reforma Agraria sobre el Empleo Rural," March 1984a, mimeo.
————, "La Revolución, la Mujer y la Alimentación," June 1984b, mimeo.
CIERA, *La Mujer en las Cooperativas Agropecuarias en Nicaragua* (Managua: CIERA, 1984a); English version available as *Tough Row to Hoe: Women in Nicaragua's Agricultural Cooperatives* (San Francisco: Institute for Food and Development Policy, 1986).
————, *La Democracia Participativa en Nicaragua* (Managua: CIERA, 1984b).
————, "La Reforma Agraria: Estratégia y Realizaciones," April 1985, mimeo.

————— , CETRA-MITRAB, and ATC, "La Feminización de la Fuerza de Trabajo Asalariada en el Agro y sus Implicancias en la Producción y la Organización Sindical," October 1985, mimeo.

Molyneaux, Maxine, "Mobilization Without Emancipation? Women's Interests, State and Revolution: The Nicaraguan Case," *Feminist Studies*, spring 1985.

Wheelock, Jaime, *Entre la Crisis y la Agresión: la Reforma Agraria Sandinista* (Managua: MIDINRA (Ministry of Agriculture and Agrarian Reform), 1984).

8

Women on the Agenda: The Cooperative Movement in Rural Cuba

Jean Stubbs
and Mavis Alvarez

Cuba embarked on a cooperative movement almost a decade ago in response to the need for modernization in the fragmented private agricultural sector. The cooperative movement also stemmed from the national need to produce an agricultural surplus for export and home consumption and to generate an infrastructural base and financial surplus for further rural investment.

Rural women were among the more ardent supporters of voluntary collectivization. The reasons women gave for joining the new agricultural production cooperatives (Cooperativa de Producción Agrícola, CPAs) included the possibility of gaining amenities in the new cooperative villages, the relative ease of working collectively as opposed to individually, and a measure of economic independence from fathers and husbands.

Under the initial agrarian reform policies of 1959, female heads of household were accorded land titles. But in practice, such awards proved to be the exception rather than the rule. Even when a woman secured a land title, a man would take on farm production responsibilities. Rural women did benefit from the numerous state development initiatives over the subsequent fifteen years. With the new cooperatives, however, for the first time in Cuban agrarian history a specific agricultural policy was spelled out encouraging women to join cooperatives and ensuring them the identical statutory rights that men had.

That such a policy was implemented testifies to the qualitative changes in the fabric of Cuban rural society that have taken place over the course of the revolution. It also reflects a major national campaign of the

Federation of Cuban Women (FMC) and the revolutionary government to redress continuing inequalities in the position of women. Increasingly under scrutiny are job and training possibilities for women and other aspects included in the Family Code of 1975 and the Family Education Campaign of the late 1970s.

The results of this concerted mobilization effort were that in 1979 over a third of cooperative farmers were women (see Table 8.1). In 1983, a peak year for the cooperative movement, the figure dropped to 28 percent, although in absolute terms the number of women had more than quadrupled. By 1985, both absolute and relative figures had dropped slightly: Women represented 25 percent of cooperative members and 12 percent of the members of cooperative executive committees.[1] The sudden visibility of women in the cooperative sector has fast outstripped the state agricultural sector; women only account for 14 percent of that sector's workforce and 6 percent of executive posts (1981 census).

What do these figures mean? In this chapter we consider why women were singled out for special policy attention within the cooperatives and what the subsequent impact was on the position of women.

Rural Versus Urban:
The Development Context

Cuba is perhaps exceptional in the Third World in that although the country is still characterized as an agro-export economy, the majority of women are not defined as rural. Over the intercensal period of 1970–1981 the proportion of the total female population defined as rural dropped from 70 percent to 31 percent. More recent figures quote 29 percent. In effect, the proportion of Cuba's population defined as rural has been falling steadily over the last few decades.

This fact is partly the result of census definitions: Cuba classifies as urban any town of 2,000 inhabitants or more; towns of 500 to 2,000 with electricity, running water, education, and health services; and also the new towns of 200 to 500 people with those amenities. This lower number of rural women, however, is much more a question of development. Since 1959, Cuba has embarked on a policy of agricultural development with marked emphasis on upgrading rural standards of living, providing sources of employment, and improving overall rural work, housing, education, and health conditions. The notion of rural urbanization was understood to cover a whole range of economic, social, and cultural amenities as the benefits of the city were transferred to small rural communities (Rojas et al. 1983; Acosta 1972 and 1973). By 1975, a total of 282 new communities had been built by the state as

TABLE 8.1
Peasant Sector by Form of Organization, 1979–1985, Cuba

Organization	1979				1981				1983				1985			
	Total	Men	Women	Women % Total	Total	Men	Women	Women % Total	Total	Men	Women	Women % Total	Total	Men	Women	Women % Total
CPA Members	14,696	9,594	5,102	34.7	36,900	25,698	11,202	30.4	82,515	60,013	22,502	27.7	71,246	53,181	18,065	25.4
CCS Members	152,794	142,473	10,321	6.8	141,376	132,176	9,200	6.5	107,972	105,276	6,696	6.2	101,193	94,632	6,561	6.5
Titleholders	111,211	105,254	5,957	5.4	101,706	96,002	5,704	5.6	77,158	76,616	4,542	5.9	72,392	67,862	4,530	6.3
Relatives	41,583	37,219	4,304	10.4	39,670	36,174	3,496	8.8	30,814	28,660	2,154	7.0	28,801	26,770	2,031	7.1
AC Members	12,885	11,784	1,071	8.2	11,643	10,507	1,136	9.8	11,064	9,816	1,248	11.3	10,129	8,943	1,186	11.7
Titleholders	10,249	9,520	729	7.1	7,987	7,253	734	9.2	8,017	7,145	872	10.9	8,602	7,593	1,009	11.7
Relatives	2,606	2,264	342	13.1	3,656	3,254	402	11.0	3,047	2,671	376	12.3	1,527	1,350	177	11.6
TOTAL	180,345	163,851	16,494	9.2	189,919	168,381	21,538	11.0	201,551	171,105	30,446	15.1	182,568	156,756	25,812	16.5

Notes: CPA (Cooperativa de Producción Agrícola) is an agricultural production cooperative in which land is owned and worked collectively; CCS (Cooperativa de Credito y Servicio) is a credit and service cooperative that brings together independent private farmers in order to acquire credit or technical assistance from the state; AC (Asociación Campesina) is a farmer association that primarily serves to coordinate independent peasant production plans with the state.

Source: Compiled from ANAP figures for the relevant years.

a direct product of integrated socioeconomic projects, whether around sugar cane, livestock, or other crop plans. The promotion of production cooperatives among small private farmers was an extension of this policy of rural urbanization; it placed greater emphasis on self-reliance and self-help in the building of similar local communities.

Two major land reforms initially paved the way for such sweeping rural change. The 1959 Agrarian Reform Law set a ceiling on the size of private farms of approximately 400 hectares; land exceeding that limit was expropriated by the state and plots of up to 67 hectares were given to tenants and sharecroppers. Decapitalization as well as overt political hostility on the part of the middle agrarian bourgeoisie largely motivated the second Agrarian Reform Law of 1963, which lowered the ceiling on all private holdings to 67 hectares.

Land reform, coupled with nationalization of all foreign enterprise (1960), and the large-scale expropriation of domestic enterprise (1961) paved the way for ambitious—and at times overambitious—state development plans with agriculture as the lynchpin. In effect, rural development was inserted into a wider process of planned socialist development. Its salient feature, sugar production, was from 1963 defined as the springboard to generate the resources for the diversification of both agriculture and industry, thus encouraging import substitution and self-sufficiency. The process was assisted by negotiated index-linked prices and markets in the socialist bloc, which today accounts for 85 percent of external trade.

In the early postrevolutionary years an attempt was made to immediately diversify the sugar-dependent economy. This attempt proved costly, however, for diversification was impossible to finance because of the relative collapse of sugar production. To restore export capacity, sugar was again accorded priority. The sugar plantations had been converted to state farms shortly after their nationalization, and subsequently state farms were seen as the model of socialist agriculture. It was assumed that they would allow for the more rapid introduction of modern technology and mechanization. State enterprises were subsequently developed in cattle, dairy, poultry, citrus, banana, and plantain production. In the 1970s the new schools in the countryside and the combined study/work program were fostered in conjunction with the expansion of the state farm sector.[2]

The attention given to the development of the state sector was inevitably felt in the nonstate sector. An all-out effort for a record sugar harvest in 1970 channeled major resources into sugar production, to the detriment of other branches of agriculture where the private sector was much larger. The 1969-1970 tobacco harvest, for example, was only 44 percent of the level of the 1965-1966 harvest, and similar, if less drastic, declines in production were recorded for other crops. These declines pointed to the need for a reevaluation of the role of small private farming; such an initiative was begun at the 1971 Congress of National Association of Small Farmers (ANAP) (Martín Barrios 1982).

From the start of the revolution the private sector had benefited from a positive state agricultural policy including improved credits, pricing, and agricultural extension work. In the 1970s, more agricultural research stations and technical institutes were built, and greater attention was paid to soil improvement, irrigation, and the use of fertilizer and pesticides. In addition to the Ministry of Agriculture, ANAP had its own agricultural extension team that catered exclusively to the private sector. The application of technical know-how was facilitated by generally improved educational standards in rural areas (all ANAP farmers today have a ninth-grade education) and a phytosanitary activist movement.

The costs of such natural disasters as hurricanes, flooding, and draught were absorbed by the state over the years through the cancellation of farmers' debts on loans and material and financial assistance for reconstruction. A more recent development has been the introduction of an extensive low-cost agricultural insurance scheme.

Since the land reform, the private sector accounted for an increasingly smaller proportion of total agricultural land (initially 30 percent, today 15 percent). However, the crops produced by the private sector continued to be either important export items (in the mid-1980s tobacco growing is still 75 percent private because of the prerevolutionary predominance of sharecropping, tenant, and subtenant farming) or items crucial to internal consumption (the private sector accounts for 82 percent of bean production, 66 percent of vegetables, 54 percent of coffee, 53 percent of fruit, and 34 percent of tubular production). Although private production was lucrative—profiting from high prices on first a black market and then a provisionally legalized free peasant market[3]—small farm production as a whole was left behind in development terms. It was fragmented, little mechanized, and labor intensive, although private farmers themselves were hard working and productive.

The key to change was seen in encouraging this dispersed private sector to pool land and resources on a gradual, voluntary, and autonomous basis. With land concentration and technification, it was hoped that productivity would increase, thereby augmenting agricultural output and undercutting high market prices. Moreover, through the formation of cooperative villages, it was hoped it would be economically feasible to further break down the social isolation of the poorer peasant household and extend the state's rural urbanization policy. The whole cooperative idea was an extension of earlier farmer's associations (ACs) and credit and service cooperatives (CCS) in line with the new state economic management and planning system which, in the state farm sector, encouraged decentralized decision-making and local initiative.[4] The goal was to attain agricultural self-sufficiency.

As a result of these policies rural Cuba, like Cuba as a whole, has been buffered to a large extent from the current world economic crisis and external debt problems. In fact, its socioeconomic indices in some respects put it more on par with the developed than the underdeveloped world.[5] It has achieved greater social equity, which has meant a significant narrowing of the urban-rural gap.[6]

Women were defined as an integral part of Cuba's development policy from the outset of the revolution (Larguía and Dumoulin 1984 and 1985). They were afforded equality before the law, employment on the basis of equal pay for equal work, and training schemes. As a result, women have begun to make inroads into new and more skilled occupations although most women are employed in health and education services in both urban and rural areas. Although agriculture is still today a major source of full-time paid employment for men, it only accounts for 10 percent of women in full-time paid occupations; a significant proportion of that 10 percent are in clerical and technical jobs.

Over the years it has become clear that the gender-based division of labor and social conceptions of male and female roles are very difficult to change, which points to the complexities and dimension of women's subordination. And studies have shown that the more rural the area, the more resistant it is to change and the more traditional the gender roles. This aspect is seen in educational differences, the low percentage of women defined as economically active, higher fertility rates, early marriages, multiple teenage pregnancies, and larger families (González forthcoming; Morejón Farnos, González, and Hernández 1982; Pérez 1979; Stubbs 1983; Catsús 1984; Cruz Vera 1985). It was hoped that the cooperative movement would bring about fundamental changes in the position of women, particularly in the more rural areas.

Women in Agriculture

The pitfalls of trying to quantify, let alone evaluate, the work of women in the rural sector include the straightforward statistical problem of whether women's labor is defined as "labor force participation." The very definition of the economically active population (EAP) is unwieldy enough in the agrarian context because of the prevalence of seasonal and unwaged labor, but it is particularly difficult to apply in the case of female family labor (Deere and León 1980).

Cuban statistics prove to be most deficient when it comes to data on women. The 1946 Agricultural Census gives a total of over 800,000 people working in agriculture—41.5 percent of the economically active population of 14 years and over. Supposedly included in this estimate are farmers, agricultural laborers, and unremunerated family labor; yet women constitute only 1.5 percent of the estimated agricultural EAP.

These figures have generally been interpreted as showing the minimal involvement of Cuban women in prerevolutionary agriculture, and they are explained in terms of the disruption of traditional peasant farming at the hands of foreign and local sugar cane plantation agriculture, land extensive cattle ranching, and, to a lesser degree, tobacco and other capitalist production. This process of capitalist development was held to have created a large class of landless laborers (Martínez Alier 1970), generating a labor surplus and minimizing subsistence agriculture and the agricultural work of women.

In recent studies Pollitt (1979, 1980, 1981, and 1983) argues that these census categories were oversimplified and obscured the existence of a sizable semiproletariat, or semipeasantry, that sold its labor power and farmed small plots. Agricultural modernization had certainly not been homogeneous. On the contrary, forms of production such as sharecropping proliferated, and agricultural capital accumulation was based on the visible seasonal exploitation of male wage labor. In male-headed households, women participated in seasonal cash crop harvest and processing activities, subsistence production, and family reproduction—all crucial to family survival. Though mitigated, this area of women's work and its invisibility continued after the revolution.

In the small farm sector, women's participation continued to go unrecorded and hence largely unheeded, though women did respond in large numbers to the FMC-ANAP (National Association of Small Producers) volunteer agricultural brigades.[7] Women were found in the (remunerated) casual and seasonal workforce, the (often unremunerated) volunteer brigades, and as an integral part of (unremunerated) small farmer family labor, much of which escaped census and yearbook statistics. For example, over the 1970–1981 intercensal period, unremunerated female family labor dropped from 1.2 percent to 0.0 percent of the EAP.

According to the 1984 yearbook, women constituted 20 percent of the rural EAP. Of the 70,000 women employed in agriculture, slightly over 60,000 worked in the state sector and some 5,000 were women cooperative farmers, whereas 607 worked as hired labor in the private sector, 505 were self-employed and 220 were reported as unpaid family labor. ANAP's own figures for 1981 show a total of some 11,202 cooperative farmwomen and 10,336 women members of CCSs and ACs;

in 1985 these figures stood at 18,065 and 7,747, respectively (see Table 8.1).

The discrepancy in the number of women enumerated as cooperative members by the yearbook and by ANAP is largely the result of differences in the definition of membership and conceptualization of economic activity. Membership in a cooperative does not automatically imply that a woman performs agricultural field work. Moreover, membership criteria vary from cooperative to cooperative. Some cooperatives automatically include women who contribute land (either in their own right or jointly with their husbands), whether they work in the fields or not. Nevertheless, whether one takes the lower or upper estimate of female cooperative membership, Cuban women clearly represent a much higher share of cooperative members than in other Latin American countries (see Chapter 9 by Deere).

The data reported for CCS and AC membership are even more arbitrary. Since the vast majority of women are family members of male small farmers, many express little need for registering as a member when they consider they can be adequately represented by the men. The CCS and AC women registered are often those who have become activists in ANAP. Thus the reported data capture political if not economic participation.

Women and the Cooperative Movement

A particular combination of social and economic factors of the cooperative movement proved the greatest attraction for Cuban women and engendered their support for cooperativization. Though male peasant farmers spoke of how wrenching it was to stop farming the land individually, women viewed the formation of production cooperatives and cooperative villages more in terms of access to running water, electricity, and amenities such as stores and schools, especially in the remote areas.[8] In this sense, women were perhaps motivated for reasons of reproduction more than production, but in the process they became part of a socioeconomic unit where individual well-being depended directly on collective economic success. Women's participation was recognized as both integral and important. The extent to which women were incorporated into production, however, varied considerably and was inevitably colored by traditional farming practices, development planning strategies, and subjective as well as objective factors at the local cooperative level.

The new agricultural production cooperatives were a more carefully organized variant of earlier moves in the 1960s to pool private holdings into collective production units owned and managed by farmers themselves. The remaining few such cooperatives provided the example, and the ACs and CCSs out of which the new CPAs grew were already versed in acting collectively on behalf of individual farmers.[9] In these "lower form" cooperatives, land was worked individually, but the cooperatives negotiated agreements on state quotas for production, inputs, and credits.

In the CPAs, land and other basic means of production are collectively owned, and each individual farmer's contribution is valued and paid off over a period of time from funds set aside by the cooperative. The cooperative is farmed and run collectively as an autonomous enterprise within the constraints of national and regional planning. It receives low interest credits from the state and preferential treatment in the allocation of certain resources. A percentage of profits goes to the state in return for services; a percentage is plowed back into production and amenities. The rest is divided between members according to their labor contribution. The cooperative elects its own president and executive committee and meets monthly as a whole. At a major end-of-the-year meeting, the members decide upon production plans, investment programs, and consumption requirements and discuss such issues as advance pay, profit sharing, and the admittance of new members.

Individual farmers not wishing to join a cooperative in a given region are not pressured.[10] However, agricultural laborers—and in exceptional cases even industrial workers—can join the cooperatives. These groups of workers make no material contribution other than labor and hence receive no compensation for means of production, although such members do have statutory rights identical to those of other cooperative farmers. The same applies to landless wives and grown children of male household heads.

Planners envisioned that once the cooperatives were under way their greater social and economic advantages would be widely recognized and others would be formed following the initial examples. They also expected that, given encouragement, women would participate in cooperative life.

The cooperative movement did mushroom beyond all expectations (Gómez 1983; Trinchet 1984). The peak year in the number of cooperatives and membership was 1983, and a less marked growth is expected over coming years. The number of CPAs has dropped because of fusions, and hence the average size of CPA land has increased. Membership, which rose to over 82,000 in 1983, has fallen to 71,000, largely as a reflection of the age structure of cooperative membership and the new social security laws, whereby for the first time cooperative farmers can take paid vacation and retire on a pension, the men at sixty and the women at fifty-five.[11] Figures for women's membership have dropped from a high of 22,000 (27 percent of the total membership) to today's figure of 18,000 (25 percent) (see Table 8.1). Age and the fact that current cooperative membership more accurately reflects women farm workers account for this drop. Even so, the figures on women's participation vary considerably from province to province according to the predominant crop, with tobacco and coffee provinces in the lead.

The current level of cooperativization generally varies from province to province and crop to crop. It is at its height in sugar production, where the CPAs account for 73 percent of nonstate land. In tobacco, cooperatives account for some 50 percent of the nonstate land, in coffee, 39 percent, and tubers, 34 percent. Cane and coffee-producing cooperatives account for 30 percent and 28 percent, respectively, of the total number of CPAs.

The hopes pinned on cooperative production, with technical and advisory services from both the state and ANAP, in terms of output in key crops were not disappointed. Yields increased significantly and cooperative members themselves reaped the benefits of improved socioeconomic conditions. However, the rapid growth of the cooperative movement has not been without problems, especially in crops like tobacco and coffee, which allow for little mechanization and are highly labor intensive.[12] Economies of scale in coffee production are particularly difficult to secure because of the particularly fragmented mountain terrain in which coffee is grown. Only in the area of Pinar del Río has lowland tobacco production been spatially concentrated to a minimal extent necessary to reap economies of scale.

Both tobacco and coffee are traditional small-farm products, whose production uses a high input of seasonal female labor and high family labor component in general. This labor structure has meant that the transition from the household farm to the cooperative farm unit, in which all labor time is computed and remunerated with guaranteed minimum wages and benefits, has significantly raised labor costs and affected the potential profitability of the cooperative sector.

Gender Patterns in Tobacco Cooperatives

Research conducted in two major tobacco-growing areas, San Luis (western Pinar del Río province) and Cabaiguán (central Sancti Spíritus province), revealed that women have played a central role in small-scale tobacco production. Nevertheless, their participation in decision-making was minimal. The household division of labor was based on male responsibility for agricultural production; men rarely took on any major aspect of domestic labor, such as washing, cooking, cleaning, caring for the children, fetching and carrying water, picking tubers, grinding corn, or feeding the chickens and pigs.

Although census enumerators may not have considered such servicing tasks to be work, peasant families, including both men and women, certainly did. Woman's work was recognized as crucial to family survival and reproduction, although within socially defined categories of what constituted women's work. The more this unpaid labor could be squeezed under capitalist productive forms, the greater was the surplus that could be extracted from sharecropping families and male wage labor alike. The same applied to child labor, which helps explain why large families were prevalent.

The general pattern before the revolution was that girls and boys started their working lives around age seven, the boys in the field with their fathers and the girls around the house with their mothers. At the height of the harvest when extra labor was essential, women and girls also cooked for the field hands. The poorer the peasant family, the greater was the need to fall back on family labor by using women and girls in the field to plant, weed, prune, and harvest the tobacco.

The type of tobacco determined to a large extent the kind and amount of work the women did. The cigar wrapper of San Luis, for example, was traditionally harvested by leaf, and the leaves were then threaded together to be strung on poles to dry. This work came to be almost exclusively women's work. It was considered particularly well suited for women because threading was carried out in the shade, with needle and thread. In contrast, the dark filler tobacco of Cabaiguán was stickier because of the black resin, and it was tougher to harvest. It was traditionally harvested by knife, on stalks of four leaves that were strung over the outstretched arm and then transferred to poles. This heavy work, along with field labor in general, was traditionally considered unsuitable for women. Also this tobacco did not need to be threaded because it was hung straight on the poles in the barns.

Regional variations were also evident in the tobacco sorting practices carried out before the harvest. In both municipalities, sorting provided temporary employment for thousands of women. The better quality wrapper tobacco of San Luis demanded greater classification into grades and therefore more skilled and better paid personnel. On average, 100 to 300 women were employed in each sorting shed in peak periods. The more select the farm, the better were the conditions of employment in this, the almost only rural paid labor for women outside the fields (*Cuba Contemporanea* 1942). But because of economic necessity many women and girls from the age of ten were forced to accept pittance wages for long hours of work in the less select sheds. In Cabaiguán, conditions of work and pay in the sorting sheds were on the whole worse. Moreover, given the lesser intensity of tobacco production in the province, larger sorting sheds employing up to 1,000 women were located only in towns, and women had to travel extensive distances, often on foot, to find wage employment.

Through the agrarian reform and rural development policies, peasant families received title to their land, family income was effectively increased, and children were placed in school. But—despite explicit government policies to the contrary—the old societal definition of women servicing the home and family was to a certain extent reinforced, especially in tobacco areas. This outcome was in part linked to the decline in production in the 1960s and the reduced demand for female labor in both the fields and sheds. The "tobacco recuperation" of the 1970s, in concert with the FMC-ANAP brigades and regularized employment for women in harvesting and sorting in the Cubatabaco state enterprise, has since helped bring women out of the home, as have the cooperatives.

Currently all tobacco farmers belong to either CCSs or CPAs. Within the CPAs, there has been a marked increased in the visibility of women and also a generally heightened awareness of women's role in production and of women's subordination even when women do not necessarily participate in either production or the day-to-day management of the cooperative. On the whole, neither the men nor the women expressed the view that women should not be working outside the home for the cooperative but rather spoke of how women's domestic responsibilities are an obstacle to their increased participation. Their dual role is by and large where the problem lies.

In the San Luis area, women constitute 31 percent of the CPA membership, compared with 1.6 percent of CCS membership and 21 percent of the workers on state farms. In the Cabaiguán area, they make up 38 percent of CPA membership, compared with 25 percent of CCS membership. As of 1983, there were no tobacco state farms in the municipality. In all three organizational forms, the figures exclude the seasonal labor participation of women, which at the height of the harvest is considerable; it runs to over a hundred on a typical large tobacco cooperative and over a thousand on a state farm. This seasonal female labor force includes women contracted from Cubatabaco, recruited among local nonworking women and from other sectors of production.

Criteria for membership differed enormously in the tobacco regions studied. On one of the older cooperatives both men and women had automatically been made members upon pooling their land, and thus membership numbers were fairly equal for the sexes. Among landless members, the application of strict criteria regarding stability of employment in agriculture often went against the incorporation of women as members. There were anomalous cases of landed women members who neither worked in the fields nor were active in cooperative business and women who worked substantially in agricultural production but whose membership was not recognized because they did not bring land into the cooperative. One working woman member lost her membership status upon divorcing because the man was considered the landed member.

In not one of the cooperatives studied was there any concept of household servicing being a part of the collective accumulation of wealth. At most, it was a semiconscious concept in discussions on such issues as eating facilities. Few cooperatives organized collective lunches for members, only for outside seasonal workers when these were employed. Women who cooked lunch on such occasions were remunerated as paid labor; those cooking for family members were not. One male accountant ventured to say that collective lunch facilities were "costly" to the cooperative, while at the same time lamenting that women's responsibilities in the home worked against their stability in field labor. On that cooperative, women constituted 50 percent of the members. Of the women members, only 19 percent actually worked in the fields; only 7 percent worked on a regular basis. Correspondingly, women worked only 11 percent of the total number of days worked by all cooperative members in the year and took a corresponding 11 percent of annual profits.

The slightly lower percentage of women members in San Luis (31 percent as against 38 percent in Cabaiguán), despite their longstanding work in tobacco, is explained in terms of its more urbanized nature; it provides other job possibilities for women. One recently formed cooperative found that the only potential woman member was the new young accountant from the area. Some wives of the cooperative farmers already worked for Cubatabaco as paid labor and would only be hired back by the cooperative during the harvest time. Other wives were older or with young children and would only work during peak harvest periods. Grown daughters were often employees of the state sector in education and health, at least until marrige, when small children interrupted work. Even then, San Luis differed from Cabaiguán in having more accessible day-care facilities. "Women in these parts don't like the fields," was the general comment about hard agricultural work there under the hot sun. In the Cabaiguán area, women often took in sewing from a nearby garment factory that could be done in the home as a "soft" option to field work.

Women's field work also varied considerably by region. In the dark filler tobacco area of Cabaiguán, where women had traditionally been less involved in tobacco production, women were organized into support brigades in such nontobacco activities as the production of roots and other vegetables for local consumption and sale to the state. This work was by no means obligatory for women, and some women took pride in working in tobacco rather than in these side-line activities. In San Luis, there was less production of other crops, women traditionally worked more in tobacco, and the division of field labor by gender was not marked.

One way in which younger women are integrated as cooperative members has to do with their studies: They may come back as the accountant or agronomist.[13] This trend can also be seen among younger men who may return as the qualified technician or tractor, truck, or combine harvest operator rather than as a field hand. Hope for the future is closely allied with technification.

Paradoxically, tobacco and coffee production, while mobilizing large numbers of seasonal women workers, has the least participation of women on cooperative executive committees, and to date no tobacco cooperative has had a woman president. Yet there are several women presidents of sugar cooperatives, even though women have not traditionally been heavily involved in that crop.

Over the last few years a concerted political effort has been made to ensure that at least one woman is a member of each cooperative executive committee. When one is a member, she still tends to be charged with the accounts or educational and recreational work while the men handle production.

One complaint from men in the Cabaiguán area was that women members not only worked in the fields less but also took less interest in day-to-day cooperative business. For example, some would not show up for the meetings. The women's complaint was that the men were going to have to change and carry their weight around the home for women to be able to participate more.

Although women's agricultural role may not have changed greatly, there is a growing questioning of gender roles. Generational change, especially between the women, is very marked and much talked about on the CPAs. "Machismo" is a current topic of conversation. The older generations feel that things are a lot easier than in their time and that new horizons are opening for women but that older women are too old to change now. The younger generations schooled away from home are beginning to challenge certain taboos. For example, Nena, now retired in her mid-sixties, remembers how from her early teens she had to help her mother by carrying food to the field hands and fetching water. Later she worked in the sorting sheds and took in washing and ironing. Now, she virtually runs her own household as well as her daughter's next door. Although her daughter, who works in the new local store, grew up in the early years of the revolution, she was quite restricted as a girl and married at seventeen. The granddaughters now have opportunities denied their mother. Nena's son, who became a college professor, continued to live with his mother in the cooperative village and did some housework even after marrying. In contrast, her daughter's husband, as president of the cooperative, has little or no time for the home. The granddaughters expressed resentment at being expected to help in the home much more than their brother did. The older granddaughter, in particular, was critical of the old-fashioned small-community gossip which limits girls' mobility, such as being out at night with boys.

Although few men currently perform housework, their participation is at least on the agenda. The women making the greatest demands on the men tend to be those who hold down jobs and political or social responsibilities. They might also be involved in the recently formed women's militia so that they are working a double or triple shift. These women are gaining confidence and questioning established mores, including the gender division of labor, male authority, and dual sexual standards.

Among the women's complaints was that men still felt that they had a right to have affairs whereas women did not. When the men in question held posts of authority, such behavior could be cause for collective action. In the case of a married couple on one executive committee, the husband went out with a younger woman member to the embarrassment of his wife and other committee women; as a result the man was suspended from his duties. Male-female tensions of this kind, both at a cooperative and personal level, cannot be resolved in the near future; however, they can be handled supportively if there is raised consciousness.

A New Crossroads
in a Decade of Transition

It has been argued here that women's work was a key component to traditional peasant agriculture. As the work and the development context in which it was placed changed, so did the nature and extent of women's work and lives. As economic pressures lessened and educational and job possibilities opened up, three marked trends appeared in women's work: (1) to seek work other than in agriculture, (2) to work on a casual, paid or unpaid basis in agriculture, and (3) to shake off field work and run the home. As a result, in a typical farm household, some peasant women show greater and others lesser degrees of agricultural participation and some engage in both agricultural and nonagricultural labor for the state. These same trends apply to the new cooperative sector but with the difference that women show a greater sense of commitment to the cooperative as such, both as a production unit and community in its own right, even if this commitment is not immediately manifest in quantitative ways.

We have attempted to show how integral women's labor is to peasant production as an economic form and the economic problems that are raised in the transition from the household to the cooperative farm. In the tobacco areas studied, the extent to which women became involved in both work and cooperative life and the resulting changes in collective and personal gender patterns depended often on technical questions such as the kind of tobacco and the way it had been traditionally harvested and on overall development factors of the region concerned. The two areas varied on both counts, and this variation, within general policy precepts and campaigns for women's equality, colored the kind of advances made.

The dichotomy between the small amount of full-time employment for women and the larger proportion of female casual and seasonal labor has meant that (1) the actual running of the cooperative fell more logically into male hands and (2) the payment of formerly "family" labor has become an increasingly costly problem, limiting cooperative profit margins.

We argued that, with strong policies and support for women at this juncture, cooperatives provide the productive structure best suited to catering to peasant women's needs in the productive and reproductive processes, ameliorating their subordinate position in both. At the last ANAP congress, in 1982, cooperative women delegates raised the issue of the obstacles limiting women's participation, the need for attention on this front, and the difference it makes once women are involved in the cooperative decision-making process.

Acknowledgments

This chapter draws on earlier papers by Mavis Alvarez (1983) and Jean Stubbs (1985). Stubbs was assisted by a grant from the Social Science Research Council and the American Council of Learned Societies, with the support in Cuba of ANAP, the Ministry of Agriculture, the Institute of Physical Planning, and the state tobacco enterprise CUBATABACO.

Notes

1. ANAP keeps detailed statistics at the national, provincial, and municipal level, and many of the private sector statistics have been taken from its records.

2. Shortage of labor was a constant throughout the 1960s and 1970s, and state agricultural enterprises relied heavily for their workforce on students from such schools spending half a day in agriculture and half a day in the classroom and from the school-to-the countryside program, whereby urban students spent from four to six weeks a year in agricultural camps. Aside from solving a labor problem, this arrangement allowed students (boys and girls) to benefit from experiencing the value of productive work.

3. Parallel state markets were introduced to sell produce at a higher price than on the rationing system but at prices that undercut the small farmer free market prices, especially as produce became more plentiful from the cooperatives. Most cooperatives took the eminently political decision to sell only to the state market and not on the free market, although they were under no obligation to do so. Free markets were finally eliminated at the request of the cooperatives after the May 1986 second national meeting of the CPAs.

4. In a sense, there has been a convergence between state farms and cooperatives. Today both enterprises rely heavily on self-management, and a direct percentage of end-of-year profits are plowed back for enterprise and local development. State farms or enterprises are still seen as a "higher form" of production. The rule of thumb generally is that in areas where there is a need for development plans with high investment, there is a preference for peasant land to pass into the state sector. Where there is no need for high investment but there is peasant specialization, then the best solution is the union of peasants into cooperatives.

5. According to Ministry of Health figures, hunger, malnutrition, and poverty have been effectively eliminated. In 1983, child malnutrition was down to 4.6 percent under the age of one, 0.7 percent for ages one to four. Infant mortality was down from 38.8 per 1,000 live births in 1970 to 17 per 1,000 in 1982, 15 per 1,000 in 1985.

6. Recent annual growth rates of around 5 percent were unquestionably more equitably distributed over society. According to official yearbook and census figures, in the last decade there has been a 48 percent increase in agricultural salaries compared with an 18 percent increase for wages in industry. In 1953 Cuba had an illiteracy rate of 10 percent, but the rate was 40 percent in the countryside, and only 34 percent of rural children aged six to sixteen were in school, contrasting with 67.7 percent of urban children. The Literacy Campaign of the early 1960s and its subsequent boost to education meant that by 1981 94 percent of urban children and 88 percent of rural children in that age group were in school. In 1958, there was one rural hospital; by 1983, there were fifty-four general hospitals, 163 medical posts, and fifty-five maternity homes in the countryside, not counting the many community polyclinics and the new family doctor plan.

7. FMC-ANAP brigades were organized in the 1960s to mobilize women in agricultural work, especially when men were mobilized for the military for distant work in the sugar harvest. By the late 1970s, with work more regularized, women pushed for their work to be remunerated, and regular production brigades of women were formed. Now, almost all work is remunerated and the brigades are virtually in abeyance.

8. This view came out strongly in the media at the time. The press ran features and interviews, and documentaries were shown such as the National Film Institute's twenty-minute documentary *Tierra sin cerca*, made by Idelfonso Ramos in 1977.

9. ACs grew originally out of prerevolutionary struggles against peasant eviction. CCSs emerged in tobacco areas where small growers needed collective access to certain resources, credits, and services. Agricultural societies went a step further by actually pooling land in the early 1960s. Some of Cuba's oldest cooperatives started out as agricultural societies. After an initial flourish, many of them disintegrated, partly because they received little expressed state support in comparison with the state enterprises. From as many as 346, there were only forty-one left at the start of the current cooperative movement.

10. A recent study by Pérez Rojas (n.d.) shows how individual (male) farmers still worry about losing their private farm and independence, being told what to do, and having to depend on others. On their own, they can make good sales on the free market and can set their own work pace. The study was conducted in a prosperous area, and individual small farmers were waiting to see if their cooperative counterparts were really better off.

11. Given that the private sector is an aging sector, cooperatives found substantial numbers of farmers retiring on pensions. A case can be made that with the age factor, migratory and generational patterns will of their own accord disintegrate the peasant economy. This is yet another reason to boost cooperativization and technification.

12. The problems (not dealt with here) include structural issues of cooperative organization, state-cooperative relations, "illicit" extra-agricultural activities of cooperatives, and the negative impact on the cooperative movement of lucrative individual farmer speculation—all of which were critically analyzed at the May 1986 second national meeting of the CPAs.

13. Ministry of Education figures for 1983 show women in the majority (51.6 percent) in higher agricultural studies for the twenty to twenty-four age group; the figure is significantly lower (15 percent) for the forty to forty-nine age group.

References

Acosta, José, "La estructura agraria y el sector agropecuario al triunfo de la revolución," *Economía y Desarrollo*, no. 9, January-February 1972.

—————, "La revolución agraria en Cuba y el desarrollo económico," *Economía y Desarrollo*, no. 17, May-June 1973.

Alvarez, Mavis, "Experiencia cubana en la promoción del rol de la mujer en la economía campesina," paper presented to the FAO/ECLA Panel on Peasant Economy Strategies: The Role of Women, Bogotá, 1983.

Catsús, Sonia, "Carácteristicas de los nucleos familiares en dos areas de estudio: Plaza de le Revolución y Yateras," Serie Monográfica 2, Centro de Estudios Demográficos, Universidad de la Habana, 1984.

Comité Estatal de Estadísticas, República de Cuba, *Censo de población y viviendas*, 1970 and 1981.

————, República de Cuba, *Anuario Estadístico de Cuba*, various issues.

————, República de Cuba, *Encuesta Demográfica Nacional*, 1979 (Havana, 1981).

Cruz Vera, Lidia Elizabeth, "Composición de la familia rural cubana," unpublished dissertation, Centro de Estudios Demográficos, Universidad de la Habana, 1985.

Cuba Contemporánea, Havana, 1942.

Deere, Carmen Diana, and Magdalena León de Leal, "Medición del trabajo de la mujer rural y su posición de clase," *Estudios de Población*, vol. 5, January–June 1980.

Gómez, Orlando, *De la finca individual a la cooperativa agropecuaria* (Havana: Editora Política, 1983).

González Quiñones, Fernando, *Cuba: participación de la mujer en la fuerza de trabajo y fecundidad. Un estudio de población y desarrollo* (Havana: Centro de Estudios Demográficos, Universidad de la Habana, forthcoming).

Larguiá, Isabel, and John Dumoulin, *Hacia una ciencia de la liberación de la Mujer* (Havana: Editorial de ciencias sociales, 1984).

————, "La mujer en el desarrollo: estratégia y experiencia de la Revolución cubana," *Casa*, no. 149, March-April 1985.

Martín Barrios, Adelfo, *La ANAP, 20 años de trabajo* (Havana: Editora Política, 1982).

Martínez-Alier, Juan, "The Peasantry and the Cuban Revolution from the Spring of 1959 to the End of 1960," *Latin American Affairs*, 1970.

Ministerio de Agricultura, República de Cuba, *Memorias del Censo Agrícola de 1946* (Havana, 1947).

Morejón Farnos, Alfonso, Fernando González, and Paul Hernández, *Las mujeres trabajadoras y los cambios demográficos en Cuba* (Havana: Centro de Estudios Demográficos, Universidad de la Habana, 1982).

Pérez Rojas, Niurka, "Análisis comparativo de las relaciones político-económicas del campesinado en does complejos agroindustriales azucareros en la provincia de La Habana," Centro de Estudios Demográficos, Universidad de la Habana, n.d., mimeo.

————, *Características socio-demográficas de la familia cubana, 1953–70* (Havana: Editorial de ciencias sociales, 1979).

Pollitt, Brian, "Some problems in enumerating the 'peasantry' in Cuba," *Journal of Peasant Studies*, vol. 4, no. 2, 1979.

————, "Agrarian reform and the 'agricultural proletariat' in Cuba, 1958–66: further notes and some second thoughts," University of Glasgow, Institute of Latin American Studies, Occasional Paper No. 30, 1980.

————, "Revolution and the mode of production in the sugar-cane sector of the Cuban economy, 1959–80: some preliminary findings," University of Glasgow, Institute of Latin American Studies, Occasional Paper No. 35, 1981.

————, "The Transition to Socialist Agriculture in Cuba: Some Salient Features," *IDS Bulletin*, 1983.

Rojas, Iliana, Mariana Ravenet, and Jorge Hernández, "Desarrollo y relaciones de clases en la estructura agraria en Cuba," in *Estudios sobre la estructura de clases y el desarrollo rural en Cuba* (Havana: Universidad de la Habana, 1983).

Stubbs, Jean, "Cuba: The Sexual Revolution," *Latin American Women Minority Groups Report*, no. 7, 1983.

_____, *Tobacco on the Periphery: A Case Study in Cuban Labour History, 1860–1958* (Cambridge: Cambridge University Press, 1985).

_____, "Gender Issues in Contemporary Cuban Tobacco Farming," *World Development*, forthcoming, January 1987.

Trinchet Vera, Oscar, *La cooperativa de la tierra en el agro cubano* (Havana: Editora Política, 1984).

Part 2
Comparative Perspectives on Development Initiatives

9

The Latin American
Agrarian Reform Experience

Carmen Diana Deere

Agrarian reform has constituted the major state initiative in Latin America with respect to agricutural development and rural income redistribution over the last several decades. In some countries, agrarian reform fundamentally altered rural class structure and the national distribution of wealth and power. In other countries, efforts at reform were minimal, sometimes only involving colonization or resettlement schemes. Whatever the form or scale, each agrarian reform has involved state intervention in the redistribution of land to formerly landless or land-poor households.

The impact of an agrarian reform upon rural women is related to the class position of each woman's household and whether that class, or segment of class, is a beneficiary of the reform. The broader the reform's redistributionary thrust, the more women it should potentially benefit. It cannot be assumed, however, that the impact of an agrarian reform on rural households is gender neutral. An increase in the household's access to land or employment or in its level of income does not necessarily mean a positive change in women's socioeconomic position. Processes of social change have complex economic, political, and ideological effects that may alter the social status of rural women as well as their position relative to men.

The central thesis of this chapter is that most Latin American agrarian reforms have directly benefited only men. It is argued that the reforms have had this result largely because households are designated as the beneficiaries of an agrarian reform but only male household heads are incorporated into the new agrarian reform structures. It is shown here that a necessary, but not sufficient, condition for rural women to benefit on a par with men is that they too be designated as beneficiaries. Women as well as men must be given access to land or the opportunity to participate in the agrarian cooperatives or state farms promoted by an agrarian reform. In this comparative analysis of the Latin American agrarian reforms it is demonstrated that this participation has taken place only in countries where the incorporation of rural women is an explicit objective of state policy.

This chapter first presents a brief overview of thirteen Latin American agrarian reforms and of the available gender-disaggregated data on reform beneficiaries. The following section analyzes the legal, structural, and ideological mechanisms that have led to the exclusion of women among the beneficiaries. The importance of state policy with regard to women's incorporation is analyzed in the next section, in which the positive experiences of rural women in Cuba and Nicaragua are compared to the contrasting ones in Chile. Subsequently, the importance of including women among reform beneficiaries is discussed. The last section examines the barriers to women's effective participation as cooperative members in those cases where they have been beneficiaries of an agrarian reform.

An Overview of the
Latin American Agrarian Reforms

To establish the context for the subsequent analysis, this section includes a brief overview of the principal features of thirteen Latin American agrarian reforms. No attempt is made to analyze the efficacy of each of the agrarian reforms with respect to its own goals or its actual impact upon the beneficiaries. Summarized in Table 9.1 are the year in which the agrarian reforms were initiated or subsequently modified, the most recent available estimate of beneficiaries and the proportion of rural households that they represent, and the predominant form of tenure and productive organization in the reformed sector.

The potential redistributive impact of an agrarian reform largely reflects the political projects that the reform represents.[1] The first three agrarian reforms carried out in Latin America—in Mexico, Bolivia, and Cuba—were the product of social revolutions. Through the agrarian reforms, the traditional hacienda was virtually eliminated and a major redistribution of landed property took place in favor of a significant proportion of the rural population.[2]

These three reforms differ, however, with respect to forms of tenancy and the organization of production in the reformed sector. The thrust of the Mexican agrarian reform was to set up the *ejido*, a form of communal-based property with production carried out either collectively and/or individually. The Bolivian agrarian reform favored the creation of individual private holdings. Although the 1959 Cuban agrarian reform also had a significant "land to the tiller" thrust (every tenant, sharecropper,

TABLE 9.1
The Latin American Agrarian Reforms

	Years Reform Initiated, Modified	Beneficiaries (Year of Data)	% Rural Households	Organization of Production
Mexico	1917, 1971	2,890,000 (1971)	69	ejidos
Bolivia	1952	217,000 (1970)	33	individual
Cuba	1959, 1963	260,000 (1963)	70	state, indiv., and prod. coops
Venezuela	1960	107,523 (1970)	17	indiv. and prod. coops
Colombia	1961, 1973	135,000 (1975)	10	indiv. and prod. coops
Costa Rica	1961	18,078 (1975)	9	individual
Honduras	1962, 1975	33,203 (1978)	8	indiv. and prod. coops
Dominican Republic	1962	11,000 (1970)	3	indiv. and some coops
Chile	1962, 1970	58,170 (1973)	20	asentamientos
Peru	1963, 1969	359,600 (1975)	37	prod. coops and some indiv.
Ecuador	1964, 1973	50,000 (1972)	7	indiv. and some coops
Nicaragua	1979, 1981	72,072 (1983)	30	state, prod. coops, and indiv.
El Salvador	1980	74,936 (1983)	12	prod. coops and indiv.

Sources for Table 9.1:

Mexico: Manzanilla (1977); percent of rural
households benefited based on estimated 4,210,877 rural
households in 1971.

Bolivia: Jemio (1973:43, 73-74); based on estimated
668,597 rural households in 1970. In 1970, 587 production
and marketing cooperatives were in existence with 25,009
members.

Cuba: Based on estimate of 110,000 new property
owners as results of 1959 and 1963 laws and permanent
employment on state farms of 150,000 by 1963 (MacEwan,
1981:53, 56). Mesa-Lago (1972:49) reports a somewhat
higher figure--200,000 new property owners--by the end of
the implementation of the 1963 agrarian reform. In 1983
there were 1,400 production cooperatives with 78,000
members (Benjamin et al. 1984).

Venezuela: Soto (1978:80); based on estimated
625,144 rural households in 1970. The figure on the
number of beneficiaries is highly disputed; other sources
put it closer to 95,000. In 1968 there were 210
production cooperatives with 78,000 members.

Colombia: Blutstein (1977:354); based on estimated
1,305,582 rural households in 1975. The beneficiaries
include the de facto recognition of squatters. Araya
(1975) reports a much lower figure for 1970--12,570
beneficiaries--amounting to only 1.1 percent of rural
households. In 1982, there were 1,284 empresas comunales
with 12,300 households (Caro 1982:196).

Costa Rica: Barahona (1980:275); based on estimated
214,516 rural households in 1975. Seligson (1980:152)
reports a much lower figure--11,306 beneficiary families
in 1976--representing only 5.3 percent of rural households
in that year. In 1977 seventeen production cooperatives
were reported in existence with 517 members.

Honduras: Callejas (1983); Honduras (n.d.:7); based
on 428,516 rural households. In 1976, 133 empresas
associativas were reported, with 10,000 members.

Dominican Republic: Weil (1973:182); based on
estimated 446,835 rural households.

Chile: Cifuentes (1975); based on estimated 290,850
rural households.

Peru: Caballero and Alvarez (1980). The number of
beneficiaries is deceptive; over one-third of the
beneficiaries enumerated in this estimate consist of
households in the officially recognized peasant
communities with adjudicated access to grazing land.
Estimate based on 971,892 rural households in 1975.

Ecuador: Franco Garcia (1976:49); based on estimated 716,447 rural households. Blankstein and Zuvekas (1973:81) report that 88 percent of huasipungo households (engaged in feudal relations of production on large estates) became landowners through the reform.

Nicaragua: The estimate includes 22,072 individuals who have received land either as individual holdings or as part of a production cooperative by December 1983 under the 1981 agrarian reform law, as well as 50,000 permanent workers on the state farms (Deere et al. 1985). The figure is an underestimation of the total number of beneficiaries because it does not include those who have gained access to land through the reform but who have not yet received land titles. In 1983, there were an estimated 238,602 rural households.

El Salvador: The estimate includes 35,000 cooperative members on the Phase I estates and 39,936 applicants for individual land parcels under Decree 207 as of December 1983 (Deere 1984). The figure is probably an overestimation of the total number of beneficiaries because only 252 applicants under Decree 207 have actually received definitive land titles. The number of rural households in 1983 was estimated as 624,386.

Data on the number of rural households were estimated from UN Demographic Yearbook (1979); 1977 Compendium of Social Statistics (UN 1980); America en Cifras (OAS, 1977), and the O.A.S. Statistical Bulletin, vol. 3, no. 34, 1981.

and squatter was given ownership of the land that he or she cultivated), the bulk of the expropriated land was used for state farms. Only in the late 1970s was emphasis placed on the promotion of production cooperatives based on peasants pooling their individual holdings.

The 1960s agrarian reforms were initiated in Latin America under the Alliance of Progress, which made U.S. development assistance contingent on Latin American countries instituting such reforms. According to U.S. policy revolutionary social change could be avoided in the Americas only if the pressing issues of rural inequality and poverty were addressed.

Launched in the wake of the Cuban revolution, the Alliance for Progress agrarian reforms aimed both at containing the peasantry as a potential revolutionary force and at breaking the power of the landed elite. The traditional landowning class was viewed as an impediment to development and its hold on political power as a barrier to modernization. Moreover, it was argued, the redistribution of land would not only satisfy the peasantry's potential revolutionary demands, but it would also spur growth by putting land into the hands of those who worked it most intensively and, through their higher incomes, lead to an enlargement of the internal market. A broader internal market, in turn, would stimulate investment and hence overall growth. Agrarian reform was thus the ideal mechanism both to contain the peasantry and to establish the preconditions for successful capitalist development.

Nevertheless, agrarian reform efforts in many Latin American countries were minimal even though agrarian reform laws were now on the books. Considered in this analysis are only those countries where relatively serious attempts at reform were made. Of the agrarian reforms initiated under the Alliance for Progress only those in Peru, Chile, and Venezuela created a significant number of beneficiaries. In Peru and Chile, this only occurred after the initial Alliance for Progress reforms were modified and implemented by more progressive governments—the Allende government in Chile (from 1970 to 1973) and the revolutionary military regime in Peru (from 1969 to 1978).

The Alliance for Progress agrarian reforms generally favored the creation of individual private property, as shown in Table 9.1. Often this was accompanied by the organization of credit and service or marketing cooperatives among individual producers. In the 1970s, a number of countries gave priority to the organization of production cooperatives (based on collective or group farming), such as the *asentamientos* in Honduras or the *empresas communitarias campesinas* of Colombia. The Allende reform in Chile and that of the Peruvian military favored collective forms of production, although some land was also distributed to individuals.

In Central America, the agrarian reform initiatives of the 1980s are the product of the revolutionary upheaval. The Nicaraguan and Salvadoran reforms represent quite different political projects. That in Nicaragua is being carried out in the context of revolutionary transformation, in the tradition of the first three Latin American agrarian reforms. Within the reformed sector, equal priority has been given to the constitution of state farms, production cooperatives, and individual producers grouped in credit and service cooperatives (Deere et al. 1985). In contrast, as a political project the Salvadoran agrarian reform is being carried out—in the legacy of the Alliance for Progress—to contain the peasantry as a revolutionary force (Deere 1984). The reformed sector includes both production cooperatives and a "land to the tiller" program.

All except the latter two agrarian reforms were initiated before feminism became an international force and before women's participation in development became a development concern. Since 1973, the Percy amendment to the U.S. Foreign Assistance Act has required all U.S.-financed development programs to take into account the impact on women. Moreover, since 1975 when the UN Decade for Women was launched, many Latin American countries have created governmental women's commissions or bureaus to oversee state policy with regard to women. To what extent have these efforts brought state policy to bear positively on the position of rural women within the Latin American agrarian reforms?

Agrarian Reform Beneficiaries
According to Gender

The majority of Latin American agrarian reforms have not produced significant numbers of female beneficiaries or even given attention to gender as a beneficiary category. As shown in Table 9.2 few Latin American countries report beneficiary data by sex. Even after a decade of "women in development" efforts, the majority of countries still publish beneficiary data according to the number of households or families benefited. For example, in the recent Salvadoran agrarian reform, potential beneficiaries applying for land under Decree 207 (the "land to the tiller" program) are not asked to report their sex.[3]

The available national-level data suggest that only in Cuba do women represent a significant number of current agrarian reform beneficiaries. In 1985, women constituted 25 percent of the 71,246 members of the country's production cooperatives; in addition, they constituted 14 percent of the workers on state farms (see Stubbs and Alvarez, Chapter 8).

In Mexico, women make up 15 percent of the ejido members. According to Arizpe and Botey (Chapter 4), however, this figure is misleading because most of these women are older widows who inherited the formal right to an ejido parcel upon the death of their husbands.

The 1982 Nicaraguan Cooperative Census revealed that 20 percent of the production cooperatives and 60 percent of the credit and service cooperatives (based on individual private holdings) had at least one woman member. However, women represented only 6 percent of the total cooperative membership of 64,891. Rural women in Nicaragua fared somewhat better than their Honduran counterparts who represent 3.8 percent of the agrarian reform beneficiaries.

Survey data for some of the other Latin American countries reveal the limited number of female beneficiaries. In a 1971 survey of eighty-three Peruvian agrarian reform cooperatives Buchler (1975) found that of 724 members interviewed, approximately 5 percent were women. But as a national estimate, even this figure may be high because the survey excluded the important coastal agro-industrial sugar cooperatives in which membership was almost exclusively male. Moreover, regional studies in northern Peru, of the cotton-producing zone of Piura (Fernandez 1982) and of the highland province of Cajamarca (Deere 1977) found that women constituted only 2 percent of cooperative membership. In

TABLE 9.2
Women in the Latin American Agrarian Reforms

	% Women Beneficiaries	Beneficiary Criteria
Mexico	15.0% (1985)	Individuals over sixteen; any age if have dependent; men or women farmers
Bolivia	--*	Individuals over eighteen if feudatario; over fourteen if married; widows with children may receive land
Cuba	25.0% (1985)	Individuals; state policy goal to incorporate women
Venezuela	--	Individuals over eighteen; preference to household heads with most dependents and most efficient farmers
Colombia	--	Individuals; point system favored farming experience, education
Costa Rica	--	Individuals over eighteen; preference to household heads with most dependents and farming experience
Honduras	3.8% (1979)	Sixteen years if single male; any age if married male; single or widowed women with children may apply
Dominican Republic	--	Heads of household
Ecuador	--	Individuals
Peru	--	Eighteen years, heads of household with dependent children, agriculturalists
Chile	--	Eighteen years and married or effective heads of household; point system, favored "aptitude" for agriculture
Nicaragua	6.0% (1982)	Individual; an objective of agrarian reform to incorporate women
El Salvador	--	Individuals

*-- = no data available

Sources for Table 9.2:
Mexico: Arizpe and Botey (Chapter 4, this book); Anaya
    (1976: ch. 9).
Bolivia: Jemio (1973:42); Article 78 of A. R. Law.
Cuba: Stubbs and Alvarez (Chapter 8, this book).
Venezuela: Guerrero (1962); Articles 104, 63 of A. R.
    Law.
Costa Rica: Escoto (1965:11).
Honduras: Callejas (1983); Honduras (1976:237-288);
    Articles 97-125 of A. R. Law.
Dominican Republic: CEDEE (1983); Castro et al. (1983).
Chile: Garrett (1982).
Ecuador: Redclift (1978).
Peru: Deere (1986); Article 84 of A. R. Law.
Nicaragua: CIERA (1984: ch. 2).
El Salvador: Simon et al. (1982), appendix 1.

Ecuador, a survey of one coastal region revealed that 6 percent of the members were women (Phillips, Chapter 6).

The findings of the available studies of the agrarian reforms in Chile, the Dominican Republic, and Colombia all suggest that the overwhelming majority of the agrarian reform beneficiaries have been men (Garrett 1982; Castro et al. 1983; CEDEE 1983; Caro 1982). No mention of women's participation could be found in the literature on the remaining agrarian reforms surveyed.

Mechanisms of Exclusion

The participation of rural women within the agricultural labor force in Latin America—both within peasant units of production and as seasonal wage workers—has now been well documented in the literature (see the Introduction to this book). Yet, as the data demonstrate, women have largely been excluded as agrarian reform beneficiaries. The mechanisms of exclusion include legal, structural, and ideological factors. Underlying almost all these agrarian reforms has been the assumption that the rural household is the primary social unit to benefit from the reform. But for purposes of implementation, in all countries except Cuba and Nicaragua, only one member of the household—the household head—has been officially designated the beneficiary. Hence, only the head of household has received land in his/her name or the right of membership in production cooperatives or credit and service cooperatives in the reformed sector.

Restricting beneficiaries to only household heads discriminates against women since throughout Latin America social custom dictates that if both an adult man and woman reside in a household, the man is considered its head. Yet in the majority of agrarian reforms examined, the beneficiary criteria either required or gave strong preference to heads of households. Even in those cases in which beneficiaries were defined as individuals, it was usually assumed, if not explicitly stated, that only one individual per household could be designated a beneficiary and that was the household head. As a result, the only women who could potentially be reform beneficiaries were either widows or single mothers with no adult male living in the household.

A related structural problem is that many agrarian reforms have benefited only the permanent agricultural wage workers employed on estates at the moment of expropriation and excluded the often large seasonal labor force from cooperative membership. In both Peru and Chile, the permanent agricultural wage workers on the expropriated estates were generally men, although women were often an important component of the seasonal labor force. Fernandez (1982) shows how on the northern Peruvian cotton plantations women represented up to 40 percent of the temporary labor force but held few permanent jobs on the plantations; as a result, women constituted only 2 percent of the cooperative membership.

The inability of many of these reforms to benefit the vast majority of seasonal agricultural workers is prejudicial to both men and women. But although men are found in both categories of workers—permanent and seasonal—the structural characteristics of women's labor force participation result in women being excluded as a social group. The few women permanent workers on the estates, and thus potential beneficiaries of the reform, were then subject to an additional criterion: that they be household heads. This requirement, of course, reduced their participation still further.

Many of the reforms instituted in the Alliance for Progress period, besides prioritizing landless workers and tenants, determined potential beneficiaries on the basis of a point system. In Colombia, for example, the point system favored those whose history of residence or work was in or near the expropriated farm and those peasants with more education, larger family size, good reputations, and farming experience (Edwards 1980:59). Women would certainly be at a disadvantage compared to men in terms of educational attainment. Moreover, female heads of household might also suffer under the reputation criterion if nonconformity with the patriarchal nuclear family norm lowered their status in the eyes of the community. Women would also be disadvantaged by the farming experience criterion if socially men are considered to be the agriculturalists and women, as unremunerated family labor, are simply regarded as the "helpers."

Ideological norms governing the proper gender division of labor—that a woman's place is in the home while a man's is in the fields—often appear in the content of agrarian reform legislation, particularly in inheritance provisions that explicitly assume that beneficiaries will be male. Article 83 of the Venezuelan agrarian reform, for example, provides that in case of death or abandonment by the beneficiary, "the Institute will adjudicate the parcel to his wife or concubine, or in third place to the son" (Guerrero 1962). A similar provision is also found in the Costan Rican agrarian reform law (Escoto 1965:12).

Ideological norms also constitute a significant barrier to the incorporation of women as beneficiaries in reforms that explicitly provide for the inclusion of female-headed households, such as Bolivia and Honduras. For example, the 1962 Honduran agrarian reform law guaranteed the rights of both widows and single women household heads but discriminated against single women without dependents as compared to single men.[4] To qualify as a beneficiary a person had to "be Honduran by birth, male, over 16 years of age if single or any age if married, or a single woman or widow if in charge of a family" (Article 68 in Escoto 1965:46).

In terms of preference ordering, the Honduran law does give female household heads priority over male heads and single men, unless the men exploited land under indirect forms of tenancy, had been previously dispossessed of their land, or had access to insufficient land as established by the zone (Escoto 1965:47). Apparently, the overwhelming number of rural men fell into one of these categories; Youssef and LeBel (1981:57) report that "in existing *asentamientos* women have last priority in being allocated land; they follow male-headed households, and single males." Yet in 1974 18.7 percent of Honduran rural households were headed by women (Callejas 1983).

An in-depth study of four Honduran asentamientos illustrates how the implementation of the law has resulted in the virtual exclusion of female household heads (Safilios-Rothschild 1983:19). Women were simply not considered to be agriculturalists. Although women's participation in certain agricultural tasks was recognized, women were not considered capable of carrying out the heavier agricultural tasks that required greater physical strength. Male cooperative members felt that women could join the cooperatives only if they had sons, preferably adult sons to replace them in agricultural field work. Thus, the predominant norms of the gender division of labor served as a barrier to women's incorporation within the agrarian reform, even though the law explicitly provided for at least female heads of household to be potential beneficiaries.

The Preconditions for Female Participation

Cuba, Mexico, and Nicaragua are the only countries reviewed in which neither sex nor kinship position has been a legal barrier in recent years to the inclusion of women in the agrarian reform process. Theoretically, not only female heads of household but also wives and daughters could qualify as beneficiaries. However, only in Cuba and Nicaragua is the incorporation of rural women an explicit state policy goal.

The Cuban agrarian reform commenced along a road similar to the processes just described in terms of rural women's participation. The numerically important small farm sector created through the first agrarian reform law (1959) was considered to benefit household units. The National Association of Small Producers (ANAP)—the principal organization charged with developing credit and service cooperatives and other associations among private producers—was constituted of household heads who were primarily men. Within the state sector, the membership of the agricultural unions was also overwhelmingly male since they organized the permanent workers on the former sugar and cattle estates, who were generally men. Although the number of permament workers within the state sector steadily increased, particularly after the 1963 agrarian reform law was promulgated, few women were employed on a permanent basis until the late 1960s.

The development of an explicit state policy with regard to the incorporation of rural women within the agrarian reform process was a response to both ideological and economic considerations. As the Cuban revolution began to develop its explicitly socialist character, the issue of equality, not just between social classes but between men and women, had to be addressed. Drawing on Marxist teachings, the Cubans accepted the theoretical premise that women's equality with men required their incorporation into the social labor force (Engels 1975). The incorporation of women into productive labor was seen as a necessary step not only for women's own social development but also for the transformation of the social relations of Cuban society (Castro 1981; PCC 1976).

This theoretical position was complemented in the late 1960s by the economic imperative of increasing rural women's agricultural participation. The expansion of sugar cane production in the late 1960s significantly increased the demand for temporary labor. At this time a concrete policy to integrate rural women into the labor force took form, largely as a result of the joint efforts of ANAP and the Cuban Women's Federation (FMC). In 1966, these two mass organizations joined to promote the FMC-ANAP brigades of rural women (FMC 1975). At first consisting of volunteer labor, these brigades provided the mechanism for thousands of rural women to participate in social production for the first time (Bengelsdorf and Hageman 1977). It was estimated that by the mid-1970s women constituted over half of the seasonal labor force for the sugar cane, coffee, tobacco, and fruit harvests (FMC 1975).

The FMC-ANAP brigades provided an important mechanism for organizing rural women and helped prepare them for the role they were subsequently to play in the development of production cooperatives in the post-1975 period. In 1975, production cooperatives received official endorsement for the first time; state incentives were given for private farmers to voluntarily collectivize their holdings. Among the incentives was the possibility of constructing a new agricultural community that allowed the socialization of many of women's domestic tasks. Of equal importance were women's right of membership and guaranteed employment in the production cooperatives.

In contrast to the Cuban case, where women's participation in the agrarian reform evolved over the course of the revolution, the Nicaraguan agrarian reform included from the beginning the incorporation of women among its objectives. In the 1981 agrarian reform law, neither sex nor kinship position is a limitation on being an agrarian reform beneficiary. And the incorporation of women into the agricultural cooperatives is an explicit objective detailed in the 1981 Agricultural Cooperative Law (Ch. II, Article 2). Moreover, the legislation requires that women be integrated into the cooperatives under the same conditions as men, with the same rights and duties.

In a recent study of women's participation in the Nicaraguan agrarian reform cooperatives it was found that many women did not await the passage of the reform legislation to begin joining the agricultural cooperatives (CIERA 1984: ch. 3). In the majority of cases, women joined the cooperatives as they were being constituted in the 1979–1981 period. This move reflects the important participation of Nicaraguan women in the struggle that defeated the Somoza dictatorship; women felt that they "had won their right" to participate in the cooperative movement. Nevertheless, the CIERA study also showed that even in a revolutionary setting, cooperatives continue to be organized without taking into account the possible participation of women (see Padilla et al. in Chapter 7). Male cooperative members assert that women are not interested in cooperatives because they do not perform agricultural work; this opinion reflects ideological biases rather than reality. Women had demonstrated their interest in joining several of the cooperatives, but the male members had ignored them. Male members were often reluctant to admit women as members because they did not believe that women could carry out a sufficient number of agricultural tasks.

Nevertheless, case studies of ten cooperatives with women members revealed that women participated in productive activities on par with the men (Deere 1983; CIERA 1984). Moreover, men in cooperatives with women members were much more positive about women's participation and contribution than men in cooperatives without women members. This finding has also been reported in the Honduran case (Safilios-Rothschild 1983). It suggests not only that a positive state policy with regard to women creates the necessary preconditions for women's participation but also that giving women a chance to participate has important effects on ideological norms regarding the gender division of labor. This result, as will be subsequently discussed, has important implications for successful cooperative development.

The importance of a clear and vigorous state policy with respect to women's participation is illustrated by the Chilean agrarian reform (Garrett 1982). Upon taking office in 1970, the Allende government broadened the criteria for defining beneficiaries. The imbalance between the situation of permanent and temporary workers on the asentamientos (who were, respectively, the members and nonmembers) was seen to be particularly problematic, so the asentamientos were reorganized to facilitate the incorporation of temporary workers.

By broadening the potential beneficiaries of the reform, the legal-structural impediments to women's participation within the new agrarian reform structures were eliminated. All individuals over eighteen years of age were eligible to become members of the general assembly of the new Centers of Agrarian Reform (CERAs). Although the conditions theoretically were in place for women to participate in the agrarian reform, the new regulations did not result in the incorporation of a significant number of rural women. This failing was partly caused by the Popular Unity government's lack of clarity on the role of women in the agrarian reform.

Garrett's (1982) analysis shows how ideological and political factors worked against the incorporation of women into the reformed sector even after their participation was made legally possible. She argues that women's participation in the CERAs was resisted by both men and women. This reaction reflected the conservative influence of the strongest women's organization in the countryside, the *Centros de Madres* (mothers' centers), organized by the Christian Democratic party under the Frei administration. The centers, which focused on and promoted women's domestic role, gave little attention to women's role in production or to social problems since these activities were considered inappropriate for women. But they did provide rural women with a social outlet that drew them away from their homes into a forum where they could discuss their everyday problems.

The centers apparently were never integrated into the structure of the asentamientos. The Popular Unity government recognized that this distance was a problem and proposed to organize rural women into social welfare committees linked to each CERA. The social welfare committees were intended to find collective solutions to social problems. But as Garrett illustrates, neither men nor women agreed that women should be concerned with problems beyond their own domestic units. Few rural women joined the social welfare committees, and the Allende government did not direct the human resources required to organize rural women along lines different from those that had been traditionally successful. This lack of support was partly the result of the difficult political conjuncture with which the Allende government was faced by 1973, but it also reflects the lack of a clear state policy. This omission served as a source of confusion and a barrier to women's incorporation.

The Importance of Incorporating Women

It is important for women as well as men to be included among the direct beneficiaries of an agrarian reform to ensure both social equity and the success of cooperative development. The exclusion of women not only has high costs for women because their position can be harmed both relative to men's and absolutely; it also has costs for cooperative and rural development programs in general. If the goal of an agrarian reform is to foster a process of social transformation, as was the case in various of these reforms, then the exclusion of one social group on the basis of gender or family position limits the breadth and depth of the reform process.

Social equity criteria would require that if both men and women are permanent agricultural workers both are entitled to become beneficiaries of an agrarian reform. An example from the dairy region of northern Peru, the province of Cajamarca, illustrates the discriminatory nature of constituting production cooperatives on the basis of only those permanent workers who are household heads (Deere 1977). In this region, women made up from 30 percent to 50 percent of the permanent workers on the dairy farms because milking (still done manually) was considered a female task. But of the fifteen agrarian reform production cooperatives in the province, only five had female members, and overall, women constituted only 2 percent of the total cooperative membership. The women workers were excluded from cooperative membership primarily because they did not qualify as household heads as a result of their kin relationship to a male permanent worker on the farm. As a result the only women who became cooperative members were widows or single mothers with children under eighteen years of age.

If a goal of state policy in creating production cooperatives is to allow the participation of workers in the decisions concerning their labor process and in the allocation of the surplus that they produce, the exclusion of one group from membership on the basis of sex and kinship is at best discriminatory. At worst, it creates the conditions internal to the cooperative for the exploitation of one social group by another.

This discrimination is also evident as a result of the distinction between permanent workers (the cooperative members) and temporary workers. In the Peruvian reform process, few temporary workers were incorporated into the cooperatives; they also were not covered by social benefits and their wages were usually lower than those of the cooperative members. Fernandez (1982) and Chambeu (1981) report that in the cooperatives in Piura and Cuzco not only were the majority of women working on the cooperatives temporary workers but the women earned lower wages than did the male temporary workers. Moreover, women's wages relative to both male temporary workers and cooperative members declined over the reform period. In the Piura cotton cooperatives, work opportunities for women also declined over the reform period (Fernandez 1982). Since women had been excluded from cooperative membership, they had no recourse to this deterioration in their economic position.

Processes of agrarian reform may also be harmful to women in terms of changes in traditional patterns of land rights. In most Andean highland areas, land inheritance has been bilateral. Women's ownership of land has assured them participation in agricultural decision-making and in the allocation of household income. Land ownership has also given women a modicum of material security for they have not been totally dependent upon their spouses. If a woman was abandoned or separated from her spouse, her inheritance assured her of a means of maintaining her family as a single woman. The Peruvian agrarian reform process represented a real setback for rural women. The individual land titles distributed by the Belaunde government (in the postreform period) were generally issued only in the name of the male household head.

Indirect participation in a reform process (through the head of household) is not necessarily equivalent to direct participation. The organization of credit and service cooperatives among independent producers on the basis of only male household heads may have important consequences for women's agricultural productivity. Providing technical assistance only to men will not guarantee that women will gain access to the information or that they will take it into account and put it into practice. The Nicaraguan cooperative study found an impressive degree of disparity in the level of technological knowledge of women members and nonmembers (CIERA 1984: ch. 5). Male cooperative members rarely shared what they were learning with their nonmember wives.

The 1979–1983 Honduran National Development plan appears laudatory in that it calls for the incorporation of 5,625 peasant women who are "direct or indirect" beneficiaries of the reform in activities leading to the economic diversification of the cooperatives (Honduras n.d.). But incorporating women as temporary wage workers or into special income-generating projects does not necessarily lead to an improvement in their material well-being or status. Without the status of cooperative membership the women are ensured neither control of the resources necessary to carry out complementary income-generating activities (Garrett 1982) nor participation in the decisions governing labor allocation, wages, or the surplus produced.

The 1971 Mexican law (Article 103) is also unusual in that it provides women who are non-ejido members access to one parcel of land for collective agro-industrial activities. Although this legal attention to women is commendable, these rights are not the equivalent to having land in one's own name or to participating in the decisions of the ejido.

Moreover, all too often special projects aimed at women fail to recognize their productive role and focus only on their domestic role. This emphasis has been evident not only in Honduras and Mexico but also in Chile, Venezuela, and the Dominican Republic. In these countries, the Christian Democratic parties have organized mothers' clubs or mothers' centers in the countryside since the 1960s; in these women are taught skills as an extension of their domestic role: cooking, sewing, flower arrangement (Callejas 1983; Garrett 1982; Soto 1978; CEDEE 1983; Castro et al. 1983).

When an agrarian reform directs state efforts and resources to benefit one group of the population through access to land, credit, technical assistance, marketing channels, and so on, it concentrates resources on only one specific group, with socioeconomic consequences for those excluded. It cannot be assumed that by benefiting the male head of household, all household members will be benefited as well. Neither can it be assumed that by organizing women into their own gender-specific activities women will not lose out relative to men. Neither the household nor the effects of a process of state intervention are gender neutral.

Women as a Positive Force
for Cooperative Development

The Nicaraguan experience thus far indicates that the incorporation of women into the agrarian cooperatives has been beneficial for cooperative development. In the cooperatives with female members women are considered to be excellent agricultural workers, and they are a force of cohesion and stability within the cooperatives. For example, proportionately more men than women left the production cooperatives as the result of personal feuds with other cooperative members or because they did not like collective work. The relatively few women who abandoned the cooperatives more frequently left because of family problems such as jealous husbands (Deere 1983).

In the few cooperative enterprises in Colombia with women members, they have been noted to be a stabilizing force. Lodoño (1975:144) reports that

> the integration of the woman and family has proven itself of real influence in the cohesiveness of the *empresa*. When the family lives on *empresa* land, when the woman participates in the assemblies and in the committees, with voice and even with vote, when she is listened to on problems of management and administration, the whole group feels itself more rooted in the *empresa*.

In Nicaragua, as in Cuba, women appear to be a favorable force behind collectivization. In Nicaragua, the strong commitment of the women members of the production cooperatives to collective work is in many ways explained by the history of discrimination against women in rural Nicaragua. The majority of women members were previously landless wage workers, and as women they had fewer agricultural employment opportunities than did the men. Moreover, in the past, women have always been paid less than men, even for the same task. Today they earn the same amount as men irrespective of the task performed, and the cooperatives offer them security of employment for the first time (CIERA 1984).

The discrimination women have traditionally faced also explains why women seem less prone than men to dream of their own private plots and why in some areas women have voluntarily pooled their private land parcels to form a production cooperative. Because women had not been taken seriously as agricultural producers in the past, they had been excluded from access to credit and technical assistance. Moreover, female household heads often found it more difficult than men to acquire sufficient labor for certain agricultural tasks and to acquire male labor for the key "male only" tasks. Pooling their land offers them the security of permanent employment and income.

In Cuba, female support for collectivization seems to be particularly tied to the advantages offered women in the realm of reproduction. Up through the 1970s, Cuban policy greatly favored workers on state farms through the development of agricultural communities. These new communities offer modern housing, with the guarantee of potable water, sanitation, and electricity; moreover, they offer health centers, schools and day-care centers, communal eating facilities, and stores provisioned with basic necessities. The principal policy change in the formation of production cooperatives was that for the first time the facilities for the construction of an agricultural community would be offered to farmers who pooled their land to form such a cooperative. The state would provide the materials and technical assistance if the new cooperative members provided the labor.

Cuban rural women are quite clear about the benefits offered by the new agricultural communities (Deere 1986). They emphasize the increase in their families' standards of living and well-being and the importance of having convenient child care. Moreover, the improved housing greatly reduces the drudgery of housework. Women's enthusiasm for the new agricultural communities has been a central factor in the successful development of the production cooperatives, and that enthusiasm is tied to the benefits offered women with respect to their responsibility for household reproduction.

Ensuring Women's Effective Participation as Cooperative Members

An explicit state policy regarding the inclusion of women as beneficiaries is crucial if women are to directly benefit from agrarian reforms. In addition, the state must give attention to the material and ideological aspects of women's subordination if women are to achieve full equality with men as cooperative members.

A fairly common observation among those who have studied agrarian cooperatives with women members in Latin America is that though women might participate in the productive activities of the cooperatives on a par with men, they play a much reduced role in cooperative decision-making. In the Peruvian cooperatives, for example, female members usually attended cooperative meetings but rarely actually participated in the discussions (Deere 1977; Fernandez 1982; Chambeu 1981; Buchler 1975).

Fernandez (1982) reports that in northern Peru women as well as men viewed women's lack of education as a central factor in their inability to participate as effective cooperative members. In rural Peru, women are disproportionately illiterate. The men reportedly viewed this deficiency as the principal reason why women were unqualified to participate in decisions regarding the cooperative. The women viewed their illiteracy as the primary reason why men showed little respect for their views and why they were afraid to speak at cooperative meetings. But women constituted a minority of the members of these cooperatives and the sheer power of numbers might also explain the women's reluctance to participate in the meetings.

In the Nicaraguan cooperatives the women members were less likely than the men to offer their opinions in cooperative meetings and to be actively involved in the affairs of the cooperative (CIERA 1984). Although the majority of women members in Nicaragua are literate (most as a result of the 1980 literacy campaign), few have confidence in their ability to deal with the complex affairs of cooperative management. Moreover, household responsibilities often limit their ability to participate in the ongoing adult education program, thereby reproducing the inequality in functional literacy levels.

The responsibility of women for domestic chores and child care limits their ability to participate as effective cooperative members in other ways. The working day of women members is much longer than that of their male counterparts. The women members commonly spend two to three hours in domestic labor before going out into the fields, and after a six to eight hour day working for the cooperative, they return home to resume their domestic tasks. In contrast, the men usually socialize with the other male cooperative members after work, often using this time to discuss cooperative business (CIERA 1984).

The problem of the double day also affects the ability of women to meet their full membership responsibilities within the cooperatives. It also explains, in the Peruvian case, the poor retention rate of women members. Chambeu (1981) reports that in a Cuzco cooperative the male members felt that women were not serious about their commitment to the cooperative because they often could not work a full day because of family problems. If the children are sick, usually women must leave work to care for them. Rather than viewing this as a social problem, this cooperative in 1980 voted not to accept any more women members. The cooperative had already lowered women's wages with respect to men's, contrary to Peruvian minimum wage provisions.

Childbearing is another factor that sometimes places women cooperative members at a disadvantage. In few countries have cooperatives made provisions for paid maternity leave. Only in Cuba are women cooperative members covered by a national social security system that includes paid maternity leave among its benefits. In the Peruvian case, cooperative members were covered by labor legislation that stipulated a woman worker's right to paid maternity leave, but the costs of such legislation fell on the individual cooperative. The male cooperative leaders considered it unjust for the cooperative to bear this cost and in at least one case pressured a pregnant member to resign.

The responsibility of women for domestic labor and child care, their relatively lower educational attainment, and their lack of authority over men are among the principal reasons cited for why women are not elected to leadership positions within the cooperatives. In Peru, only a handful of cases have been reported of cooperatives with women officers (Bronstein 1982; Chambeu 1981). The data on women in cooperative leadership positions in Cuba and Nicaragua are more encouraging. In Cuba, women occupied 12 percent of the cooperative leadership positions in 1985 (see Chapter 8). Case studies of ten Nicaraguan cooperatives with women members revealed that in half a woman was a cooperative officer (CIERA 1984). In most cases a woman had been elected to a leadership position as a result of an explicit consensus within the cooperative that the women members should have a representative.

Of all the reforms in Latin American countries, the agrarian reform process in Cuba shows the most impressive gains for women. But even there, women do not participate in production on equal terms with men. Benjamin et al. (1984) report that women's earnings on the cooperatives are substantially lower than the men's. There is still a marked gender division of labor in productive tasks, and men's tasks are often better paid. Further, women cooperative members often work fewer days and fewer hours per day than the men because of household responsibilities. And women are still disproportionately represented among the temporary workers who provide seasonal labor to the state farms and production cooperatives.

Cuban state policy has recognized the burden of the double day for women and its role in limiting women's full participation in production. The 1975 Family Law requires men to share equally in childrearing and in domestic maintenance tasks when the wife works in social production (see Stone 1981: Appendix 2). This step is most innovative in terms of social policy. Its importance lies in state recognition that women's participation in social production alone is not enough to guarantee women's equality with men as long as women carry the burden for reproduction. If domestic labor cannot be fully socialized, the only alternative—if women's equality is to be achieved—is for men to share the reproductive burden. Although Cuban society has not yet eradicated the subordination of women, important legal and economic preconditions, necessary to achieve the goal of social equality, are in place.

Conclusions

This comparative analysis of the Latin American agrarian reform experience has demonstrated that processes of socioeconomic change are not gender neutral. It cannot be assumed that state policies designed to benefit rural households will necessarily benefit the women.

Rural women in Latin America have not benefited from agrarian reform on a par with men. Lack of attention to the incorporation of women as direct beneficiaries has resulted in women losing access to resources and/or being displaced from productive activities. The consequences are both economic—leading to lower female productivity or lower incomes—and social—contributing to a decline in female status and well-being. The failure to include women within new agrarian reform structures has also created new barriers to achieving male-female equality, barriers that serve to perpetuate women's subordination. Moreover, the lack of female participation has led to less successful processes of cooperative development and of agrarian reform and certainly of social transformation.

This comparative analysis of agrarian reform processes suggests that how rural women fare in an agrarian reform is closely tied to state policy. At a minimum, the state must pay attention to the legal and structural barriers that preclude female participation. As demonstrated, the criteria for selection of agrarian reform beneficiaries are very important in this regard. A crucial precondition for an egalitarian agrarian reform is that all adults within the targeted group be legally entitled to be beneficiaries.

The right to acquire land in one's own name or the right of cooperative membership is a necessary but not sufficient condition for women to participate on par with men in an agrarian reform. State policy must also be directed toward creating sufficiently attractive incentive and support structures for women to want to participate, to overcome the possible resistance of men, and to participate effectively. Attention to women's domestic responsibilities within the household and to their compatibility with productive work is an important component of both the incentive and the support structure. Other policies that enable women to participate more effectively within the new agrarian structures include adult literacy programs and agricultural and leadership training courses specifically for women.

This comparative analysis of the Latin American agrarian reforms also suggests the important role that rural organizations can play in either promoting or discouraging women's participation in the new agrarian structures. The Cuban experience is most instructive for in it the mass organizations provided the crucial mechanism to link macro policy with local-level processes of change. Moreover, the coordination between the women's organization and the small farmer's organization proved effective in integrating women into the overall process of agrarian reform while paying attention to the specific needs of women.

Acknowledgments

This is an abridged and updated version of an article published in *World Development*, fall 1985. The author is grateful to Hannah Roditi for skillful research assistance and to numerous colleagues for providing references and comments and criticism on earlier versions of this chapter.

Notes

1. An excellent class-analytic overview of the Latin American agrarian reforms is provided in de Janvry (1981: ch. 6).

2. The short-lived Guatemalan agrarian reform also fits into this category. Between 1952 and 1954, 33 percent of the peasantry benefited from the reform (de Janvry 1981: Table 6.1); the reform was subsequently undone.

3. See Beneficiary Application Form, Appendix 3, in Simon et al. (1982). The Agency for International Development, currently funding this agrarian reform, informed Deere that data on the sex of beneficiaries were not available for either Phase I or Phase III of the reform. Nevertheless, compliance with the Percy amendment requires that all U.S. foreign assistance programs take into account the impact of such programs on women.

4. The 1942 Mexican agrarian code was similar to the Honduran in this respect, but it was subsequently modified in 1971 to give single women similar legal rights to ejidatario status as single men had (Alcerreca 1974; Chavez 1960). However, as Arizpe and Botey report (Chapter 4), few single women have availed themselves of this opportunity. The Bolivian agrarian reform law explicitly provided that only widows could be beneficiaries (Article 78, in Jemio 1973:42).

References

Alcerreca, L., *Análisis Crítico de la Ley Federal de Reforma Agraria* (Mexico, 1974).

Anaya, P., *Los Problemas del Campo* (Mexico: Editorial Jus, 1976).

Araya, J.E.A., et al., *La Política Agraria en Colombia 1950-1971* (Bogotá: Fundacion para la Educación Superior y el Desarrollo, 1975).

Barahona Riera, F., *Reforma Agraria y Poder Político, el Caso de Costa Rica* (San Jose: Editorial Universitaria de Costa Rica, 1980).

Bengelsdorf, C., and A. Hageman, "Emerging from Underdevelopment: Women and Work in Cuba," in Z. Eisenstein, ed., *Capitalist Patriarchy and the Case for Socialist Feminism* (New York: Monthly Review, 1977).

Benjamin, M., J. Collins, and M. Scott, *No Free Lunch: Food and Revolution in Cuba Today* (San Francisco: Institute for Food and Development Policy, 1984).

Blankstein, C. S., and C. Zuvekas, Jr., "Agrarian Reform in Ecuador: An Evaluation of Past Efforts and the Development of a New Approach," *Economic Development and Cultural Change* 1, no. 2 (1973):73-94.

Blutstein, H. I., et al., *Area Handbook for Colombia* (Washington, D.C.: American University, 1977).

Bronstein, A., *The Triple Struggle: Latin American Peasant Women* (Boston: South End Press, 1982).

Buchler, P., *Agrarian Cooperatives in Peru* (Berne: Sociological Institute, 1975).

Caballero, J. M., and E. Alvarez, *Aspectos Cuantitativos de la Reforma Agraria (1969–79)* (Lima: Instituto de Estudios Peruanos, 1980).

Callejas R., Cecilia, "Examination of Factors Limiting the Organization of Rural Women in Honduras," M.A. thesis, University of Florida, 1983.

Caro, E., "Programas de Desarollo y la Participación de la Mujer en Colombia," in M. León, ed., *La Realidad Colombiana* (Bogotá: ACEP, 1982).

Castro, A., N. Grullón, and M. León, "Instituto Agrario Dominicano," report prepared for the Primer Seminario Nacional de Métodos y Técnicas de Investigación sobre la Mujer Rural, CIPAF, Santo Domingo, August 1983.

Castro, F., "The Revolution within the Revolution" (1966), in E. Stone, ed., *Women and the Cuban Revolution* (New York: Pathfinder Press, 1981).

CEDEE (Centro de Estudios Dominicanos de la Educación), "Historia y Situación de la Organización de la Mujer Campesina en R.D.," paper presented to the Segundo Encuentro Nacional de Educación Popular, CEPAE, Santo Domingo, December 1983.

Chambeu, F., "Participación de la Mujer Rural en Acciones y Cambios Ideológicos en un Contexto de Reforma Agraria," unpublished research report, Lima, 1981.

Chavez de Velazquez, M., "La Mujer y la Reforma Agraria," *Filosofía y Letras* 60 (1960–62):235–244.

CIERA, *La Mujer en las Cooperativas Agropecuarias en Nicaragua* (Managua: CIERA, 1984).

Cifuentes, E., "Land Reform in Chile," Background Paper, Studies in Employment and Rural Development No. 15, International Bank for Reconstruction and Development, June 1975.

Deere, C. D., "Changing Social Relations of Production and Peruvian Peasant Women's Work," *Latin American Perspectives*, vol. 4, nos. 1 and 2, 1977.

————— , "Cooperative Development and Women's Participation in the Nicaraguan Agrarian Reform," *American Journal of Agricultural Economics*, December 1983.

————— , "Agrarian Reform as Revolution and Counterrevolution: El Salvador and Nicaragua," in R. Burbach and P. Flynn, eds., *The Politics of Intervention* (New York: Monthly Review, 1984).

————— , "Rural Women and Agrarian Reform in Peru, Chile and Cuba," in J. Nash and H. Safa, eds., *Women and Change in Latin America* (South Hadley: Bergin, 1986).

————— , P. Marchetti, and N. Reinhardt, "The Peasantry and the Development of Sandinista Agrarian Policy, 1979–1984," *Latin American Research Review*, fall 1985.

de Janvry, A., *The Agrarian Question and Reformism in Latin America* (Baltimore: Johns Hopkins University Press, 1981).

Ecuador, *Ley de Reforma Agraria y Colonización—Decreto Supremo No. 1480* (Quito: Talleres Graficos Nacionales, 1964).

Edwards, W. M., "Ten Issues in Carrying Out Land Reform in Colombia," *Inter-American Economic Affairs* 34, no. 3 (1980):55–68.

Engels, F., *The Origins of Private Property, the Family and the State,* (New York: International Publishers, 1975).

Escoto León, *Leyes de Reforma Agraria en America Central* (Bogotá: IICA-CIRA, 1965).

Fernandez, B., "Reforma Agraria y Condición Socio-Económica de la Mujer: El Caso de dos Cooperativas Agrarias de Producción Peruana," in M. León, ed., *Las Trabajadoras del Agro* (Bogotá: ACEP, 1982).

FMC, Federacion de Mujeres Cubanas, *Memories: Second Congress of Cuban Women's Federation* (La Habana: Editorial Orbit, 1975).

Franco Garcia, J. M., "Nueva Ley de Reforma Agraria en el Ecuador," *Derecho y Reforma Agraria* 7, no. 7 (1976):35–54.

Garrett, P., "Women and Agrarian Reform: Chile 1964–1973," *Sociologia Ruralis* 22, no. 1 (1982): 17–28.

Guerrero, T., *La Cuestión Agraria* (Caracas, 1962).

Honduras, "Ley de Reforma Agraria: Decreto Ley No. 170," *Derecho y Reforma Agraria* 7, no. 7 (1976):237–288.

—————, Secretaria Técnica del Consejo Superior de Planificación Económica, *Plan Nacional de Desarollo 1979–1983*, n.d.

Jemio, A. E., *La Reforma Agraria en Bolivia* (La Paz: MNR, 1973).

Lodoño, A., *Las Empresas Comunitarias Campesinas, Realidad y Perspectivas* (Bogotá: Centro de Investigaciones y Acción Social, 1975).

MacEwan, A., *Revolution and Economic Development in Cuba* (London: MacMillan, 1981).

Manzanilla, V., *Reforma Agraria Mexicana* (Mexico: Editorial Porrua, 1977).

Mesa-Lago, C., *The Labor Force, Employment, Unemployment and Underemployment in Cuba: 1899–1970* (Beverly Hills, Calif.: Sage Publications Professional Paper, 1972).

PCC, Comité Central del Partido Comunista de Cuba, *Sobre el Pleno Ejercicio de la Igualdad de la Mujer, Tésis y Resolución*, La Habana, 1976.

Redclift, M. R., *Agrarian Reform and Peasant Organization on the Ecuadorian Coast* (London: Athlone Press, 1978).

Safilios-Rothschild, C., "Women and the Agrarian Reform in Honduras," in *Land Reform: Land Settlement and Cooperatives* (Rome: FAO, 1983), pp. 15–24.

Seligson, M., *Peasants of Costa Rica and the Development of Agrarian Capitalism* (Madison: University of Wisconsin Press, 1980).

Simon, L., J. Stephens, and M. Diskin, *El Salvador Land Reform, Impact Audit* (Boston: Oxfam America, 1982).

Soto, O. D., *La Empresa y la Reforma Agraria en la Agricultura Venezolana*, Madrid, 1978.

Stone, E., ed., *Women and the Cuban Revolution* (New York: Pathfinder Press, 1981).

Weil, T. E., et al., *Area Handbook for the Dominican Republic* (Washington, D.C.: American University Press, 1973).

Youssef, N., and A. LeBel, "Exploring Alternative Employment and Income Generation Opportunities for Honduran Women: Analysis and Recommendations," ICRW report to USAID/Honduras mission, October 1981.

10

Women's Components in Integrated Rural Development Projects

Elsa M. Chaney

As always, Marthy slowed up her walk as she came to her gate. Her house glowing blue and pink always pleased her. Every square inch of her property was used. Hot pepper, sweet pepper, beans and peas, Irish potato, sweet potato, yam. Marthy frowned at her tomato plants, they looked sickly and spotty. Reminded her of the Agricultural Expert who'd come round. Told them to grow one crop and sell it for a good price instead of growing little, little all around. She kissed her teeth in new vexation remembering his schoolified voice. "The experts has done whole heaps of tests on this soil and tomatoes is just the crop for this area."

Marthy popped off a dead leaf and crumbled it in disgust. Just as well she had planted only a few. The fellow so stupid. What was the point of growing whole heaps of one thing to go and hassle yourself to sell it to get enough money to turn around and buy the very things you could grow yourself?

"Then suppose now," Marthy mumbled to herself, "Just suppose I did plant out in tomatoes and dey never thrive. I woulda did en up wid no money an nothing to eat neither." Marthy kissed her teeth and pushed open her door.
—From "Story" by Christine Craig (1977)

This chapter makes a preliminary effort to explore some of the questions posed by women's components in large integrated rural development projects. It examines the implications of women's projects that emphasize the production of use values over exchange values.

Lacroix (1985) defines integrated rural development as a type of rural development project "that tries to integrate a number of otherwise unrelated components, each of them addressing one aspect of rural underdevelopment . . . and [tries] to bring a basket of goods and services,

191

consisting of production, social and infrastructure components, to poor rural areas" (1985:15).

Integrated rural development projects (IRDPs), which emphasize production, particularly of domestic food crops, are also designed to help the poor meet their basic needs by delivering to them directly certain welfare benefits, including improved health and sanitation, increased access to education, housing and rural electrification, and potable water and improved roads.

Thus because IRDPs include both productive and reproductive[1] components, they provide many points of entry for women to participate at the staffing, farming, and household levels. There is a well-documented tendency to ignore women's productive activities in projects that focus on agricultural production. But there would be less reason to ignore women's stake in projects designed to deliver the kinds of benefits and services that impinge directly on women's recognized domains.

Nevertheless, most IRDPs in Latin America, like rural projects everywhere, have focused principally on productive aspects and thus on male activities. As Tendler (1982:7) points out, measurable economic rates of return in rural projects tend to be highest for directly productive activities—mainly, investments in irrigation, livestock, or staple crops—and lower for social activities and services. Thus, because equity benefits are difficult to trace and measure, she says, productive activities with readily quantifiable output increases are made the centerpiece of projects.

At best, such projects have introduced special women's components to enhance women's participation and contribution. The argument in this chapter is that, though not ideal, such components in large projects are far superior to the small, often-isolated income-generating projects that have been the other major alternative in women's programming.

The purpose of this chapter is to compare and contrast two women's components that were added to large rural development projects in the early 1980s—to the II Integrated Rural Development Project (II IRDP) in Jamaica and to Plan Sierra in the Dominican Republic. Both women's components were afterthoughts in that neither was included in the original project designs or mentioned in the project documents.

The two women's components initially centered on nutrition/gardening interventions: intensively cultivated, family-sized vegetable plots, planned so that the selection of vegetables complemented the starchy staples produced on most farms thus providing a more balanced diet. Crops were to be cycled and rotated so that a year-round selection of food from the family plot was anticipated. Nutrition education—based on foods that households actually had available from their fields and gardens[2]—was included in both components.

The rationale for concentrating first on family food production is clear. Not only is food an obvious first priority, but also projects should focus on a limited number of activities, particularly during their first years. Women, their groups, and their communities can absorb only so much information, and the people who are to instruct and transfer techniques will also be able to master only a few things well, at least at the beginning. Learning basic nutrition and principles of family and community health, linking this knowledge to the cultivation of even a fairly limited number of vegetables, and mastering the art of teaching adults represent a large undertaking.

Another potential benefit of intensive gardening projects was the time savings they signify for women. The existence of a backyard garden ensures that basic foods for cooking are at hand rather than in a distant store or provision field. Moreover, good nutrition means less illness and therefore less expenditure of time and money. Educating children about nutrition and responsible agricultural and conservation practices by including them in the work of a family garden plot is another economic use of the mother's time. A backyard garden also is an economic and efficient method of "storing" vegetables because food in the earth, unlike vegetables bought in the market, retains its nutritive value for a long time. In addition, family gardens are ecologically more sound than commercial plots that require regular irrigation and extensive pesticide applications.

In Jamaica, a corps of twenty extension officers was trained to work with the women in the project. In the Dominican Republic, the women's efforts are fostered through ten *promotoras de la mujer* (women's promoters) who work with the extensive network of 123 *campesina* (peasant women's) groups—most of which predate Plan Sierra—the result of some twenty years of organizing effort by the Catholic Church. In Jamaica, a project in solar drying and vending of fruits was a later addition to the women's component. In the Dominican Republic, along with the nutrition/gardening focus, animal husbandry (cows, pigs, and chickens) recently has been incorporated into the women's program.

In their initial stages, both women's components were deliberately aimed at improving women's productivity in subsistence-generating, rather than income-generating, activities.[3] The important question to be addressed here is whether subsistence-generating activities are detrimental to women's situation and status because such projects increase women's reproductive tasks but provide little or no income in cash. The argument usually made is that as women take on ever greater responsibility for providing the family food, men's monopoly of the cash crops and control over cash income is reinforced. Proponents of this argument insist that cash income and control over that income are essential to any improvement in women's status whether they live in rural or urban areas, or developing or industrialized countries. They cite many studies that demonstrate the importance of women's economic autonomy in giving them a stake in decision-making at both the household and community levels.

In this chapter, I will argue that the cash-over-subsistence position may not always be defensible. Women with access to land make a valuable contribution to family food production—and improvement of family nutrition, including their own—that may outweigh any advantages they could gain from earning cash. Indeed, it may even be a serious error to encourage women's participation in income-generating activities if these are the usual undercapitalized, labor-intensive endeavors— weaving, sewing, embroidering—that often are the only possibilities for cash earning in remote and isolated rural areas.[4]

By working all day, a woman in the sierra of the Dominican Republic can weave a bag from *guano*, a local fiber, to sell for transporting tobacco, for which she receives 46 Dominican centavos (in 1985 about US$0.20). In contrast, for less than a day of labor per week, a woman can have a flourishing vegetable garden.[5]

Blas Santos (1983), director of Plan Sierra, made much the same argument. Because countries such as the Dominican Republic are articulated to the world economic system through an unequal exchange of primary products for industrial inputs and manufactured goods, he says, there also is an unequal remuneration for the hours spent in the production of the exchanged product. In the Third World, unequal exchange is based on low-salaried workers and requires a policy of cheap food that puts agricultural producers at a disadvantage.

As a consequence, according to Santos, the campesino family's income is far below the level necessary to sustain a minimum standard of living, and the family survives through a series of strategies in which the rural woman, as the principal producer of use values, has the major role. The preeminence accorded to exchange values over use values determines the undervaluation of women's work and the subsequent domination of men in the rural household. He suggests that

> as there is great prominence given to exchange values over use values, society, including the *campesino* families themselves, does not value women's work. More crudely, the woman "doesn't work" unless she is producing goods for the market, measurable in cash. Even though the devaluation of use values may not be the only cause of the predominance of men over rural women, one can be sure that it is indeed a factor of primary importance. (Santos 1983:4; translation by Chaney)

Benería (1982) notes that during the past few years, there has been a reevaluation of the significance of nonmarket production, based in great part on the burgeoning feminist and Marxist literature on unpaid household production that has challenged conventional economics. She therefore proposes

> that any conceptualization of economic activity should include the production of use values as well as of exchange values, . . . and that whether this production is channeled through the market and whether it contributes directly to the accumulation process are questions that can be taken up at a different level of analysis, and should not bias our understanding of what constitutes economic activity. That is, the argument is far from implying that there is no difference between commodity and noncommodity production, . . . but that the latter is also part of the realm of economics, and must be analyzed and valued accordingly. (Benería 1982:129)

In other words, the opportunity cost of women's labor time in rural areas may not be zero, as sometimes is assumed. Rather, if the amount of income conserved in the production of use values is taken into account or if the production of use values could be monetized, then in many cases rural women's time would turn out to be too valuable to be spent on weaving and sewing. On the latter point, the maintenance of a household garden, since it takes a minimal amount of time once it is established, does not prevent women from engaging in other activities.

The remedy for women's oppressed condition thus may not lie in removing them from their important and necessary work in the rural household. Instead the solution may lie (1) in finding a way to make explicit women's contribution to rural households and to place a value on subsistence production and their other activities and then (2) in communicating the importance of women's contribution to their communities, their families, and themselves. In the short term, until there are drastic structural changes in the organization of the society and the economy, who else would perform these household tasks?

For these reasons, the first objectives suggested for the family food production programs in the II IRDP in Jamaica and in Plan Sierra revolved around the recognition of women's contribution to family and community through

1. helping women develop some notion of self-worth;
2. giving men and children new perspectives on the value of the work women do;
3. increasing community appreciation of women's economic, social, and cultural contributions, especially emphasizing women's role

in the family economy, both in income generation and income conservation.

A second research issue to be explored in this chapter is the set of conditions under which women find it beneficial to participate in these projects. These conditions must permit women not only to realize the short-term goals set for the women's component but also to lead them to greater participation in other aspects of the larger project. A key ingredient in success appears to be the existence of women's organizations able to negotiate and bargain on the women's behalf.

Women in Integrated Rural Development

From the late 1960s to the early 1970s, development experts grew increasingly concerned that the benefits of development were not reaching the poor majority in rural areas of Third World countries. Community development efforts, which dominated the approach to rural modernization and betterment in the 1950s, were later discovered to have delivered their major benefits to local elites, reinforcing their political and economic dominance.

By the early 1960s, a reaction led to major attempts at agrarian reform and land distribution, but most of these efforts foundered because national political systems were dominated by alliances of large landowners and urban commercial and industrial leaders. In all these attempts, there was little of the trickle-down effect that had been anticipated and that would, it was thought, deliver to the poor—if only indirectly—the benefits of progress.

The Green Revolution, which brought dramatic increases in the production of cereals in many countries, also left a series of distressing problems in its wake: Benefits appeared to accrue mainly to farmers who had sufficient land, and the employment-creating possibilities of highly-mechanized technologies were extremely limited.

Therefore, the climate was receptive for the enunciation in 1973 by the World Bank of a "new style" strategy to reach the world's poor. New development strategies were to be "aimed at the satisfaction of basic human needs of the entire population rather than fulfilling market demand" (Haq 1980). By 1975, the full program was set out in the World Bank's *Rural Development Sector Policy Paper*. Similar concepts were enacted into law in the United States through the "New Directions" legislation included in the Foreign Assistance Bill of 1973 (Mickelwait et al. 1978). The new approach was an attempt not only to emphasize increased productivity—adapting and bringing the benefits of the Green

Revolution to poor farmers—but also to address directly the problems of access to basic welfare goods and services. The attempt to accomplish both ends—productivity and welfare, growth with equity—within the framework of a single project gave birth to integrated rural development.

Nowhere in the key documents setting forth the new style approach, however, was the participation of women mentioned, even though the main thrust of the World Bank and other agencies' attack on rural poverty was to raise incomes of small farmers and domestic food producers—and a large proportion of these were women. From the mid-1970s onward, the World Bank, the United Nations, the U.S. Agency for International Development, and other First World development agencies did enunciate policies to include women in the development process. As one policy pronouncement put it,

> Although it was not clearly recognized at the time, the evolution of World Bank lending toward the "new style" projects has inevitably led to a far more explicit consideration of the role of women in economic and social development than had been the case in the past. . . .
>
> In implementing these [new] projects, it has become evident that measures to raise the production and income of small farmers must often take explicit account of women if they are to be successful. . . . The persons often responsible for the cultivation of subsistence crops and domestic live-stock are women in many rural societies (World Bank 1975b:5,7).

Women in the Caribbean also participate at high rates in agriculture, as evident even in the official statistics that consistently underestimate women's rate of activity in both the rural and urban labor force (Chaney 1984:ch. 5).[6] But studies of women in the agricultural sector include few published accounts of women's participation in integrated rural development projects.[7] As Charlton (1984:181) remarks, the challenge of responding to the diversity of female roles has not yet been met in integrated rural development, any more than in other approaches to development.[8] We now turn to an analysis of two attempts to incorporate a women's component into integrated rural development programs in the Caribbean.[9]

Plan Sierra

Plan Sierra, a rural development project covering 2,500 square kilometers in the Cordillera Central of the Dominican Republic, was begun in 1979 under the sponsorship of the Dominican government. However, it functions independently and is codirected by the private sector, with a board of directors presided over by the Catholic bishop of Santiago. The program has two main objectives: (1) to improve the quality of life of the poor, and (2) to conserve the natural resources of the region, particularly the soil.

Of the 105,000 inhabitants of this central mountainous region east of Santiago known as El Sierra, 82 percent earn the principal part of their living from farming. Only 23 percent of the 17,000 families in the project area have sufficient land, however, to support themselves entirely from their farming activities. Thirteen percent have 50 to 100 tareas (equal to about 3 to 5 hectares), whereas 10 percent own 100 to 200 tareas and can be classified as rich peasants. Another 38 percent are semiproletarianized, owning less than 30 tareas, and 18 percent are landless. One-half of the land in the project area is in the hands of large landowners.

In the Dominican Republic, according to 1970 census figures 44 percent of women in the labor force participated in agriculture (Chaney 1984: Table 5.10). The country is characterized by heavy outmigration. Fortmann and Rocheleau (1985:257–58) observed that women share with men the harvesting of the annual crops and the coffee harvest (as owners and/or hired farmworkers); they raise the small animals (hogs and chickens) for meat and egg production, usually milk the cows, and tend home gardens with vegetables, fruits, and herbs. Women also gather the fuelwood and carry water, with some help from the children.

Women also participate in the scant industry of the Sierra. In addition to weaving tobacco sacks from guano, they weave seats and backs for chairs, a specialty of the region. For manufacture of the chair frame, which takes one-half the time necessary to weave the seat and back, men receive about three times the amount that women are paid for their work. Although shaping the wood pieces on a lathe takes skill, it is very light work—but I was told that "women never do this work"; indeed, the idea was greeted with laughter at one workshop.

Most of the people of El Sierra scratch out a living in an area where slash-and-burn agriculture has denuded the mountains of their forest cover and accelerated the loss of topsoil—with consequent silting of the rivers and dams. Median income of the people in Plan Sierra is US$311 per year. The process of soil erosion not only has drastically lowered production in Sierra agriculture but also has deprived the lowlands of vital water for irrigation.[10]

The government of the Dominican Republic hopes to increase production of food in lowland agriculture—fresh vegetables, rice, and other products—to feed the Dominican people, to reduce the millions currently spent in importing food, and to generate foreign exchange through agricultural exports. To accomplish these objectives, Plan Sierra is assisting peasants to adopt new systems of crops and new methods of cultivation centered around tree culture (including coffee, fruit, wood, and forest varieties) that not only keep soil intact but also promise better returns to farmers for their labor.

Intensive programs to improve rural health and primary education also are under way; ten new rural health clinics are functioning, and 380 persons have been trained as promotores of health in their communities. Nearly 500 primary teachers (about one-half of them women) participated in courses each summer for four years to receive their teaching certificates; most did not have sufficient training and were teaching without their degrees. Plans now are under way to work with teachers, under a special dispensation from the Ministry of Education, on ways to incorporate the "culture of conservation" into all phases of the school curriculum. About 70 percent of the Sierra inhabitants are illiterate, and many children drop out of school because they have access to only the first three primary grades in their local communities.

In the beginning, Plan Sierra did not envision the inclusion of a women's component: It was assumed that women would benefit if men participated. During the first period of work, however, the staff became concerned that women were not finding the project responsive to their special situation and needs. Initially, women's participation was confined to health services, home hygiene, and home economics (Fortmann and Rocheleau 1985:258). Of course, women also participated in the agricultural aspects, but they acted principally as laboring hands for their fathers and husbands, with apparently little control over the returns or over the decisions on crops to be planted, retained for household use, or sold.

Caught up in a system in which the man has the major decision-making role both in the fields and in the house, women live as dependents of their menfolk—first their fathers, then their husbands, and, finally, their own sons. They work long hours in both housework and fieldwork, but their contribution is not assigned much value by their families, communities, or themselves.

For the past two decades, several organizations, including some sponsored by the Catholic Church, have been at work consciousness-raising and organizing farmers (all of them male agriculturists), women who define themselves as housewives, and youth. Although mistrust is evident between the leadership of some groups and Plan Sierra, many of the base organizations collaborate with the project. Plan Sierra also works through committees of local representatives formed to deal with the project.

Plan Sierra carries out its program through teams of promotores or rural development workers and agronomists, most of them young men with the equivalent of a high school diploma in agriculture. At first, women were included specifically only in health component and in the retraining offered to primary school teachers. Then in 1981, the women's program, centered around gardening and nutrition, was added. The program is in the hands of women's promotores (always female) and social workers who may be either men or women. The project was decentralized after the first two years into three zonal offices and nine suboffices, each with a team of ten or twelve persons with different responsibilities for the project's work at the local level (see Flora and Santos 1986 for more details).

The Jamaican IRDP

The Jamaica IRDP was a government/USAID effort in the hills of central Jamaica, which operated from 1978 to 1983. (Although the project was designed to run for five years, extensions were denied and it closed because of corruption and mismanagement.) Soil erosion and destruction of water resources were particularly severe in the region. The stated project goals were to increase food for the nonfarm sector; to create a rural market for industrial goods and services; to improve Jamaica's trade balance by cutting down on food imports; and to improve the overall welfare of rural people.

The project concentrated its efforts on soil conservation, agricultural extension services, and credit for 4,000 families living on 30,000 hilly acres in the project area. Of the farm households, 79 percent had 5 or fewer acres, accounting for only 15 percent of the acreage in the project. Per capita income of the potential project participants was estimated at about US$200 per year. Another 1,000 families in the project area were landless.

There was a high proportion of female farm heads in the project area, about 22 percent, approximately the same proportion as in national statistics. A sample survey at the beginning of the project showed another 47 percent of the women regularly worked in cash crop production, and an additional 21 percent joined their menfolk at least during planting and harvesting.

The women's component grew out of concern that one of USAID's major efforts in the Caribbean ought to include attention to women who were not farm operators (those who managed farms were included in the main project efforts, although they were underrepresented as compared with male operators). The project made scant provision for women's interests and contributions. Project officers became convinced that the IRDP would remain strictly a soil conservation effort unless women were involved in such elements as health, nutrition, education, and housing.

The women's component in the II IRDP was run from a central office, but the extension workers were assigned to the project's twenty sub-watershed officers. The women's component officers worked alongside agricultural extension and soils conservation personnel and field assistants. In theory, the best qualified and most senior person in the team was designated team leader. The women's officer could occupy this position if she had the prerequisites. In fact, only one team was ever led by a member of the women's component. Some of the agricultural extension officers and other technical personnel were women, and they occasionally led a subwatershed team; a woman was in charge of the major demonstration plot. Most of the initial project workers were recent graduates of the Jamaica School of Agriculture (roughly two years beyond secondary school), and six of the first women's component officers were graduates of this institution in home economics. None of these had received agricultural training, and the project itself prepared the first officers in a month-long training course. The rest of the women's component officers were high school graduates from the project area.

Rationale for Intensive Gardening

Today, many observers believe that the small farm sector shows the greatest potential for development in the Caribbean. A development project that enables people to obtain inputs for the kinds of productive activities in which they already are engaged makes much more sense than investing in new activities, particularly if these require large capital investments. These considerations, linked to the concern over food availability and food security in the Caribbean, led to the decision to focus the women's components in the two projects on intensive gardening, without ever suggesting that women's participation would always be limited to that activity. In both projects, the decision to make intensive gardening the centerpiece of the women's efforts was based on the following reasoning:

1. Many women already had access to the major resources required. Indeed, a recent study of poverty in Plan Sierra has identified a serious underutilization of resources, particularly land, as one cause of the extreme poverty in which the people of the Sierra are living.

2. Family gardens were in line with the overall project goals to increase productivity in food crops and thus did not isolate the women from the main project thrust.

3. An immediate and critical need—the precarious state of nutrition and family health—could best be addressed through a nutrition/family gardening effort.

4. Rural families that are not self-sufficient, or nearly so, are vulnerable. If they cannot buy the food required for good nutrition, either the incidence of malnutrition rises or the national economy can be drained by importing and distributing subsidized foods.

5. Any improved cash position of peasant families from development projects might not translate into improved nutrition but might be used to purchase less nutritious, processed foods or might not go into food purchases at all if men control income.

6. The intensive gardens themselves become demonstration models for soil conservation, an interesting and important side effect. Through techniques of intensive, organic cultivation, concentrated application of inputs and soil conditioning techniques, and frugal use of water resources, the potential for a modicum of self-sufficiency is available for all to see. This is especially important in a soil conservation project—to see the effects of restoring and building soil.

7. Some women expressed an interest in eventually selling vegetables. The family food projects were valuable in providing experience in efficient cultivation as well as resource conservation. Some women did, in fact, begin to sell their small surpluses; others had vegetables to use in barter or to give away.

Accomplishments

The first priority in each of the projects, then, was to establish small, family-sized gardens with a continuous cycling of vegetables. The suggested schedule for planting provided for rotation, and an attempt was made to plant a variety that would put back into the soil the nutrients the previous vegetable selection had taken out. During the IRDP's first year, 822 gardens were set up. Serious drought conditions during most of 1981 reduced the number of gardens. The Vosseler study (1982) indicated that only 42 percent of the households surveyed had a garden at that time. During 1982, gardening conditions improved, but the high point in number of producing gardens at any one time never reached 1,000 of the 5,000 project families. Emphasis also was placed on forming women's groups, and each of the twenty officers was to be working with at least one by March 1981.

With respect to Plan Sierra, 6,525 gardens were established by the end of 1984. A scheme to provide a cow to each family (with the proviso that milk may not be sold, but the surplus may be given away) was well launched: One hundred and ninety-three cows had been distributed under the plan and 66 calves had been recuperated (the women "pay" for the cow with its first female offspring). To receive a cow a family is nominated by its local women's group, but its selection must be approved by the plan on the basis of need. The women's associations decide and handle the distribution of pigs, and in 1984 365 families received pigs (for which they give back two female offspring).

In Plan Sierra, the women's component is in the process of becoming fully integrated into the rest of the project. A new approach in Plan Sierra for the women's activities is being tested in La Celestina, a forest reserve purchased by Plan Sierra and settled by 100 families. The aim is to make the families as self-sufficient as possible in food, although there will be work for the men in forest management and lumbering activities and, in the future, for women and men in wood artisan activities.

Each family has been allotted sufficient land to accomodate a complete farming system. Besides a house and separate cookhouse, the parcel contains land set aside for a plot on which the main subsistence crops are grown (primarily the responsibility of the male) and a vegetable garden, pasture for animals, compost pile, fishtank, and poultry yard, all the responsibility of the female (assisted by older children). Each part of the system sustains and feeds back into the next: The farm provides fodder for the animals, they in turn provide compost material, and the areas for pigs, chickens, and ducks are arranged so that their wastage drains into the fishtank.

Evaluation

The two projects provide an interesting opportunity to study, under roughly similar agricultural and ecological conditions, two women's components that began with very similar designs; to trace their development (one toward complete integration into the larger project, and the other toward oblivion); and to test the economics of subsistence generation versus income generation.

Analyses of the situation in rural Jamaica and the Dominican Republic suggest that the economic value of home-produced food needs to be reevaluated. Food prices are rising in rural areas of the Caribbean and cannot realistically be expected to decline. Food will be in ever greater demand because of population growth and improved economic well-being, if development efforts are successful.

As a result, improved cash position of the campesino family may not translate into improved quality of life if people become totally dependent upon the market economy for food. At the same time, any food produced by the family will have increased cash value. Moreover, the potential food price inflation is increased as new cash-crop income competes for a smaller quantity of locally produced food—again enhancing the value of home-produced food.

Additional factors contribute to rising food prices. Local market prices must reflect increasing costs of distribution and delivery, based on increased energy costs—which are not diminishing in most Caribbean countries. Other energy costs to the family include human time and exertion as well as fuel costs expended in getting food home over difficult terrain. Thus in evaluating energy required for home food production, the total energy expended in alternatives must be considered. To my knowledge, no effort has been made to measure the exact cash savings in a family food production effort, but the validity of the argument should be evident.

The experience in these two projects suggests that intensive gardening is a far more economic use of time and inputs than artisan activities or sewing. In these days of mass-produced, reasonably well-made and durable garments, purchased food may be relatively more expensive than purchased clothes. Although hard data are not available, a planner must ask if it is not more reasonable for women to use the available labor time to produce food and to spend cash for clothes. In terms of the materials needed—especially the initial investment in sewing machines—and the time expended, making clothes at home may be a luxury within the reach of only the middle class.

Why was one of the two components so much more successful? The existence of the large network of women's groups in the Plan Sierra region may explain why the women's efforts there have been more successful than those in Jamaica where rural women were not highly organized. Indeed, one of the project goals in the Jamaica IRDP was to work toward organizing women not only to grow vegetables but to engage in income-generating activities, including a family-to-family tourist enterprise (which did not go beyond the planning stages). Also, because the project director was changed, the women's component was given low priority after the first two years.

In the Dominican Republic, the seven-person project directorate supported the women's component wholeheartedly and arranged for one of the project leaders to go to Jamaica to see firsthand the schemes being developed there for women in the IRDP. Subsequently, a workshop held in January 1981 with representatives of the peasant women's groups formed the basis for planning of the women's component.

The final outcomes on these two projects are not known since surveys have not been carried out to assess the results; such studies are planned.[11] In Jamaica, it will be of interest to see to what degree the gardening and solar-drying efforts are still being carried out and whether they have been picked up by the Ministry of Agriculture, which inherited the IRDP activities. The degree to which the women's groups fostered by the project are carrying on its aims also needs to be explored. In contrast, the women's efforts in Plan Sierra can be termed highly successful. This outcome appears to be largely the result of the high degree of organization among the women that antedated the project and, therefore, may outlast it. Indeed, the women's organizations were seen by one observer as the key:

> Once project personnel began to realize the importance of women's activities, primarily through the enthusiasm women showed for their grassroots homemakers' organizations, as well as their quick adoption of the offered technology, the plan shifted to an overt attempt to design and implement projects for women. The gardens are the most successful.
>
> The garden project, which was initiated two years after the plan was underway and received much less financial support than the agronomic project, has spread much more rapidly. By January 1983, there were 6,000 household gardens. Their cultivation involves the use of some of the same methods of soil conservation suggested for other crops. (Flora and Santos 1986:222)

The Jamaica IRD women's component also received generally favorable reviews while it was still in existence. Harris-Williams (1983:22–23) found several positive aspects: the intensive contact of the female extension officers with farmers; the practical experience the women participants were afforded in business skills; the improvement in nutrition of farm families; and the conservation of family income through vegetable production. She also found the component cost-effective, "with low investment costs and demonstrable returns."

Nevertheless, there were some dissenting voices. Gillings' (1983) appraisal is almost completely negative, not only on the women's component but also on the IRD project in general. She especially criticizes the implicit assumption that only women should be responsible for own-consumption food production and finds the activities "a set of conventional 'women's activities,' all related to their reproductive domestic roles" (Gillings 1983:16). She also criticizes the project for not providing employment that offers independent income. Harris-Williams (1983:23) notes some shortcomings in the Jamaica project. She points out that the component was never thoroughly integrated with the other components, and, while introducing the women to some business skills, the project did not sufficiently prepare them to manage their own groups. She also mentions the lack of adequate resources and the difficulties the women had in getting inputs and tools.

The signal advantage of situating a women's component within a larger development project is the abundance of experts and advisers attached to these projects and available to the women's component. The knowledge of these advisers can be tapped at every step: for help with soil preparation, including the necessary conservation measures; for appropriate varieties for a particular zone, which may not always be consistent across the entire project region; for proper cultivation techniques and pest control, as well as the most effective ways to process, prepare, and store crops to retain maximum food value. In contrast, women's projects often are set up in isolation and initiated with little or no technical assistance in production, management, and marketing.

Initially, planners hoped that some of the abundant project resources might be diverted to the women, but this strategy proved hard to implement. In the Jamaica IRDP, for example, the women's component waited months for hand tools (when large tractors and shiny new trucks were seen everywhere); consultants finally provided these by bringing in a set, having them hand-cast at a local foundry, and hiding the cost in their own budget. In Plan Sierra, the needs of women for fuelwood species and palm fiber for weaving were overlooked. Additionally, although women were included in the training exercises for coffee planting, they found that obtaining credit depended on their marital status (Fortmann and Rocheleau 1985:260).

The ultimate test of any project must be whether the women at least make some steps forward. Did this happen in either of the projects under discussion? Until the evaluation study is carried out, the answers must be qualified. Nevertheless, going back to the questions posed in the chapter introduction, in a preliminary way it would seem that the cash-generating over subsistence-generating position in projects for women has at least been challenged by these initiatives—even though the savings realized by growing rather than buying food still needs to be documented, as do the returns to alternative income-earning activities.

As for the women's components realizing their respective short-term goals, the activities in the II IRDP in Jamaica were cut off before they had a chance to become institutionalized. Although two of the project officers were hired by the Women's Bureau with the notion that they would carry on several of the project's activities—particularly those with the women's groups—this approach did not materialize.

In the case of Plan Sierra, the garden/nutrition program "took hold much more strongly than did the production changes required of the men" (Flora and Santos 1986:218). Flora and Santos explained this success not only because the male-oriented changes were more radical but also because of the good prior organization of the women's groups and the women's strong desire to maintain a separate, complementary source of income and subsistence for their families.

In the case of Plan Sierra, the activities of the women's component also led to greater participation in the larger project. However, in Jamaica, the women's activities had little or no carryover into other aspects of the II IRDP.

The women's components had as their objective to improve women's status in terms of greater participation in decision-making as well as an increased appreciation of the value of their work in the eyes of their communities, their households, and themselves. Whether women's status in this sense improved is something that cannot yet be answered.

Acknowledgments

I am grateful to Martha Lewis for the opportunity to talk over many of the ideas in this chapter and other papers on women in agriculture; to Jasmine McPherson, coordinator of the Jamaican women's component; and to Beverly Samuels Bennett and Novlette McPherson, regional officers of the project; and in the Dominican Republic, to Martha Fernández and Inmaculada Adames.

Notes

1. Reproductive labor includes all those activities that produce and reproduce the labor force, including childbearing and child rearing—the myriad tasks that come under the rubric of "housework" and subsistence production. Recent analyses insist that domestic labor has both productive and reproductive aspects; see Benería (1982) and McIntosh (1981).

2. For persons interested in the Family Food Production Plan, the vegetable varieties and rotation schedule are available from Elsa Chaney. There is a small but growing literature on the utility of women's gardens for nutrition; see Borremanns (1983); Brierley (1976); Campaña and Lago (1982); Chaney and Lewis (1980a and 1980b); Cleveland (1984); Cloud (1978); Immink et al. (1981); Laumark (1982); Niñez (1984); Pacey (1978); Soon (1983); Stavrakis and Marshall (1978); Yang (1976 and 1981). See also bibliographies on gardening projects throughout the world, edited by Brownrigg (1985).

3. Alternative terms might be self-sufficiency or income conservation.

4. For discussion on women in handicraft projects, see Buvinic (1984); Chaney (1982); Dhamija (1983) and Dixon (1978:78–104).

5. Once established, estimates on the amount of time required to maintain two 15 foot by 15 foot plots range from three to five hours per week, or fifteen to twenty hours per month. Cleveland (1984) estimates two to three hours per week.

6. It is important to remember when looking at the levels of female labor force activity registered in the countryside that the underestimation probably runs about 20 to 30 percent in the Hispanic areas. In the Eastern Caribbean, women form 20 percent or more of the agricultural labor force in St. Lucia, St. Vincent, Dominica, and Grenada; their numbers in Trinidad and Antigua are 8 and 7 percent, respectively; in Barbados they represent only 1 percent of those

working in agriculture, according to census data (not allowing for undercounting) (Chaney 1984).

7. Studies on women and agriculture in the Caribbean include those by Knudson and Yates (1981), one of the few field research projects carried out to date on women and farming in the region, and by Henshall-Momsen (1981), also based on survey research and covering Montserrat, Nevis, and Puerto Rico. Another contribution is that by Odie-Alie (1982), carried out as part of the Women in Caribbean Project and dealing with Guyana. There also is a Master's thesis on women and agriculture in Trinidad by Harry (1981).

8. Charlton (1984) includes a short assessment of integrated rural development projects based on secondary materials. A fuller treatment of the issues is contained in Palmer (1985). A full-scale study on the IRDP project in Bangladesh (Abdullah and Zeidenstein 1982) shows that the women's program had a lower status and fewer resources than other IRD activities.

9. Five studies touch on the two women's components under discussion in this chapter: A survey of women in the Jamaica IRDP was carried out by Harris-Williams (1983) as part of a regional project to assess the impact of development schemes on rural households and on the role of women, a collaborative effort of the Population Council and the Women and Development Unit of the University of the West Indies, Barbados. Vosseler (1982) carried out a survey of the Jamaica IRDP area, and Gillings (1983) looked at the women's component for her Master's paper at the Institute of Social Studies in The Hague. An examination of women's participation in Plan Sierra by Fortmann and Rocheleau (1985) looks particularly at their activities in the agroforestry component of the project. There also is an excellent article by Flora and Santos (1986) on the women in Plan Sierra.

10. The fourteen rivers of the Sierra form the most important water system of the country, annually delivering 2 billion cubic meters of water for irrigation and human consumption in the Cibao valley.

11. In Plan Sierra, the survey to be undertaken this year will probe next steps in the women's programming. An in-depth study of women in integrated rural development, with emphasis on the two projects discussed in this chapter, will get under way in 1986, carried out by Chaney in collaboration with Scarlette Gillings, a Jamaican social scientist.

References

Abdulla, Tahrunnessa A., and Sondra A. Zeidenstein, *Village Women of Bangladesh: Prospects for Change* (Oxford and New York: Pergamon Press, 1982).

Benería, Lourdes, ed., *Women and Development: The Sexual Division of Labor in Rural Societies* (New York: Praeger Special Studies, 1982).

Borremanns, Valentina, "Appropriate Technology Which Lightens Women's Heavy Task," *GATE-Questions, Answers, Information* 3 (September 1983):3–7.

Brierley, J. S., "Kitchen Gardens in the West Indies, with a Contemporary Study from Grenada," *Journal of Tropical Geography* 43 (December 1976):30–40.

Brownrigg, Leslie, *Home Gardening in International Development: What the Literature Shows* (Washington, D.C.: League for International Food Education, 1985).

Buvinic, Mayra, "Projects for Women in the Third World: Explaining Their Misbehavior" (Washington, D.C.: International Center for Research on Women, 1984), mimeo.

Campaña, Pilar, and Soledad M. Lago, ". . . Y las mujeres tambien trabajan," Resultados de Investigacion No. 10 (Santiago de Chile: Grupo de Investigaciones Agrarias, Academia de Humanismo Cristiano, 1982).

Chaney, Elsa M., "Proposal for a Continuation of Women in Development: II Integrated Rural Development Project, Christiana," Christiana, Jamaica, April 30, 1980, unpublished.

———, "A Women in Development Project in Swaziland: Skills Training for Income Earning," New York, UN Department of Technical Co-operation for Development, 1982, unpublished.

———, *Women of the World: Latin America and the Caribbean*, U.S. Department of Commerce, Bureau of the Census, and U.S. Agency for International Development, Office of Women in Development, 1984.

———, and Martha W. Lewis, "IRDP Women's Programme: Suggestions and Recommendations for Expanding the Women in Development Components in the II Integrated Rural Development Project, Christiana, Jamaica, September 18, 1980a, unpublished.

———, and Martha W. Lewis, *Creating a "Women's Component": A Case Study in Rural Jamaica*, Washington, D.C., Office of Women in Development, U.S. Agency for International Development, 1980b.

Charlton, Sue Ellen M., *Women in Third World Development* (Boulder, Colo.: Westview Press, 1984).

Cleveland, David, "The Potential for Household Fruit and Vegetable Gardens as a Nutrition Intervention in the 'More and Better Foods Project,' Egypt," Tucson, Arizona, Department of Family and Community Medicine, University of Arizona, 1984, mimeo.

Cloud, Kathleen, "Sex Roles in Food Production and Food Distribution in the Sahel," in Ann Cowan, ed., *Proceedings and Papers of the International Conference on Women and Food* (Tucson, Arizona: Consortium for International Development, University of Arizona, 1978).

Craig, Christine, "Story," *SAVACOU, a Journal of the Caribbean Artists Movement* (Jamaica), Special Issue on Caribbean Woman, 13 (1977):53–56.

Dhamija, Jasleen, *Women and Handicraft: Myth and Reality* (New York: SEEDS No. 4, 1983).

Dixon, Ruth B., *Rural Women at Work: Strategies for Development in South Asia* (Baltimore: Johns Hopkins University Press for Resources for the Future, 1978).

Flora, Cornelia Butler, and Blas Santos, "Women in Farming Systems in Latin America," in June Nash and Helen I. Safa, eds., *Women and Change in Latin America* (South Hadley, Mass.: Bergin and Garvey, 1986).

Fortmann, Louise, and Diane Rocheleau, "Women and Agroforestry: Four Myths and Three Case Studies," *Agroforestry Systems* 2 (1985): 253–272.

Gillings, Scarlette Ilene, "Impact of Rural Development Projects on Women: A Case Jamaican Case Study," Master's research paper, Institute of Social Studies, The Hague, 1983, mimeo.

Hag, Mahbub ul, "Changing Emphasis of the Bank's Lending Policies," in *The World Bank and the World's Poorest* (Washington, D.C.: World Bank, 1980).

Harris-Williams, Sonja, "The Second Integrated Rural Development Project (IRDP-II) of Jamaica: A Review of Clients' Experiences and Responses to the Project," in *Planning for Women in Rural Development: A Source Book for the Caribbean* (New York: Population Council, and Barbados: Women in Development Unit, University of the West Indies, 1983).

Harry, Indra Sita, "Women in Agriculture in Trinidad," Master's thesis, University of Calgary, Canada, 1980.

Henshall-Momsen, Janet D., "Women in Small Scale Farming in the Caribbean," in Oscar C. Horst, ed., *Papers in Latin American Geography in Honor of Lucia C. Harrison* (Muncie, Ind.: Conference of Latin Americanist Geographers, Department of Geography, Ball State University, 1981).

Immink, Maarten, Diva Sanjur, and Mirta Colon, "Home Gardens and the Energy and Nutrient Intakes of Women and Preschoolers in Rural Puerto Rico," *Ecology of Food and Nutrition* 11 (1981):191–199.

Knudson, Barbara, and Barbara A. Yates, *The Economic Role of Women in Small Scale Agriculture in the Eastern Caribbean—St. Lucia* (St. Michael, Barbados: Women in Development Unit, University of the West Indies, 1981).

Lacroix, Richard L. J., *Integrated Rural Development in Latin America*, Washington, D.C., World Bank Staff Working Papers, No. 716, 1985.

Laumark, Sandra, "Women's Contribution to Intensive Household Production in Bangladesh: Vegetable Cultivation," papers presented at the Third Annual Seminar, Maximum Production from Minimum Land, Bangladesh Agricultural Research Institute, February 1982.

McIntosh, Maureen, "Gender and Economics: The Sexual Division of Labour and the Subordination of Women," in Kate Young, Carol Wolkowitz, and Roslyn McCullagh, eds., *Of Marriage and the Market: Women's Subordination in International Perspective* (London: CSE Books, 1981).

McNamara, Robert S., "Address of the Hon. Robert S. McNamara, President of the World Bank Group, at the Annual Meeting of the World Bank Board of Governors, Nairobi," September 24, 1973.

Mickelwait, Donald, Charles F. Sweet, and Elliott R. Morss, *New Directions in Development: A Study of U.S. Aid* (Boulder, Colo.: Westview Press, 1978).

Niñez, Vera K., *Household Gardens: Theoretical Considerations on an Old Survival Strategy*, Lima, Peru, Training and Communications Department, International Potato Center, Potatoes in Food Systems Research Series, Report No. 1, 1984.

Odie-Alie, Stella, "Women in Agriculture: the Case of Guyana," Cave Hill, Barbados, Women in the Caribbean Project, Institute of Social and Economic Research, University of the West Indies, 1982, mimeo.

Pacey, Arnold, *Gardening for Better Nutrition*, 5th ed. (London: Intermediate Technology Publications Ltd. for Oxfam, 1978).

Palmer, Ingrid, *The NEMOW Case, Women's Roles and Gender Differences in Development, Cases for Planners* (West Hartford, Conn.: Kumarian Press, 1985).

Population Reference Bureau, *World's Women Data Sheet*, in collaboration with UNICEF (Washington, D.C.: Population Reference Bureau, 1980).

Roberts, George W., *Recent Population Movements in Jamaica* (Kingston, Jamaica: Herald Ltd. for the Committee for International Coordination of National Research in Demography (CICRED) Series, 1974).

Santos, Blas, "Consideraciones sobre el rol de la mujer campesina dominicana en las estrategias de supervivencia," San Jose de las Matas, Plan Sierra, 1983, unpublished.

Soon, Young Yoon, "Women's Gardens in Casamance, Sengal," *Assignment Children* 63/64 (1983):133–153.

Stavrakis, Olga, and Marion Louise Marshall, "Women, Agriculture and Development in the Maya Lowlands: Profit or Progress," in Ann B. Cowan, ed., *Proceedings and Papers of the International Conference on Women and Food* (Tucson, Arizona: Consortium for International Development, University of Arizona, 1978).

Tendler, Judith, *An Interpretation of the World Bank's New-Style Rural Development Projects* (Washington, D.C.: World Bank Staff Working Papers No. 532, 1982).

Vosseler, Harriet, "Survey of Home Economics/Women in Development Component," II Integrated Rural Development Project, Two Meetings and Pindars Watersheds, Jamaica, 1982, mimeo.

World Bank, *Rural Development Policy Paper* (Washington, D.C.: World Bank, 1975a).

————, *Integrating Women into Development* (Washington, D.C.: World Bank, 1975b).

Yang, Y. H., "Home Gardens as a Nutrition Intervention," in H. J. Roberts and T. A. MacCalla, eds., *Small Scale Intensive Food Production Proceedings* (Washington, D.C.: League for International Food Education, 1976).

————, "Nutritional and Environmental Considerations in Small Scale Intensive Food Production," in *Small Scale Food Production: The Human Element*, Proceedings of the Third International Conference on Small Scale and Intensive Food Production (Washington, D.C.: League for International Food Education, 1981).

11

Income Generation Projects for Rural Women

Cornelia Butler Flora

Peasant women traditionally have generated income either directly by earning money or indirectly by providing expenditure-saving goods. Moreover, when asked, peasant women stress the need for increasing income generation opportunities (Nelson 1980:8). Despite the historical and contemporary evidence of Latin American peasant women's productive activities and the clear need articulated by them, both external and national development assistance programs have tended to ignore the importance of separate income sources for women within the household. The resulting programs often have even decreased women's income-generating options rather than increasing them (Nash 1983).

Organized external political pressure by various factions of the U.S. women's movement and internal insurgence by feminists within development institutions (Flora 1982; Staudt 1985), as well as mobilization of women in developing countries fueled by the UN Decade for Women, pushed concern for women to the foreground of major development efforts. The rationale for the inclusion of women included (1) equity— it was unfair to leave women out of the development process; (2) welfare—development could be detrimental to children if women, as their primary caretakers, were not given resources directly; and (3) efficiency—projects worked better when women were included.

At the margins of development assistance, private voluntary organizations (PVOs) have for some time promoted small micro enterprises run by women. These have allowed peasant women to augment their incomes, thereby meeting their needs and those of their families in the ever more precarious economic situation chronic in Latin America. The success of these projects, as measured by the income generated and levels of well-being achieved, is in part a function of project design and implementation. In this chapter, alternative ways for rural women to increase income are discussed. First, I analyze how women's income generation projects got on the development agenda. Then, I present three different models that have served as strategies for women's income generation projects and analyze cases illustrative of these. Finally, the lessons learned from the projects are summarized in terms of economic, organizational, and welfare goals.

Alternative Ways to Increase Income

Rural women's need for income in cash or in kind could be met in a variety of ways. Neither land reform (Deere 1985; de Janvry 1981; Barsky and Cosse 1981), import or export substitution industrialization, nor labor organizing included rural women to any significant degree (Fernandez-Kelly 1983). Even though government policy does not encourage women to increase their income by mechanisms that imply a redistribution of existing resources, such as land reform and labor organizing, rural populations continue to seek access to land and to form labor organizations. Land invasions still occur in many Latin American countries, and rural women are often a vital part of such invasions. However, governments move swiftly to repress such land occupations, and land reform is no longer part of the policy dialogue.

In the 1970s, government policy shifted to less radical development tactics. The economic situation in many developing countries also changed during that time. An increasing proportion of the people were in the informal sector in both rural and urban areas—a change having major implications for class structure and class struggle (Portes 1985). The high inflation of the 1970s helped articulate the informal sector with a slightly expanding formal sector. Inflation also put more economic stress on families that required more and more cash to purchase basic necessities. As the result of the growth of the informal sector, class struggle turned from the realm of production, focused around place of work, to the arena of reproduction, focused around the home. Because of this change in the locus of struggle, women became involved in class struggle in greater numbers than ever before. The focus of protest shifted from land distribution and conditions of the workplace to the provision of housing, education, and services and the rising cost of living. The antagonists became government officials and housewives rather than owners and workers. In rural areas, grassroots protest began to focus more on the cost of living and service delivery by the government than on access to land or working conditions (Flora et al. 1985; Hirschman 1984).

Demands from grassroots groups to direct resources toward basic needs corresponded well with the integrated development programs of the 1970s, a period that coincided with the "New Directions" program orientation in the U.S. Agency for International Development (USAID) and the emphasis on the "poorest of the poor" by the World Bank. Infrastructural investments in roads, water, and electricity received the bulk of external financing. Nonformal education, maternal and child health, and housing also were addressed. Such policies on the part of governments were acceptable in the years of expansionary monetary and fiscal policy. In such an economic context, welfare programs did not necessarily mean redistribution of existing resources. Instead, new resources directed to marginal populations were provided through increasing international indebtedness on the part of governments. That indebtedness was encouraged by the international banking system and sanctioned by local elites, who rightly calculated that such government commitment deflected further class struggle.

The economic crisis in Latin America in the 1980s was triggered by lower commodity prices, higher real interest rates, and a world-wide recession. International lenders no longer tolerated the expense of welfare measures and looked less enthusiastically at state investments in infrastructure and attempts to increase human capital. Led by the International Monetary Fund (IMF), such programs, which included subsidized food as well as housing, health, transportation and education programs, were systematically curtailed in rural and urban areas in Latin America. Yet the economic crisis put increased burdens on the poor. The situation of poor women, in particular, was made even more difficult by the very measures put into effect at the urging of international lenders to correct the fiscal difficulties. Traditional survival strategies of subsistence agricultural production and petty commodity production were no longer viable. What kind of program could meet the political need of legitimation of the government yet remain low in cost and not challenge the existing distribution of resources? And what programs would be acceptable to the international donor community and the international lenders?

From 1981 on, the official U.S. policy has been to emphasize private sector development approaches. This strategy has been echoed by the UN Development Programme (UNDP) (1982), the World Bank, and British, German, and Canadian donor agencies (Bremer et al. 1985). The private sector thrust includes (1) policy reform, (2) project assistance to the private sector, (3) project assistance using private sector delivery mechanisms, and (4) mobilization of the developed country private sector for development (USAID 1982).

Women's income generation projects thus meet the demands of both national governments and international donors in the mid-1980s. They can be mounted with minimal governmental input (usually by PVOs or private for-profit development groups). The use of PVOs generally ensures relatively dedicated, low cost staff. Although such groups serve a relatively limited number of clientele with each project, "they are the only institution that has proven itself consistently capable of serving this group at all" (Bremer et al. 1985:54).

The private sector initiative shifts the source of responsibility for change. Under the assumptions of the new model, governments impede rather than facilitate or implement changes. The onus of success is placed on women concerned about income generation and their organizations rather than on the larger social structure. Structure, under private sector development reasoning, is addressed by changing policies that distort the functioning of the market and thus serve as impediments to growth.

Women's income generation projects have been attempted by nongovernmental groups for over thirty years. During this period, they have taken on the character of the dominant development modes of each era: community development in the late 1950s and early 1960s, cooperatives from the mid-1950s through the 1960s, and the delivery of goods and services in the 1970s. As a result of their roots in the community development era of the 1960s and the Food for Peace funding that early on financed them, women's income generation projects include a holistic emphasis on participatory and welfare goals. This evolution has left a mixed set of goals for women's income generation projects: increasing income, building participatory organizations, and creating welfare delivery systems. Only in the 1980s have the income-generating aspects of the projects become paramount and the major project criteria. Buvinic (1984), for example, criticizes the tendency of women's projects to fall back on organizational or welfare delivery modes. The private sector initiative has delegitimized the organizational and welfare goals of women-oriented development efforts, while giving legitimacy and directing resources toward small enterprise development.

Grassroots participation and organization are no longer on the development agenda. Official declarations that individuals, through the private sector, must be unleashed for development to occur relieves political and economic pressures by marginal groups on states, which now have other priorities and other pressures. Emphasis on the private sector by donor agencies is particularly strong in Latin America, where the private sector is viewed as stronger than in lesser developed areas of the world. Development assistance, which is destined for military and economic support to client governments, has shifted from the public sector to the private sector. Private groups, nonprofit and for profit, are receiving ever-greater incentives to develop income generation projects for women and appear to be doing so in increasing numbers.

Implications of the Economic Opening

Past income generation projects differ from job creation activities carried on by either public or private sector. A job creation activity assumes a straightforward, formal, contractual relationship between capital and labor. One works a given period of time, or produces a stated quantity of goods, and receives payment (Portes and Walton 1981). The activity is considered successful if the employer can then sell the goods or services produced for more than the costs of production and thus continue to pay wages regularly. Weber (1978) refers to this process as formal rationality, in which the measure of success is the balance between profit and loss, using capital accounting procedures. Although profit maximization may not be the single standard on which the enterprise is judged, profit generation is recognized as the primary requisite for enterprise continuance. Income is assumed to come only from the sales of goods and services rather than from employee assessments (taxation) or donations.

Women's income generation projects, in contrast, have had multiple goals and multiple standards for success. Ideally, the women themselves participate in the creation of the opportunity to generate income. They take part in planning and management, as well as provide labor. Income generation projects, as they have evolved within the development community, imply empowerment as well as income as a goal. Weber (1978) refers to consideration of such social well-being criteria as substantive rationality. An income generation project, given these organizational criteria, can fail if either the goal of income or that of organizational empowerment is not met.

Rural women's income generation projects usually have emerged between intervals of major industrial activity. Those interstices are growing as the people having capital seek to increase profits by substituting informal labor relations for the more costly formal ones. The fact that such enterprises are outside formal capital relations does not mean that they are destined to become formal or that they are unimportant to those mainstream economic enterprises. Portes and Walton (1981) point out the growing importance of informal enterprises and informal labor relations in generating employment in Latin America. Instead of conflicting with major industrial and service enterprises, the informal sector increasingly articulates with them. Women's income generation projects must compete either with major industry, which is difficult because of the scale involved, or with the informal sector, which negates the capacity to provide an adequate return to the labor and management of the women involved.

The extensive literature on the informal sector (Portes and Walton 1981; Portes et al. 1985; Portes 1983; Tendler 1983; Flora et al. 1985) has demonstrated that the profitability of informal sector enterprises is based on their ability to exploit family labor and to hire workers at rates below the minimum wage and without fringe benefits. As a result, those employed in the informal sector are considerably less well off than the enterprise owners or their counterparts in the formal sector (Portes et al. 1985).

When a collective enterprise attempts to compete with one in the informal sector, it faces several disadvantages. The collective enterprise must eliminate the cost-saving aspects of informal sector production. Labor relations must be formalized through contractual relationships, including the payment of social security and other social benefits and the establishment of regular working hours. For a women's income generation project to follow the informal sector pattern of cost savings through self-exploitation or exploitation of labor would be contrary to the ideals of substantive rationality of the women's organizations. On the other hand, to compete under the existing market conditions the collective enterprise either must operate at a loss or charge higher prices than its informal sector competition. If the collective income generation enterprise is to meet its social justice goals, it becomes an economic failure.

Not surprisingly under such circumstances, projects that naively began as income generation projects for women have turned into concessional projects that offer social welfare services, such as free food, health programs, community sanitation, and education, rather than projects that continue to attempt to mount a successful economic enterprise. The shift from an enterprise creating goods and services to one directly distributing goods and services has been referred to by Buvinic (1984) as the tendency for women's projects to "misbehave." Such a trajectory is an attempt to save the substantive goals in order to maintain a viable organization. If economic efficiency is the only goal, projects tend to either fall back into simple commodity production or become one more rural sweat shop.

By examining a number of women's income generation projects we can analyze these contradictions in more depth. Three basic approaches to women's income generation projects are presented in the following sections: (1) the cooperative approach, (2) the community development approach, and (3) the service delivery or welfare approach. We will compare the cases in terms of initial goals (including both formal and substantive rationality), degree of integration into the formal sector, and final outcome. I have selected cases that represent a range of outcomes in hopes of illustrating the possibilities and pitfalls of this facet of private sector development.

Illustrative Cases

The following cases are drawn from studies in a variety of Latin American countries of projects carried out by the Peace Corps, the InterAmerican Foundation, and USAID and its contractors, including the Pathfinder Fund and the Organization for American States. Projects by charity and church organizations are underrepresented because they tend to be poorly documented and to undergo few formal evaluations.[1] A further complication in documentation is that many projects have multiple funding sources, and a major funder may not come on the scene until the basic organization is established and the project is under way. Intermediary organizations may be linked to funders at a variety of points in project development and may enter the project at a variety of stages—from forming the organization to providing take-off capital or adding more capital once a project seems successful. Because of the current stress on income generation projects, competition often develops among donor agencies to fund those projects already in existence—indeed, competition by international donors is sometimes a reason for project failure.

The projects described here have existed from two to twenty years. They show how collective enterprises face a series of difficulties in attempting to meet the twin goals of economic viability (formal rationality) and social justice as a viable grassroots organization (substantive rationality). Two of the three basic strategies used are the cooperative model, which stresses income over organization, and the community development model, which stresses organization over income. Both have welfare as a stated goal, although it is more important in the community development model. The third strategy uses the welfare model or service delivery model in which the primary goal is the delivery of specific services aimed at increasing the well-being of the target group. In this strategy, the organization is a facilitator for distribution. (Income generation, when it is attempted, often was not originally planned.) Unfortunately little documentation exists for projects with welfare as a primary goal.

The Cooperative Model

The cooperative model has a long history of application in rural areas of Latin America. Since at least the 1920s, the Catholic Church and many PVOs, as well as national governments, have actively promoted this kind of income generation activity. Functional types of cooperatives vary from saving and loan (the most common) to input procurement and marketing to production cooperatives (the least common). Often several functional types—input procurement and marketing, for example—are combined. Such units allow the aggregation of resources to provide economies of scale for the individuals involved and for the agencies servicing those individuals with credit, technical assistance, and legal services. The 1960s were the high point for use of the cooperative model as an international development strategy, although it continues to be applied, particularly in conjunction with land reform programs and by PVOs.

The Ecuadorian sweater industry cooperative, described by Gladhart and Gladhart (1981), provides a good example of the strengths and weaknesses of this model. In 1965, two Peace Corps volunteers started a sweater knitting cooperative in the northern part of Ecuador, in the small community of Mira. They initially formed a cooperative of forty women; they set up the organizational structure, obtained legal recognition, and established markets and sources of inputs. In addition, the project included enhancing the knitting and design skills of the women of the community. With the technical assistance of the volunteers, the cooperative functioned reasonably well. A number of women in the rural village learned the business and artisanry skills necessary to make a profit. While the volunteers were present, the cooperative maintained formal labor relations and collective input to management, production, and marketing decisions.

Once the volunteers left, the cooperative was taken over by a locally powerful family group, which was accused by the others of stealing from the cooperative. In short order, the cooperative was dissolved. The sweater making went on, however; many of the original members of the cooperative set up their own businesses, bought the raw materials from the already identified spinners, farmed out the lesser skilled parts of the production process to other women, often from other villages, and then finished the products and controlled the marketing channels. By 1979, a cottage industry had emerged with 1,000 families producing 6,000 sweaters a month.

The income generation aspects of the project continued to be successful. Knitting previously had been one of many relatively low-paying activities women in the villages used to "ensure themselves access to their own economic resources, the distribution of which they control" (Gladhart and Gladhart 1981:2). The new method of organizing production and distribution redefined and greatly broadened the categories of women involved in artisanry production. Most of the women in the community, who became the wholesalers (*mayoristas*), and even women in the surrounding communities who knitted on a piecework basis increased their incomes. The extended family, rather than the cooperative, became the organizational base for production. The credit once provided by the cooperative is now supplied by the mayorista. The mayoristas provide permanent loans to the wool spinners to ensure provision of the wool they need to produce yarn. They provide credit to the women who work on a piece basis, paying them immediately rather than waiting for the sweater to be sold. Finally, they provide credit in the form of merchandise to the Indian traders who sell a portion of the sweaters produced in the regional markets.

The income generation activity articulated well with the agricultural cycle because it allowed peasant women to utilize the difference between labor time (the time actually needed for cultivation, planting, and harvesting) and production time in agriculture (the time between initial cultivation and harvest) to engage in a cash-producing activity. In the cooperative the women learned the production, marketing, and business skills necessary for continuing profitable production. Sweater production was flexible enough to respond to changing demands of foreign markets, where most of the sweaters were sold but individual enough to withstand competition from other regions that might seek to imitate the product.

Women's control over at least a portion of the funds they generated is indicated by increasing substitution of kerosene, propane, and electricity for firewood and by the purchase of pressure cookers. Young women who had completed their formal schooling in the villages were encouraged to stay at home to knit rather than to go to the cities as domestic servants. Women's options certainly increased. Most of the income generated through the extended family network enterprises of credit, production of inputs, sweater manufacturing, and distribution was invested in purchasing more agricultural land, a male-controlled resource. Family welfare thus increased. Viewed from this perspective, the activity was a success. Women had more income and some control over its use within their families. But at the same time, a new set of class relations emerged and a new set of inequalities may be developing. Further, a potentially politically viable organization—the cooperative—was destroyed.

The second example—a poultry cooperative in Honduras—was initiated by the Pathfinder Fund.[2] The peasants of the area of Sorata (a pseudonym) near the Nicaraguan border had worked as day laborers with usufruct rights to hacienda land to grow subsistence crops. The hacienda's refusal to continue to recognize those rights triggered a confrontation that led to the forced sale of some of the hacienda lands to the peasants as part of the Honduran agrarian reform program. The men organized a very unified production unit, which experienced high productivity on its intensively cultivated collective hectares. However, the families still depended on seasonal wage work as coffee harvesters to meet expenses because most of the cooperative income went to pay off a loan from the National Agrarian Institute for the land purchase.

Several outside institutions responded to the publicity given to the men's cooperative and set up a variety of both welfare and productive projects in the community. They were, however, poorly planned and coordinated and tended to focus resources on a single leader. As a result, community divisions increased.

The women's income generation project was implemented by the Honduran Instituto de Investigación y Formación Cooperativista (IFC), a small private organization that provides education, skills, technical assistance, and research to the beneficiaries of Honduras's land reform. The IFC introduced the idea of a poultry project. The women found poultry and egg production attractive because, unlike the other scattered projects, it would lead to a legally established women's cooperative. The IFC also determined that it would be an income generation project (instead of a nutrition project aimed at home consumption) that would produce for the market.

Sixty-one women were initially involved. The capital to build the required poultry barn and water supply shed were provided by Pathfinder through IFC. Training was a key part of the project. All members participated in a basic course on cooperatives and organization especially geared to semiliterate learners. Other training focused on poultry production, management, literacy (taught by the literate women in the cooperative), and beekeeping. The latter two activities were initiated by the women and organized by them.

Delays in the delivery of inputs and the natural cycle of poultry production impeded an early and regular flow of income to the women. Thus other projects to provide more regular income in kind were instituted, including goats, bees, and gardens. In addition, work time in the cooperative conflicted with the women's seasonal work time in the coffee harvest to generate cash income. Because of the unpredictability of availability of day-old chicks, it was impossible to coordinate the labor demands of the cooperative with the labor demands of the agriculture cycle in which the peasant women were immersed. The bulk of the cooperative's earnings had to be saved to be reinvested in baby chicks and feed. The nondisbursal of apparent profits occasioned some community dissension in the face of a disastrous crop year in 1983. Little money was available for the men to pay off their loans or for families to eat. Many wanted to use the reserves to meet those pressing needs, but the IFC insisted they be saved for their original purpose, thus allowing the enterprise to continue. Although this outside intervention was typical of IFC style, it was also necessary for enterprise survival.

The organization maintained its solidarity when confronting enemies outside the community. The women were able to organize effectively to get an obstructionist government official to allow them access to water. They also lobbied the government to ensure that the price of eggs covered the costs of production.

The project was highly dependent on external inputs. The chicks, which had to be repurchased for each cycle, and the special ration that such hybrid chicks required, as well as the medicines necessary to ensure bird survival in enclosed conditions, also had to be purchased. The presence of the Nicaraguan contra forces and an increasing war climate in the country, combined with general scarcity of imports, increased the costs of feed and medicines. The increased input costs, combined with a sharp drop in the price of eggs, endangered the economic viability of the project.

When the project was evaluated in 1984, it was continuing without the presence of the IFC. The women were using the cooperative structure to demand contraceptives and sex education. A pattern was established of women in the community teaching each other. The project had generated more income than the men's cooperative in 1983, although the return to the women was still low because most of the profits (and a growing proportion of them) had to be saved to be reinvested. By law, cooperatives must set up a rotating credit fund, and the women were taking advantage of it, particularly to fund children's education. The women also loaned money to the men's cooperative. The women seem to have greater control over resources than before, both collectively, and, to a degree, individually.

The Community Development Model

Community development was an international theme during the late 1950s and early 1960s (Holdcroft 1978). Although not antithetical to the cooperative model—indeed, cooperatives were often justified as a means of community development (Alvarado-Greenwood et al. 1978)—the goals of the community development model were broader and not limited to economic growth. In its early years, participation was highly stressed. As a model of development, however, this model took on a cold war flavor, especially as applied by the United States in such Latin American countries as Guatemala. The participatory aspects were a demonstration of the U.S. "heritage of democracy and idealism" (Poston, 1962:26) in contrast to authoritarian, top-down development efforts. In Latin America, the participatory aspects of the approach appealed to those who saw the need for broad-based grassroots organization to deal with local problems and to present a coherent voice for the disadvantaged at the national level.

The Appropriate Technology for Rural Women Project (PTAMC) best exemplifies the use of the community development model as applied to women's income generation projects.[3] Income generation projects were just a portion of PTAMC's mandate. PTAMC was designed to create women-based organizations as a mechanism to introduce a variety of appropriate technologies. Those technologies were to provide mechanisms whereby the women and men of the communities could better perform their daily tasks of production and domestic upkeep, as well as expand their options to improve the quality of their lives. The project was first implemented in Bolivia and Ecuador by the InterAmerican Commission of Women of the Organization of American States, in cooperation with the Ministries of Agriculture and Livestock of those countries.

Women in Ecuador and Bolivia are active in agricultural production, and their role in decision-making is increasing because of temporary male migration. The indigenous cultures of these countries are relatively egalitarian internally, although contact with Hispanic culture has caused men to be favored in access to education, productive resources (land, credit, and technology), and wage labor opportunities. Because of the extensive poverty in rural areas in both countries, women's domestic chores are heavy, and women must serve as the major shock absorber for the economic instability and natural disasters that permeate the Andean region.

PTAMC's process of establishing women-based community organizations and income generation projects was based on traditional community development methodology, which combined technical assistance (Gamm and Fisher 1980) and self-help (Littrell 1980) approaches. Two examples of the application of this model—chosen because of varying degrees of success in terms of equity, efficiency, and welfare goals—are the communities of Chawirapampa and Corpata in highland Bolivia.

Chawirapampa is a highly unified, nucleated farming community of about 120 families in the rich farming area near Lake Titicaca. It requested to work with PTAMC, having heard about it from other communities. PTAMC's usual approach was to initially set up in a community "appropriate" development technologies, which were created by technicians who used local materials but not local contexts. In Chawirapampa a greenhouse and a windmill were constructed with community participation. Although the greenhouse no longer functions, the windmill, now operated as a handpump, helps take advantage of the high water table to provide water for the main income-generating activity, cheese making.

This area has traditionally produced milk and cheese, with cheese production being an arduous daily task of the women. The cheese is consumed domestically or sold to intermediaries who resell it in local markets. Because of its initial emphasis on technology, PTAMC's first efforts focused on cheese-making technology rather than on establishing new, locally controlled marketing channels. PTAMC purchased (and partially donated) the equipment to mechanize the procedure and hired a Swiss technician to train the women to make cheese. The technician had worked many years in Andean countries, but this was the first time he had trained women in cheese making. Although always a female activity when performed domestically, the process has almost universally become male when mechanized. The technician was surprised by the speed with which the women learned and reported that they taught him a number of helpful techniques. The quantity of cheese produced thus far has been limited only by the availability of milk. Since pasture land is limited and can only support a certain number of cows, pasture and herd improvement were introduced as complementary activities.

Men have been appointed managers of the cheese factory because of Spanish language skills, deemed necessary by the community for purchasing inputs. The community feels strongly that the posts should rotate (but only among the men) to maintain their participatory character. Managerial skills, at the urging of the (all male) peasant union of the community, are de facto confined to males.

Currently each of the thirty women participating in the project works twice a month in the cheese factory in two-day shifts. Upon completion of the shift, one of the women or her husband takes the cheese to La Paz to be marketed at the offices of the Ministry of Agriculture, UNICEF, and PTAMC itself—offices community members learned about in the course of the project. This marketing strategy has certain limitations because it depends on the good will of a few key bureaucrats, but in a primarily informal economy, such direct marketing has major advantages because it avoids intermediaries. Cheese curds are sold locally to school children and members of the community.

The women's organization tried various forms of dispersing the surplus generated by their cheese sales. After experimentation, they decided not to pay the male manager or the women for making cheese. Rather, the surplus capital was to be used to finance the organization.[4] Women earn income from the enterprise by selling milk to it. All the member households own cows, although some of the unmarried women get only a small portion of the family product to sell to the factory. Members are the primary source of milk for the factory, although a person does not have to be a member to sell it milk.

Collective cheese making has opportunity costs for the women involved because it involves time taken away from private cheese making. Women still like to control their own production, despite the hard daily work cheese making at home entails. The absence of wages for factory work means that women have no direct incentive to work. The spill-over effects from the organizational activities of pasture improvement and milk purchasing are high, meaning that one does not have to be a member and contribute labor to benefit from the organization's activity. Thus many women enter and leave the organization, going from individual to collective cheese making according to their own wishes and those of their husbands. This fluctuating membership has weakened the organizational strength of the women's group. As a result major decisions concerning the cheese factory are made by the peasant union. Women have increased their voice in community activities and have established a low but regular income source for themselves through the sale of milk. Community welfare has increased. Yet many of the resources generated by this project remain in male hands.

The second example of the community development model is drawn from Corapata (population 1,500), located on a main highway less than an hour from La Paz. It is a small trading center made up of agriculturalists and merchants. In response to the efforts by a PTAMC promoter, a community group was formed consisting primarily of young unmarried women anxious to generate income and much less interested in organizational and expenditure-replacing activities. The group was small, with little male participation, although the promoter sought to include men. At the insistence of the young women, the project chosen was handicraft knitting. The promoter purchased the raw materials, designed the objects to be made, and marketed the items, with little community participation. The quality of the knitted items produced varied enormously.

Tightening market conditions for hand knitted items because of currency valuation policies made export difficult, so an attempt was made to industrialize the product in order to make both cost and quality appropriate for the local market. PTAMC and the community organization signed a contract with a private handicraft dealer, who agreed to teach machine knitting and to lend machines to the project. The young women had hoped to purchase their own machines but could not accumulate enough surplus. The dealer took over purchasing the inputs and marketing.

This project had few community development spin-offs. After two years, PTAMC withdrew from the community. The young women continued to knit on a putting-out basis for the dealer. They in effect became industrial workers in the informal sector. For PTAMC, the project was a failure. Nevertheless, the incomes of the young women and their families increased as a result of the project.

The Welfare Model

The model of service delivery has generally been directed at those people who cannot provide for themselves goods or services others in the society can procure through the market. Beneficiaries are traditionally children, the aged, women, or victims of a natural disaster. Although such projects were originally concerned solely with service delivery, they were increasingly criticized for their paternalistic nature and the depoliticized dependency they built up (see, for example, Rodríguez et al. 1973 and CIDEM 1985). As a result, income generation activities were added to the basic delivery model.

There is little documentation of income generation projects based on this model. Two case studies are presented here: The one from Muruamaya in highland Bolivia represents a project started on the welfare model that was transformed into a community development project and the one from San Pedro Pita in subtropical Ecuador illustrates a project started on a community development model that was transformed into the welfare model.

Muruamaya is a dispersed agricultural community of sixty families located along a secondary road about an hour and a half from La Paz. The women's organization had been started as a mothers' club to receive food from the World Food Program. Under that program, women formed groups to receive food and sell it to the members at prices below market costs. Membership was limited to pregnant women and those with children under five, effectively excluding unmarried women, older women, and men. Profits from the sales of the donated food were deposited in an account of the mothers' club and were to be used for community benefit (Duran-Sandoval 1985). Unfortunately, high inflation and the unwillingness of the national mothers' club organization to allow the community organization access to the money rendered the savings worthless.

The Muruamaya group wanted to start a bakery but lacked the capital. At that point, it was "delivered" to PTAMC, along with four other mothers' clubs. It was the only one of the five service delivery organizations that was able to change from a recipient mode to a production mode, despite PTAMC's efforts.

After expanding the organization to include men and other women in the community, PTAMC and the community organization worked to construct a bakery. PTAMC immediately attempted to get official flour rations from the Bolivian government because rationed flour cost about a third as much as black market flour. Those efforts were unsuccessful. Baking techniques, marketing, and pricing were taught, but in order to make a small profit, the community had to charge more than bakeries that had the flour ration. The new Bolivian government, inaugurated after the field work was completed, has eliminated subsidized, rationed food, which may increase the competitive position of the bakery.

San Pedro Pita is a community of wage laborers in the province of Bolivar, Ecuador, which produces coffee, cacao, citrus, and other fruits. PTAMC formed a community group in 1980 whose first activities included a vegetable garden and classes in various handicrafts and in health, and it refurbished the community locale. Community participation involved a minimum input of labor.

Citrus processing seemed a natural basis for an income generation project since citrus was the major product of the area. However, no labor use study of the agricultural cycle was carried out by PTAMC. The group and PTAMC chose marmalade production. PTAMC, after careful identification of appropriate technologies, provided rustic but serviceable tools and developed a cooking procedure that used local firewood. But the citrus fruit had to be processed before it rotted, during the time when many women and men in the community worked as day laborers gathering fruit for local landowners. As a result, women who worked in the fields found it difficult to also work in the factory. Although labor in the project was voluntary, it was also hard; members were required to spend most of one day each week making marmalade.

To participate in project activities, members had to give up a day's wages, which, for the 1985 harvest, was 400 sucres (S/400) in that area. Profits from marmalade production in previous years amounted to no more than S/150 per day worked. The opportunity cost of participation in the project was thus high, especially for the poorest women and men. Understandably, the number in the group decreased substantially, and only those from the upper stratum of the community participated.

The group is now composed about equally of males and females, but men do most of the traveling for input purchases and sales—a distinction that is resented by the women. Oranges for marmalade are purchased locally; other inputs such as sugar and jars are purchased in small quantities in Guayaquil or Quito and involve long trips. PTAMC arranged for marketing through state stores, but sales were also made locally. The organization increased prices from time to time because "everything is getting more expensive" rather than as a result of systematic calculation of production costs.

Plan Internacional (formerly Foster Parents' Plan) entered the community in 1983 with much needed disaster relief in response to a disastrous flood. In 1984, it signed an agreement with the community organization and with PTAMC to establish a larger project. Over sixty children in the community now have godparents in developed countries who send money regularly. In addition, the plan made resources available to the community to build a completely new kitchen with expensive new equipment—equipment that can only tangentially be used to make marmalade (and as a result is not used at all). The fact that the simpler technology supplied by PTAMC is still being used suggest its appropriateness to the local situation.

The infusion of outside funds led to further disintegration of the women-based community organization. The leaders, both male and female, now make almost all the decisions without consulting the group. Like the garden, the factory seems to be developing into the property of a few members; the remainder participate little and see few profits.

This project suffered because of an inadequate feasibility study: The major income generation activity occurred at the point in the agricultural cycle that demands for wage labor were highest. As a result, the participation was limited to the wealthier members of the community. But even more important, PTAMC failed to develop a viable project in terms of profit generated or organization formed because a well-financed charity project established a recipient mentality as opposed to one of participatory responsibility.

Lessons Learned

1. Projects have to be carefully designed for them to benefit women. Projects must be run on sound business principles no matter what the setting. The generation of a surplus is critical for such projects to succeed; sufficient surplus must be generated for reinvestment in productive capacity, as well as for distribution to the members so that the return to labor is positive. The group collectively needs to be able to calculate how much surplus is generated as well as to determine what will be done with it. For this to occur, simple capital accounting procedures need to be instituted and all participants instructed in how to read monthly profit and loss statements and to calculate costs of production. Members must also understand the need to reinvest in the enterprises.

2. Female control over their enterprises is more likely when hand, rather than mechanized, production is used (Table 11.1). In the case of the Bolivian cheese factory, the strong male organization and the guidance of PTAMC kept the technology in female hands, but the enterprise was run by men. In similar projects in the Andean region, industrialized cheese making has become a male activity.

3. Projects that achieve both economic and social goals articulate with the existing division of labor by sex, age, and class within a community. It is important for planners to understand not only what women do—the important production activities in which they are engaged—but also how the activities of women of different ages and social classes differ. The successful craft projects all recognized that some women were currently engaged in a domestic production activity.

TABLE 11.1
Income Generation Projects for Women:
Project Business Structure

	Product	Substitute Capital for Labor; Increased Labor Efficiency	New Source of Inputs	Marketing Channels	Introduced New Product	Surplus Reinvested
Cooperative Model						
Ecuadorian Sweater Industry	Sweaters	No	Yes	Yes	No	Yes, individually
Honduran Poultry	Eggs and chickens	No	Yes	Yes	Yes	Yes, collectively
Community Development						
Chawirapampa, Bolivia	Cheese	Yes	Yes, some	Yes	No	Yes
Corapata, Bolivia	Sweaters	Yes	Yes	Yes	Yes	No
Welfare Model						
Muruamaya, Bolivia	Bread	Yes	Yes	Yes	Yes	Unclear
San Pedro Pita, Ecuador	Marmalade	Yes	No	Yes	Yes	No

By providing better quality supplies, ensuring quality control, and establishing marketing channels, the range of women involved in these activities was greatly expanded. And men were less likely to try to take over and control these activities because they were traditionally female activities.

4. Projects that work best are those that ensure that women actually control the income they generate (Table 11.2). Some of the projects allowed women to earn money by selling inputs to the production enterprise, whereas others allowed the women to sell the products produced as petty traders and to earn a commission on the sales. Such income has traditionally been in the female domain, whereas wage income has been in the male. In the same vein, women often choose to disburse profits in the form of physical products such as cookware— permanent items for their own use. And bulk purchases save money over individual buying. However, the main function of such in-kind profit disbursals seems to be to ensure that the women control the surplus that they generate. Further, their productive activity is symbolically reaffirmed whenever they use those household goods. Finally, giving women a portion of the product produced, to sell or consume domestically, also provides them with a hidden source of income that can be bartered for either consumption or savings items, such as hogs. Formal economic evaluations often overlook such nontraditional methods of remuneration, which are usually derived and decided upon by the women themselves. Women's control over the income generated is crucial both to a project's success and to female empowerment.

5. Planners must understand how a project fits into the existing farming system to ensure its complementarity with the current survival strategies of rural women (Table 11.3). For example, the marmalade factory and the poultry enterprise both required intense labor at the same time seasonal agricultural wage work was at its peak. The opportunity cost of women's labor at that point in the agricultural cycle was so high that only the upper stratum of women could participate. Only a highly profitable project could result in a shift in time allocation for most women.

6. It is difficult to turn a welfare organization into a productive organization. Further, the entrance of a welfare-model promotional group can destroy an income generation project. The organizational structure and the centralized control of resources of intermediary groups often mean that they have difficulty transferring responsibility to the members of the groups that they have formed. Group responsibility is thus never formed. Paternalism is difficult to break.

7. Projects need to be multifaceted (Table 11.4). The multiplicity of needs of rural women—of which income may be the most important—

TABLE 11.2
Project Design and Process

	Recognition of Actual Division of Labor by Age and Sex	Resources Controlled by Women	Benefits Outweigh Costs	Multifaceted	Flexible
Cooperative Model					
Ecuadorian Sweaters	Yes	Yes, in part	Yes	No	Yes
Honduran Poultry	Yes	Yes	Somewhat	Yes	No
Community Development Model					
Chawirapampa, Bolivia	Yes	Partially	Not for individual	Yes	No
Corapata, Bolivia	No	No	For unmarried women	Originally, then no	
Welfare Model					
Muruamaya, Bolivia	No	Unclear	Unclear	Yes	Yes
San Pedro Pita, Ecuador	No	No	Yes	Yes	Yes

TABLE 11.3
Project Design Consideration

	Participatory Structure	Provision of Capital	Fit with Existing Farming System	Source Funding	Change Agent
Cooperative Model					
Ecuadorian Sweaters	No	Initially loan from Peace Corps, later from mayoristas	High	Peace Corps	PCV
Honduran Poultry	Yes	Grant	Med. Low	Pathfinder/USAID	National Groups
Community Development Model					
Chawirapampa, Bolivia	Moderate for women	Grant	Yes	CIM/USAID	National Groups
Corapata, Bolivia	No	Grant	No	CIM/USAID	National Groups
Welfare Model					
Muruamaya, Bolivia	Yes	Grant	No	World Food Program CIM/USAID	National Groups
San Pedro Pita, Ecuador	No	Grant	No	CIM/USAID Plan Internacional	National Groups

TABLE 11.4
Project Goal Achievement

	Increase Income	Strengthen Organization	Increase Well-Being
Cooperative Model			
Ecuadorian Sweaters	Yes	No	Yes
Honduran Poultry	Yes	Yes	Yes
Community Development Model			
Chawirapampa, Bolivia	Some	Yes	Yes
Corapata, Bolivia	Yes	No	Only of workers
Welfare Model			
Muruamaya, Bolivia	Unclear	Yes	Yes
San Pedro Pita, Ecuador	No	No	No

means that projects must address welfare and empowerment goals as well as income goals. Because of the economic crisis in many Latin American countries and the difficulties of carrying out many of the projects, organizations work best when they have a variety of project goals so that success can be obtained in at least one area.

8. Projects are more successful when they maintain characteristics of the informal sector and do not replicate the formal rationality of the formal sector (Table 11.5). Becoming part of the formal sector can often lead to take over by a few or to financial failures.

Conclusion

The organizational goals of women's income generation projects are critical to their economic success. Such projects cannot succeed unless some surplus is generated; that requires careful analysis by the women of what constitutes their current farming systems and how potential enterprises would articulate with it. The cost involved in each stage must be made explicit and linked to the benefits the women themselves will gain. Many income generation projects become paternalistic even when they generate income because women have been empowered only with the techniques of production, not with the techniques of administration and business.

Buvinic's (1984) analysis points out the weakness of the welfare model, as the two case studies presented here validate. However, her implicit criticism of the community development approach, which stresses organization as a goal, must be reconsidered. The case studies demonstrate that women derive power when they form multipurpose organizations. Indeed, the most successful cooperatives tended to expand into the community development model. Those groups can meet their immediate subsistence requirements, address their medium-term productive needs, and ultimately provide a vehicle for challenging the structures that determine the solutions to their long-term productive and reproductive problems.

The difficulties of competing with the informal sector when creating collective units of production must be recognized. If the units are geared only for production, they will have little chance of success within dominantly market-oriented economies. A multifaceted project that imparts administrative, marketing, political, and production skills will either allow women in the short term to create their own private enterprises that can function better in the existing structures or help collective organizations survive until a better economic and political conjuncture arises for more concentrated collective action to take place.

TABLE 11.5
Aspects of the Formal Sector Incorporated in the Project

	Separation of Household and Enterprise	Formal Task Assignment	Wages Paid	Benefits Paid	Capital Accounting Procedures
Cooperative Model					
Ecuadorian Sweaters	No	No	No	No	No
Honduran Poultry	Yes	Yes	No	No	Yes
Community Development Model					
Chawirapampa, Bolivia	Yes	Yes	No	No	No
Corapata, Bolivia	Yes	Yes	Yes	No	No
Welfare Model					
Muruamaya, Bolivia	Yes	Yes	Unclear	No	No
San Pedro Pita, Ecuador	Yes	No	No	No	No

Income generation projects for rural women have emerged as a residual strategy for a variety of macro-development models. They are generally considered only because more heroic development strategies are politically or economically difficult. On the one hand, they do not question international or national resource distribution. On the other, they mean recognition, often for the first time in development programs, of the importance of women as producers, not just as another beneficiary group such as children, the blind, and the aged. And the organizations created as mobilizers for production can become mobilizers in the social and political area as well, particularly when the economic goals of the international donors are combined with the political goals of the local groups that implement the projects to facilitate structural change. Until that happens, women's income generation projects, if properly designed and implemented, can meet some of rural women's immediate needs.

Notes

1. See American Home Economics Association, *Generacion de Ingresos para Mujers Rurales*, (1981) for a large number of cases. However, the work leaves key questions about the process unanswered.

2. This case is part of the Pathfinder Fund's "Women in Development: Projects, Evaluation and Documentation Program (WID/PED)," funded by USAID. Under this program, Pathfinder funded and monitored five women's research and action programs in Latin America and the Caribbean. Two were urban, one was semiurban, and two were rural. All were group-owned productive enterprises, and all operated in the formal economic sector (Crandon 1985). The monitoring and evaluation were carried out to identify factors leading to project self-sufficiency. As a result, the degree of documentation of the process is much richer than in most project evaluations.

3. The following cases are drawn from my field visits to evaluate the Appropriate Technology for Rural Women Project (PTAMC) of the Interamerican Commission of Women of the Organization of American States (CIM).

4. A 1983 PTAMC-commissioned evaluation estimated that the profit of the organization was 43,500 Bolivian pesos ($B43,500) a month, even when labor was paid. At that rate, the organization could repay its share of the costs of equipment and installation in six months (Myers 1983). Profitability is difficult to maintain in a setting of hyperinflation (it approached 14,000 percent in 1985), however, since costs and income are difficult to reconcile. But even though prices are changing at least every month, the enterprise is accumulating capital.

References

Alvarado-Greenwood, William, Steven Haberfeld, and Lloyd C. Lee, *Organizing Production Cooperatives: A Strategy for Community Economic Development* (Berkeley, Calif.: National Economic Development and Law-Center, 1978).

American Home Economics Association International Federation for Home Economics, Region of the Americas, *Generacion de Ingresos para Mujeres Rurales,* Taller de Adiestramiento, Jamaica, November 22–27, 1981.

Barsky, Osvaldo, and Gustavo Cosse, *Tecnologia y Cambio Social: Las Haciendas Lecheras del Ecuador,* (Quito: Facultad Latinoamericana de Ciencias Sociales, 1981).

Blumberg, Rae Lesser, "A Walk on the 'WID' Side: Summary of Field Research on 'Women in Development' in the Dominican Republic and Guatemala" (Washington, D.C.: USAID, LAC, and PPC/CDIE, June 1985).

Bremer, Jennifer, Elizabeth Cole, William Irelan, and Phillip Rourk, *A Review of AID's Experience in Private Sector Development,* AID Program Evaluation Report No. 14 (Washington, D.C.: USAID, April 1985).

Buvinic, Mayra, *Projects for Women in the Third World: Explaining Their Misbehavior* (Washington, D.C.: International Center for Research on Women, April 1984).

CIDEM (Centro de Informacion y Desarrollo de la Mujer), "Donacion de Alimentos y Projectos Productivos. Sus Consequencias sobre la Organizacion de la Mujer," paper presented at the workshop, Food Aid and Productive Projects, La Paz Bolivia, February 1985.

Crandon, Libbet, *Women, Enterprise, and Development: The Pathfinder Fund's Women in Development: Projects, Evaluation, and Documentation* (Washington, D.C.: Pathfinder Fund, 1985).

Deere, Carmen Diana, "Rural Women and State Policy: The Latin American Agrarian Reform Experience," Michigan State University, Women in Development Working Paper No. 81, March 1985.

de Janvry, Alain, *The Agrarian Question and Reformism in Latin America* (Baltimore: Johns Hopkins University Press, 1981).

Duran-Sandoval, Marie, "Los Clubes de Madres en Bolivia: Participation y Desarrollo Socio-Economico," paper presented at the meeting of the Latin American Studies Association, Albuquerque, New Mexico, April 1985.

Fernandez-Kelly, Maria Patricia, *For We Are Sold, I and My People: Women and Industry in Mexico's Frontier* (Albany: State University of New York Press, 1983).

Flora, Cornelia Butler, "Incorporating Women into International Development Programs: The Political Phenounology of a Private Foundation," *Women and Politics* 2 (winter 1982):89–106.

Flora, Jan L., Cornelia Butler Flora, Humberto Rojas, and Norma Villareal, "Consumer Stores in Colombia," *Grassroots Development* 9 (spring 1985):16–25.

Gamm, Larry, and Frederick Fisher, "The Technical Assistance Approach," in James A. Christenson and Jerry W. Robinson, Jr., eds., *Community Development in America* (Ames: Iowa State University Press, 1980), pp. 48–63.

Gladhart, Peter Michael, and Emily Winter Gladhart, "Northern Ecuador's Sweater Industry: Rural Women's Contribution to Economic Development," Michigan State University, Women in Development Working Paper No. 81/01, June 1981.

Hirschman, Albert O., *Getting Ahead Collectively: Grassroots Experiences in Latin America* (New York: Pergamon Press, 1984).

Holdcroft, Lane E., *The Rise and Fall of Community Development in Developing Countries, 1950–65: A Critical Analysis and An Anotated Bibliography* (East Lansing: Department of Agricultural Economics, Michigan State University, 1978).

Littrell, Donald W., "The Self-Help Approach," in Christenson and Robinson eds., *Community Development in America* (Ames: Iowa State University Press, 1980), pp. 64–72.

Myers, Barbara, "Analysis de Formularios Evaluativos: Proyecto de Technologia Apropriada para la Mujer Campesina," report prepared for PTAMC, La Paz, May 1983.

Nash, June, "Implications of Technological Change for Household Level and Rural Development," Michigan State University, Women in Development Working Paper No. 37, October 1983.

Nelson, Nici, "Actividades Productivas y Generadoras de Ingreso para Mujeres del Tercer Mundo," Documento de Trabajo UNICEF/TARO/PM/80/4 Marzo de 1980.

Portes, Alejandro, "Latin American Class Structure: Their Composition and Change During the Last Decades," *Latin American Research Review* 20, no. 3 (1985):7–40.

————, "The Informal Sector: Definition, Controversy, and Relation to National Development," *Review* (summer 1983):151–174.

————, and John Walton, *Labor, Class and the International System* (New York: Academic Press, 1981).

————, Silvia Blitzer, and John Curtis, "The Informal Sector in Uruguay: Its Internal Structure, Characteristics, and Effects," paper presented at the meeting of the Latin American Studies Association, Albuquerque, April 1985.

Poston, Richard W., *Democracy Speaks Many Tongues: Community Development Around the World* (N.Y.: Harper and Row, 1962).

Rodríguez, Alfredo, Gustavo Riofrio, and Eileen Welsh, *De Invasores a Invadidos* (Lima: DESCO, 1973).

Staudt, Kathleen, *Women, Foreign Assistance, and Advocacy Administration* (New York: Praeger Publishers, 1985).

Tendler, Judith, *Ventures in the Informal Sector and How They Worked Out in Brazil* (Washington, D.C.: Office of Private and Voluntary Cooperation, USAID, 1983).

UNDP (United Nations Development Program), "Policy Review: Measures to be Taken to Meet the Changing Technical Cooperation Requirements of the Developing Countries," report to the Administrator of the Governing Council of the United Nations Development Program, April 1982.

USAID (United States Agency for International Development), *AID Policy Paper: Private Enterprise Development* (Washington, D.C.: USAID, May 1982).

Weber, Max, in *Economy and Society*, Guenther Roth and Claus Wittich, eds. (Berkeley: University of California Press, 1978).

12

Rural Women and Migration in Latin America

María de los Angeles Crummett

Studies of migration in Latin America have proliferated in recent decades. The significant contribution of migratory flows to the rapid growth of major urban centers in Latin America as well as the continued importance of international migration, particularly to the United States, have inspired an extensive and varied literature spanning several disciplines. Yet, despite the large body of research and varied policy strategies designed to reduce rural-urban migration, analyses of women's roles in the migratory process have been notably lacking (Castro et al. 1984; Thadani and Todaro 1979). This omission is particularly surprising as many studies show that Latin American women migrate to the cities in greater numbers than men (Elizaga 1966; Boserup 1970; Youssef et al. 1979; Cardona and Simmons 1975; Jelin 1977; Alba 1977; Arizpe 1978). Moreover, little attention has been paid to the impact of migration on the women who remain behind in rural communities (Butterworth and Chance 1981; Chaney 1982). And almost no research exists on the ways in which state development programs have influenced female migration.

In this chapter I assess some of the research findings on rural women and migration and consider the implications, both in research and in development policy, of failing to include the category of gender in the analysis of migration. I concentrate mainly on rural-urban migration because, although a variety of migratory patterns can be established (rural-rural, urban-urban, urban-rural, international), the most significant numerical flow in Latin America is from rural to urban areas (Cabrera 1975). Also women predominate in this flow.

The first section of this chapter provides an overview of early studies on internal, largely permanent migration in Latin America. Here I look at the types of information provided by these studies and discuss their underlying conceptual approaches. In the second section I argue that sufficient gender-related differences exist in the process of socioeconomic change in the countryside to warrant a specific analysis of women's participation in migration. This section provides an overview of the impact of development processes on rural women and offers initial thoughts on the linkages between state development policies and women's migration.

In the third section, I examine several case studies that explicitly consider why women tend to predominate in rural-urban migration in Latin America. In this section I assess the usefulness of the concepts of class, the gender division of labor, and the household in examining the differences between migrant men and women and the impact of migration on the women who remain behind. Finally, I provide preliminary conclusions on the status of research on women and migration and suggest several areas where additional work needs to be done.

Early Research Questions and Approaches

Demographic Studies

The first research studies on internal migration in Latin America that shed light on the migration of women were undertaken largely by demographers, and they relied heavily on census and survey data (see, for example, Alba 1977; Elizaga 1966 and 1970; and Cabrera 1975). The major concern of this early research was to determine the volume and rate of the migrant flow from rural to urban areas. A secondary motivation was to identify the basic socioeconomic characteristics of the migrant population (sex, age, education, marital status, occupation). For these reasons, population studies have tended to treat migrant men and women solely in terms of demographic categories. The information is limited to descriptive statistics and often focuses on global trends for Latin America as a whole.

The 1940s—a period of intense migration and urbanization in Latin America—marked the starting point for demographic research on migration.[1] At this time two salient trends characterized migratory flows in Latin America: (1) Women went to urban areas in greater numbers than men; and (2) women migrated at a younger age than men. Although these trends have not been constant over the last forty years and vary widely among Latin American countries and regions, Orlansky and Dubrovsky (1978) in their overview of migration research show that demographers documented this pattern clearly for the countries of Argentina, Chile, Colombia, Brazil, Ecuador, and Costa Rica. The exceptions to this pattern of female-dominated migration were found in Paraguay, Guatemala, and Peru.[2]

The early studies described the similarities and differences between male and female migrants and between migrants and nonmigrants in terms of age and civil status. Researchers found that a significant percentage of women migrants were young girls and that women migrated at an earlier age than men did. For example, by 1970 in Mexico City and Buenos Aires, female migrants were prevalent in all age groups but especially in the ten to nineteen age range (Oliveira and García 1984). With regard to civil status, several studies revealed that the proportion of unmarried women in urban centers is higher than in rural areas, and it is also higher among migrant women than native urban women. These studies also indicated that the majority of female migrants were single—either unmarried, separated, divorced, or widowed (Orlansky and Dubrovsky 1978:14).

In short, the demographic studies showed that young single women formed the largest group in rural-urban migration. However, no comprehensive analytical framework emerged with which to satisfactorily understand the migration phenomenon itself. A number of studies have suggested that varying patterns of labor absorption along with uneven economic development at different historical periods have led to the successive waves of migration (see, for example, Oliveira 1976 and Alba 1977).

More often, however, demographers have sought the causes of migration in the experiences of individual migrants (Orlansky and Dubrovsky 1978:16). The decision to migrate is then seen as an individual choice with economic motives; the impetus for migration is primarily the search for work. In this respect, demographic studies are closely allied with microeconomic models of labor transfer (see, for example, Fei and Ranis 1961 and Todaro 1969) where the individual's economic behavior constitutes the primary level of investigation. Moreover, in emphasizing individual behavior, this framework makes the implicit assumption that the determinants and consequences of female migration mirror those of male migration (Thadani and Todaro 1979:1).

Consequently, demographic approaches could not pose, much less answer, an obvious question raised by their research findings: Why do more women than men migrate to the cities in Latin America? The next generation of migration research provided some initial answers.

Migrant Women and Work in the Cities

During the late 1960s and early 1970s, research on women and migration emerged in the context of the growing visibility of urban problems. Such themes as "urbanization without industrialization," "hypertertiarization," and the issues of poverty, integration, and marginality among migrants were of primary importance to researchers of urban-ization in Latin America (Lattes 1984).[3] An influential point of view was that rural-urban migration was the major factor contributing to serious imbalances in the growth of urban centers: causing high and chronic unemployment, "disguised" unemployment, underemployment, low productivity, and other urban problems (Lattes 1984; Jelin 1977).

Although these sweeping appraisals of the impact of migration on the urban economy were subsequently challenged, the issue of migrant women's employment persisted, primarily because of the tremendous concentration of women in the tertiary sector. In fact, one outstanding feature characterized the entire Latin American region: Migrant women were overwhelmingly concentrated in unskilled service occupations, the primary occupations being domestic service or street vending.[4] In fact, one of three women who work for a wage in Latin America are employed as domestics (Fernández-Kelly 1983:70).

Various studies illustrated the significance of this phenomenon. In 1970, 29.5 percent of the female labor force aged eight and over in Mexico City were employed in domestic service, and half of these women were rural migrants (García et al. 1979:5). A similar pattern was evident in the data for Greater Santiago, Chile, for the period 1955–1966: Fifty-seven percent of the economically active female migrant population gained employment in domestic service. Smith (1973:205) reported that approximately 30 percent of all female migrants to Lima, Peru, between 1956 and 1965 entered domestic service in the city. Moreover, migrant women were more likely to be engaged in domestic service than native urban women (García et al. 1979; Orlansky and Dubrovsky 1978).

The new generation of research that thus came to the fore was devoted to exploring migrant women's economic participation in the urban labor market. Three trends were noted for the industrialized cities of Buenos Aires, Mexico City, and Santiago. First, more rural women than native urban women participate in the labor market. Second, the participation of women in economic activities is lower in rural areas than in urban areas.[5] Third, the degree of women's participation increases with the degree of urbanization (Orlansky and Dubrovsky 1978:9).

In these empirical studies on labor force participation, women lacked the occupational mobility within the urban labor markets that men enjoyed. Research by Muñoz et al. (1977:85) on Mexico reported that in all migrant categories (recent, intermediate, and established) the proportion of women engaged in "marginal" occupations was greater than that of men. Marshall (1980:456), examining the case of Argentina, states that migrant-native differences in the type of labor force participation are much greater among women than men. Unlike women migrants, the male migrants tended to be more spread out in the urban occupational structure and not concentrated in any single economic activity. Jelin (1977:134) tentatively concluded that "the differences in the profiles of migrant and native women's occupations are considerably larger than those of males and are more consistent across various cities and countries in Latin America."

The literature not only described the type and extent of migrant women's economic participation in urban labor markets but also examined the living and working conditions of domestic servants (Rutte García 1973); domestic service as a means of upward mobility (Smith 1973); the economic role of paid domestic labor in "dependent" capitalist development (Goldsmith 1981); and changes in migrant women's social status (Whiteford 1978), values (Harkess 1973), and domestic relations (Buechler 1976).

Although these studies clearly addressed an important aspect of female migration, they did not explain fully why more women than men in Latin America migrate to the cities. The analysis of the causes and consequences of migration is based on a "push-pull" model of rural-urban migration. Pull, or demand factors, in urban areas (new industries, employment opportunities and expectations of better wages) draw the rural population to the cities, whereas push, or supply factors, in the rural sector (stagnation and the reorganization of agricultural production) provoke outmigration. Women predominate in cityward migration because of the greater demand for female labor; that is, more job opportunities (in domestic service) are available for women than are for men. The impact of push factors on the situation of women in rural areas is not explicitly considered except to suggest that "the economic role of females is relatively minor in the rural areas" (Jelin 1977:136); therefore, women are the first to be "freed" to migrate to the cities (García et al. 1979:5).

The push-pull model thus provides some insights into the phenomenon of female migration. It underscores a process of uneven development and its impact especially on urban areas. And, it is sensitive to the fact that migration affects men and women differently. Nevertheless, this framework, like the demographic approach, is drawn from a microeconomic model of labor migration. It assumes that the decision to migrate is based upon individuals' considerations of economic opportunities and constraints but does little to illuminate the different contexts in which these decisions are taken or to explain the group dynamics involved. It therefore fails to fully account for the specific effects of development processes on male and female migration.

Historical-Structural Perspectives

During the 1970s other theoretical and conceptual approaches emerged that, in relation to internal (and international) migration, presented strong criticisms of earlier models concerned with individual motivations and preferences (Lattes 1984). These approaches adopted a macro-analytic framework and are referred to as "historical-structural." They emphasized class conflict and uneven regional development between rural and urban areas within countries.

In analyzing migration, the historical and macro-social school of thought argued that population movements from rural to urban areas can only be understood as part of the broader effects on the countryside of social, political and economic change and conflict (see Stern 1979; Singer 1974). Capital accumulation, in particular, is seen to contribute toward and exacerbate rural poverty, the unequal distribution of income, and stagnation in the peasant sector—all of which provoke rural out-migration. From this perspective, the most important expulsive factors include the decreasing viability of peasant agriculture; the concentration of agricultural resources, particularly land, among a small number of capitalist producers; and outmoded forms of land tenure.

This analysis remains exclusively at the level of macro processes although it is comprehensive in its consideration of the historical and structural dimensions of migration. The micro-demographic approach, as previously discussed, places an unrealistic emphasis on the role of individual choices. By contrast, the structural framework is overly deterministic in that it totally ignores the significance of the dynamics of local cultural and individual preferences. It views local processes as completely governed by the requirements of capital (Berg 1985). As such, the specificity of the migration process is almost completely lost. As Lattes (1984:77) points out, it has not yet been determined how observations at the structural level tie in with the behavior of individuals.

In summary, these two broad research traditions—the microdemographic and the historical-structural—have generated information about migration processes at different levels of analysis. The micro model provides a plethora of detail on the socioeconomic characteristics of individual migrants and the macro-social school analyzes the larger processes of migration. Neither school integrates the analytic advantages of the other. Also, neither microeconomic nor structural perspectives have addressed gender issues in migration. This omission leads to a further criticism: The analyses are incomplete as they fail to consider that micro- and macro-structural forces may affect men and women differently. In fact, in the macro-structural framework women are invisible (Long 1983:1). Consequently, neither model accounts for the gender specific character of migration.

Rural Women, State Policy, and Female Migration

The strong incidence of women in rural-urban migration in Latin America calls for a deeper understanding of women's roles in rural areas. The socioeconomic conditions prevailing in rural areas explain to a great extent the differential effects of migration on the sexes (Orlansky and Dubrovsky 1978:8). However, analysis must go beyond empirical or theoretical generalizations of macro-structural forces within the rural sector and include an investigation of the way in which these forces affect women's circumstances. Evidence from various studies shows that rural women have a subordinate position in Latin America and that particular forms of capitalist development affecting production organization in rural areas appear to create conditions that foster the migration of women rather than of men (Young 1978). And by the extent to which state development policies ignore women's productive roles, they may induce increased female migration.

Historically, the development of capitalism within the Latin American countryside has reduced the demand for a permanent labor force and replaced these workers with temporary, seasonal laborers (Blumberg 1979). The mechanization of agriculture, in particular, has resulted in fewer permanent job opportunities, and on the whole, women workers have been disproportionately displaced from the permanent labor force (Garrett 1976; Prates 1980).

Tadesse (1979:8) explains that women are the first to be displaced by the introduction of technological innovations because men are relatively more privileged in terms of access to essential resources such as land, labor, cash, education, and know-how. Consequently, women are more easily displaced from tasks that can be mechanized or remunerated. Increasingly, then, women work in agriculture only on a temporary basis, during peak seasons, and often in the most labor-intensive tasks of agricultural production (Tadesse 1979; Díaz and Muñoz 1978; Crummett 1984).

Studies have also shown that where capitalist development has resulted in a decrease in the number of small family holdings, women are further marginalized in agricultural production. They work more in secondary or less important household income-generating activities than in agricultural production on subsistence or below-subsistence minifundios. These trends have been noted in Chile (Garrett 1976), Brazil (Vásquez de Miranda 1977), Peru (Deere 1976), and other Latin American countries. With the relative weight of the agricultural sector and the rate of wage employment in agriculture declining steadily, rural women are left without productive roles in agriculture.[6] This is one hypothesis of why the rural-urban migrant stream in Latin America tends to be predominantly female (Youssef et al. 1979; Prates 1980; Sen 1981).

Compounding the problem of declining work opportunities for women in rural areas is the unequal distribution of land resources on the family farm itself, which works against female children. For example, older daughters in rural areas are responsible for numerous tasks within the household including care of younger siblings and helping with domestic chores. Additionally, they participate in a variety of economically productive activities on the family farm. However, once younger sisters are able to take over some of these activities, older daughters are expected to marry or are encouraged to enter the wage labor market, often through cityward migration. Among poor and landless households, the shortage of land often make migration the only option available for women (Sen 1981).[7] Sons are also expected to find paid work; yet in contrast to the encouragement to daughters to leave, they are discouraged if not prevented from leaving (Young 1978). Overall their economic opportunities in the rural sector are greater than women's, not only because of better local opportunities in paid labor but because in many cases land rights are passed on to sons.

In short, the unequal gender division of labor within the household and the marginalization of women in agricultural production contribute toward the creation of a surplus female population that has little or no place in rural production (Prates 1980). This situation has caused both sex and age differentials in migration.

The public policy measures implemented to foster rural development in Latin America are relatively well known. A wide variety of agricultural development programs, including land reforms and rural development projects, have emerged at different periods in response to the growing agrarian crisis.[8] The stated aim of many of these projects has been to improve the productivity and welfare of the rural poor. An additional, if unspoken, motivation has often been to curtail rural outmigration.

An implicit goal of many land reform and rural development programs has been to halt the flow of migrants by encouraging rural families "to stay on the farm" (Laquian and Simmons 1975:3). The effect of these programs on rural-urban migration is unclear, and little information is available on how women are being affected.[9] Have women been targeted as a key component of these strategies? And what percentage of state funding is allocated to women? Indirect evidence suggests that most of these plans, programs, and policies are being designed without an awareness of women's roles and the gender and class differences in the rural sector. The effect may be, therefore, to exacerbate the already high levels of female migration. The following example illustrates this point.

Most agrarian reform programs in Latin America have made no explicit attempt to integrate women into the reform process. In fact, women's control over land has been undermined by ignoring traditional use rights. Men benefit directly from reform measures that designate households as the beneficiaries of agrarian reform. In practice this distinction means that only male heads of households are incorporated into the new reform structures (see Chapter 9 by Deere). Even when a woman is the sole head of household she is rarely considered a possible beneficiary. Because of this practice, the distribution of land in some countries has actually resulted in a deterioration of women's economic standing (Arizpe 1981). As noted, rural-urban migration is one way in which women, particularly daughters, respond to their growing economic marginalization in the countryside.

State policies affecting women and migration are more explicit in certain types of rural employment programs. Women are the preferred workforce for export agriculture, which has become an increasingly attractive strategy for raising foreign exchange earnings in many developing countries. Women rather than men are considered cheap labor. In Colombia, women constitute approximatly 70 percent of the labor force in the cultivation of flowers for export (Arizpe 1981). Women from both poor urban zones and depressed rural areas migrate to the area in search of employment. The Mexican government has also promoted rural employment programs in support of agro-industrial enterprises. In Zamora, migrant peasant women from neighboring rural areas constitute the bulk of the workforce in strawberry production for export to the United States.

Existing data show sufficient gender-related differences in development processes to warrant an analysis of the determinants of female migration. Such analysis is essential if we are to understand both why more women than men participate in rural-urban migration and what the impact is on the women who remain behind.

Recent Developments, Concepts, and Approaches

In the late 1970s and early 1980s the primary concern among migration scholars was to overcome the limitations of micro and macro perspectives. They argued that a comprehensive analysis of population movement must encompass both the determinants of behavior and the structural factors that motivate individual actors (Wood 1982:312). This approach led various authors (Wood 1982; Pessar 1982; Dinerman 1982) to search for analytical bridges that related the atomistic behavior of individuals to the overall process of macro-economic change. The approach taken, then, represented an effort to integrate two different levels of analysis into a single conceptual framework.

In these studies, the household unit emerged as an intermediate variable, and its study would bridge the gap between individual and social levels of analysis. Pessar (1982:3) argues that the household is "an evolving nexus of social relations which originates within a larger field of social relations and institutions through which it is transformed and which it may in turn modify." This notion of the household captured the dynamic character of the linkages between micro and macro levels. By shifting the unit of analysis to the household, migration can be viewed as a group decision-making process in which individuals take part, as well as a process related to the overall condition of households linked to one another through larger community and regional ties (Dinerman 1982). There is also a recognition that, in the rural sector, households typically serve as units of both consumption and production, thereby providing an additional link between micro and macro approaches (Wood 1981). Thus, this definition of the household unit contains the necessary conceptual and methodological tools to combine the best of the two reigning theoretical models for the study of migration (Pessar 1982:2).

Attempts to revise existing theories along these lines more thoroughly capture the autonomous actions of individuals and locate these actions in the context of larger economic structures. Moreover, they have sensitized researchers to the fact that the study of migration requires a more complex and varied approach than those suggested by traditional studies (Lattes 1984). Indeed, one major advance was to draw attention to issues of gender in the migration process. In this framework, the internal dynamics of the family and the household provide the basis for understanding potential differences in the patterns and characteristics of male and female migration. Women's dual roles as wage laborers and unpaid family workers in the household division of labor are highlighted as key components shaping and defining migration patterns.

Several recent studies argue that more work needs to be done before concluding that the household constitutes the most appropriate unit from which to integrate micro and macro perspectives on migration (Bach and Schraml 1982; Crummett 1984; Schmink 1984). In particular, the linkages between different levels of analysis—individual, household and societal—require greater analytical and empirical treatment. In a growing number of studies on migration (Crummett 1984; Arizpe 1978; Young 1978), an analysis of class relations has enriched the household focus by locating women's roles in the household division of labor within the broader context of social relations of production. These approaches emphasize that only within the context of local and regional structures and relations does the household become a useful analytical tool in the investigation of the differential impact of migration on the sexes (Crummett 1984).

Class, Household Structure, and Sex Selectivity in Migration

In the Latin American context, applying analyses of class to household structure in the rural sector has been particularly successful in linking micro and macro perspectives to explain gender-specific migration. This type of analysis not only has illustrated the social, economic, and historical processes within capitalist agriculture that generate a migratory labor force but also has attempted to show how these processes vary over time—affecting some classes, households, and individuals and not others. These studies have shown that the diversity in migration patterns—men are the migrants in some cases and women in others—can be explained by such factors as the household's access to means of production (that is, class position) and the sex and age division of labor within the household. In short, if the impact of capitalist production relations in the countryside varies significantly from region to region and by class, then who is selected for migration varies accordingly. Consequently, the question, "Why do more women than men migrate?" becomes "Under what circumstances do migratory pressures have a greater effect on women than men or vice versa?"

Deere's (1978) case study of the Cajamarcan peasantry of Peru, for example, shows that the extent to which rural producers are integrated into capitalist relations of production impacts upon the sex and age division of labor within rural households and, consequently, upon the gender composition of the migrant stream.

The social and economic differentiation of the peasantry contributes to differential migration by class, sex, and age. Among the poor peasantry, demographic pressures on the land coupled with a growing dependence on wage income form a strong inducement for working-age children of both sexes to migrate either temporarily or permanently. From the age of twelve or thirteen, sons are involved with their fathers in local wage work; by the time a young man reaches fifteen or sixteen he is migrating with his father on a temporary basis. Daughters, also pulled into migration, confront a different situation. A younger woman has fewer possibilities for local employment while very young but can capture the wage of an adult woman (as a domestic servant) at a younger age than a young man can. By the time a girl is sixteen she will have migrated permanently to the coast or the capital city to work as a domestic (Deere 1978:30).

Young (1978), working in Oaxaca, Mexico, finds that migratory pressures are far greater on women than men, not only because of young women's economic opportunities in the cities but primarily because they have been the most affected by changes in the household's productive base. Like Deere, she postulates that the transformation of agrarian structures has led to class stratification, which in turn has resulted in a new division of labor by sex within and outside the peasant household. Although this restructuring of women's roles permeates all classes of the peasantry, the most severely affected are poor and landless women. These women work long and hard days as they struggle to meet basic subsistence requirements. In addition to domestic production and other household tasks, these women work as wage laborers for wealthier families.

In Oaxaca, one of the consequences of the social transformation brought about by the penetration of capital has been an increase in family size among the poor peasantry. With the disappearance of reciprocal labor exchange, these households have to depend to a greater extent on their own labor resources, thus placing greater emphasis on women's reproductive capacities. For households dependent on wage labor for survival, a large family may increase the number of potential income earners, thus benefiting the household as a whole. This situation, however, has potentially deleterious effects on women of the poor peasantry by accentuating their workload in both wage and nonremunerated domestic labor.

As in Cajamarca, the need for money income among the poor peasantry of Oaxaca has led to the expulsion of working-age children, but young single girls overwhelmingly constitute the rural-urban migrant stream. Young (1978) hypothesizes that in the 1940s and 1950s increasing poverty within the peasant community led to the expulsion of daughters rather than sons for two main reasons. First, the gender division of labor within the household placed the burden of agricultural production on men. Second, and more important, the fact that many of the economic activities that women and their daughters carried out—the making of food and clothing and the preparation of products for sale on the local market—were being undermined by more efficiently produced manufactured goods.

The 1970s, however, witnessed a diversification of the migration pattern. Greater economic constraints on the poor to acquire money income and increased opportunities for wealthier households led to a situation where people of all ages were leaving. Nevertheless, the majority of migrants were young, between the ages of ten and twenty-nine, and more migrants were female than male. So, though over time more and more household members from different classes were drawn into migratory wage labor, young women of the poor peasantry continued to be the most vulnerable to migratory pressures.

Other factors help explain the continued predominance of women in migration. With the destruction of domestic manufacture, unmarried, abandoned, or widowed women find it difficult to maintain themselves economically; women are not agriculturists nor do they have land rights in the majority of cases. For many women in this situation, migrating to the city is preferable to remaining in the rural community (Young 1978:298–299).

In Aguascalientes, Mexico (Crummett 1984), transformations in the rural sector as well as new opportunities in manufacturing activities have affected the gender composition of the migrant pool. In this region, the commercialization of agriculture, beginning in the 1940s, seriously eroded the economic viability of smallholding rainfed agriculture and provoked an increase in the number of landless agricultural wage workers. A major consequence of this process was an outflow of rural inhabitants. Between 1940 and 1960, the migrant stream was composed largely of young single women from poor peasant and landless laborer households migrating to the cities, especially to Mexico City. Between 1960 and 1970, however, young men constituted a far greater percentage (62.5 percent) of the migrant population; this change reflects the effects of mechanization within irrigated areas of the state, which reduced the demand for permanent agricultural workers.

In Aguascalientes, as in Oaxaca, the erosion of women's productive activities in the rural area and the demand for female labor in the cities partially explain the early tendency for women to dominate the migrant stream. In this region, however, the sharp decrease in female migration after 1960 appears to be a result of increasing opportunities for women in both rural and urban areas in the state. Women's participation in agricultural wage work increased in those phases of production calling for temporary seasonal labor. The cultivation of grapes, the state's most important fruit crop, employs women during the harvest—the most labor-intensive period of production. More important, the growth of the textile and garment industries in Aguascalientes City in the 1960s increased the demand for a permanent female labor force. These industries also flourished in numerous rural communities and employed a predominantly young and female workforce. The textile and garment industries in turn promoted the growth of *maquila doméstica* (piecework in the home of women's and children's clothing)—an activity exclusively employing women.

Migration and the Women
Who Remain Behind

Analyses of class and household structure have been equally important in addressing the impact of migration on the women who remain behind. Available evidence, largely drawn from studies of international migration, suggests that women are affected in a variety of ways when husbands, fathers, daughters, and sons migrate. The age and sex selectivity of migration, for example, can have profound effects on the household division of labor by transferring work roles from the young to the old and by increasing the work burden of women and children in rural areas where male outmigration prevails (UN Secretariat 1984). Again, research shows that the extent to which women are affected by migration invariably relates to the household's economic standing within the rural community.

Where migratory pressures are greater on sons or the male head of household, a new gender division of labor emerges within the household. A common result of this migration pattern is that women are relegated to the subsistence sector in agriculture. An example taken from a study of rural outmigration from Guanajuato, Mexico, to the United States gives evidence of this result. In this community, subsistence agriculture has become the exclusive activity of women, older persons, and children as the result of male outmigration to the United States (Margolis 1979). Deere's work also shows the effects of male migration on the household division of labor. Women of the poor peasant stratum assume greater responsibility for agricultural production—an activity previously dominated by men—as men leave the household in search of temporary wage work elsewhere.

In addition to greater workloads in agriculture, available evidence suggests that poor peasant women are most adversely affected by changes in the gender and age division of labor brought about through migration. Young (1978) finds that the expulsion of young daughters from smallholder households increases many mothers' unpaid household chores. The care of younger children, traditionally a responsibility of older daughters, is added to the mothers' already heavy workloads. A number of tasks traditionally entrusted to children such as animal care and wool collecting also became the mothers' charge.

Transformations in the division of labor in the household and in production brought about through male migration often impact upon the economic structure of the household unit, which in turn may affect its composition. For example, findings from my field research in Aguascalientes show that remittances from international migration, in particular, have served to supplement household income substantially, bringing it above a bare subsistence level. The cash influx from husbands in the United States has allowed women from landless laborer households to purchase a variety of consumer goods as well as to pay children's health and educational expenses. On the other hand, if remittances are low or unreliable—more often the case for migration within Mexico—women are left with the primary, if not sole, economic responsibility of the household. This situation may alter the composition of the domestic unit. Weist's (1973:205) study of a Mexican town suggests that recurrent wage-labor migration, characterized by male absenteeism and low re-muneration, leads to the formation of female-headed households.

Women are not always the "victims" of migration; they often take active parts in the migration process even when they do not go themselves. In Aguascalientes, women's roles in the household division of labor interact with other economic parameters to condition and perpetuate a specific migration trajectory. In the region of Calvillo, temporary cyclical migration to the United States has constituted the dominant migrant pattern among landless households for several decades, and migrants are overwhelmingly male heads of households. I suggest that the tem-porary character of the migrant stream and male selectivity in migration are related to the sexual division of labor both within and outside of the household unit. Two key factors operate here: the lack of permanent, steady employment for men in the region and women's dual roles in productive and reproductive activities.

The majority of landless households in Calvillo depend on wage work to meet consumption needs. Wage income is primarily obtained from work in the guava fields or through *maquila doméstica*. (Overall, more than 75 percent of households depend on either guava or maquila production for employment.) These two activities reflect the rigid gender division of labor prevalent in the region and in the household. Guava, a labor-intensive crop, employs a male workforce; maquila, on the other hand, exclusively employs women, and almost all female children from the age of seven or eight who work in maquila production are unpaid family laborers. The nature of maquila work—paid work in the home— means that day-to-day responsibilities of household maintenance and child care can be performed simultaneously with wage work.

The limited range of salaried work available to male household members shapes the pattern and intensity of migration. Employment in guava production is seasonal (the harvest period extends from late September through early February). Few jobs are available in guava during the off-season, and other employment opportunities—in con-struction, petty commerce, or odd jobs in the community—are sporadic. During the off-season, temporary migration is at its highest, with migrants leaving after the harvest and returning in the fall.

Yet despite the strong incentive to migrate, men could not leave without women's contribution to household income. Their work in maquila provides the household with a dependable source of income throughout the year. Indeed, the availability of steady, though poorly remunerated, work allows the male head of household to migrate knowing that basic needs are being met in the interim before his remittances arrive. In short, in this case study, women's activities ensure the ongoing economic as well as social reproduction of the domestic unit during periods of male outmigration.

In all the studies presented, the gender-specific character of migration has reinforced key components of class. Among landless and poor peasant households, in particular, male migration had important consequences for the household division of labor: Women increased their participation in agricultural production and wage work while retaining their traditional responsibilities for child care and family welfare. Thus the intensification of women's labor in paid and unpaid work and productive and reproductive activities sharpens not only the analysis of migration but also of class and household relations. On the one hand, it reveals how and which household members are most vulnerable to and marginalized by changes in the household's productive base. On the other, it shows how these household members actively respond to changing circumstances.

Directions for Research

In the past twenty years of migration research some progress is evident on the issue of women and migration. We have an idea of the relative importance of women in the rural-urban migrant stream during the initial stages of industrialization in Latin America; of the concentration of migrant women in domestic service in urban areas; and of the pressures on young women of the poorer stratum of the peasantry to migrate. Initial research efforts on the impact of migration on women have also shown that women's roles in the household division of labor are both responses to and results of migration. Nevertheless, more analytical and empirical research is needed to better understand women's participation in migration. This section attempts to outline several research areas requiring further analysis and elaboration.

By using class and household as independent variables to explain migration researchers have begun to illuminate the special characteristics and circumstances that distinguish female from male migration. Yet the concepts of class and household require greater analytical clarity than existing studies provide. Although the determination of social classes in the agrarian sector has been the subject of heated debate in Latin America, scholars tend to share a conceptualization of the household as a harmonious, undifferentiated economic unit. More attention needs to be paid to gender and age-based inequalities within the household and their relation to wider social and economic conditions. Reference to "household interests" and "household decisions" obscures the unequal conditions under which different household members migrate. Household inequalities help explain who in the household is selected for migration.

The household as a conceptual tool in attempting to bridge the gap between studies focusing on structural factors and on individual behavior, though useful, has fallen short of fulfilling its aim. The integration of the two levels of analysis in migration research—micro and macro—has not been satisfactorily accomplished. Nor has a consensus been reached on how much relative importance should be accorded to micro and macro factors in the analysis of migration. As Parkin (cited in Thandani and Todaro 1979:11) states, "How much analytical emphasis should be placed on the individual migrant as being free to decide between alternative courses of action, and how much on the wider political, economic, and ecological factors directing and constraining migratory flows of particular groups?"

Another task for future research involves pursuing more comparative, cross-cultural studies on women and migration. Much of the recent work presented here, though careful in its attention to the historical and regional influences in the migration process, is based on case studies focusing on one or two communities. Although this approach has been useful in generating hypotheses, these hypotheses now need to be tested in a broader context. Few researchers have undertaken comprehensive studies involving major regions within or across countries. Such studies are necessary if we are to understand more fully the migration process and women's roles in it.

Another area of research involves documenting and accounting for changes in women's migratory patterns over time. Early demographic research on migration trends indicated a clear pattern of permanent female migration to the cities. The case studies, however, provided some evidence that the intensity of women's involvement in migration does not necessarily follow a unidirectional rural-urban course. If these case studies are correct, then a variety of patterns in terms of both direction (rural, urban, international) and type (temporary, permanent, circular, and return) may now characterize female migration. If there has been a shift over time in women's migration trajectories, what accounts for the heterogeneity of the current migrant stream?

The effects of the current economic crisis in Latin America must also be taken into consideration in a discussion of changing migratory patterns.

If return migration is indeed a significant trend in the 1980s, to what extent is it gender differentiated? If the demand for domestic servants continues, pressures may be even greater to send young women to the cities so that reverse migration may be primarily male.

A major shortcoming in migration research, as we have seen, is the absence of an analysis of gender in the migration process. The lack of attention to gender in migration studies leads to the erroneous assumption that the differences between male and female migration are insignificant. Analyses now generalized to both male and female migration actually are gender-specific theories—specific to male migration (Thadani and Todaro 1979:4).

Although a variety of rural development plans and projects have been designed to reduce rural-urban migration, women are not targeted as a key component of these strategies. And though much more work needs to be done on the state's role in promoting or inhibiting migration, a systematic evaluation of the indirect effects of these programs on women and migration must concurrently be undertaken. It is of great practical importance that such studies be initiated to evaluate the particular impact of rural development projects on women. Any strategy designed to improve the condition of women in rural Latin America must take into account the state development policies that shape the pattern of female migration.

Notes

1. Since the end of World War II, almost every country in Latin America has experienced a massive redistribution of its population through migration. For the region as a whole, 5.3 million peasants migrated to the cities between 1950 and 1960; another 4.5 million migrated between 1960 and 1970 (de Janvry 1981:121). According to Jelin (1977:130) the annual urbanization rate in Latin America as a whole was 1.26 percent from 1920 to 1930 and 2.5 percent from 1950 to 1960.

2. In the period 1960 to 1970, Alba (1977) states that female migration was greater than male migration to the metropolitan area of Mexico City, but the opposite trend prevailed in the migrant stream toward northern Mexico.

3. The literature on urbanization in Latin America is far too extensive to cite here. The book compiled by Cornelius and Trueblood (1975) provides an overview of some of the main issues and problems.

4. A far more extensive literature exists on domestic servants in Latin America than on street vendors. Arizpe's (1979) study on the Marías of Mexico City and a recent work by Bunster and Chaney (1985) for Lima, Peru, are two good case studies of street vendors.

5. Recent studies have challenged the assumption of low participation rates for Latin American women arguing that women's productive work is seriously

undervalued and underestimated in census data. The economic contributions of women are particularly undercounted in rural areas, and there are few estimates of women's work in the urban informal sector. Wainerman and Lattes (1981) provide an excellent review and critique of the ways in which Latin American census data underestimate women's work.

6. Between 1950 and 1980, there was a massive recomposition of the labor force in Latin America from the primary sector—that fell from 56 percent of the economically active population in 1950 to 36 percent in 1980—to the secondary and tertiary sectors (Ramos 1984). Between 1950 and 1970, agricultural wage employment increased by only 0.5 percent per year, accounting for 24 percent of the total agricultural labor force (de Janvry 1981:121).

7. Increasing demographic pressure on the land in the face of fixed or decreasing resources adversely affects sons as well. Work in Aguascalientes, Mexico (Crummett 1984), showed that in poor ejidatario households only one son, usually the oldest, inherits his father's plot. Migration to the cities or in some cases across the northern border is the usual employment option for younger sons.

8. See de Janvry (1981) for an anaysis of land reform, integrated rural development, and basic-needs programs in Latin America.

9. Pereira Reis (1976:85) and Laquian and Simmons (1975) argue that the long run effects of land reform have been to increase rural emigration.

References

Alba, F., *La población de México: evolución y dilemas* (México: El Colegio de México, 1977).

Arizpe, L., "Mujeres migrantes y economía campesina: análisis de una cohorte migratoria a la ciudad de México, 1940–1970," *América Indígena* 38, no. 2 (1978):303–326.

————, *Indígenas en la Ciudad de México. El caso de las "Marias"* (Mexico City: Secretaría de Educación Pública, 1979).

————, *La migración por relevos y la reproducción social del campesinado*, Cuadernos del CES 28 (Mexico: El Colegio de México, 1980).

————, "La participación de la mujer en el empleo y el desarrollo rural en América Latina y el Caribe," paper presented at the ILO Seminar on Women and Rural Development, Michoacán, Mexico, 1981.

Bach, R. L., and L. A. Schraml, "Migration, Crisis and Theoretical Conflict," *International Migration Review* 16, no. 2 (summer 1982):320–341.

Berg, R., "The Contribution of Return Migration to the Growth of Rural Capitalism in Peru," University of Notre Dame, 1985, unpublished manuscript.

Blumberg, R. M., "Rural Women and Development: Veil of Invisibility, World of Work," *International Journal of Intercultural Relations* 3, no. 4 (1979):447–472.

Boserup, E., *Women's Role in Economic Development* (New York: St. Martin's Press, 1970).

Buechler, J., "Something Funny Happened on the Way to Agora: A Comparison of Bolivian and Spanish Galician Female Migrants," *Anthropological Quarterly* 49, no. 1 (1976):62–68.

Bunster, X., and E. Chaney, *Sellers and Servants: Working Women in Lima* (New York: Praeger Special Studies, 1985).

Butterworth, D., and J. Chance, *Latin American Urbanization* (New York: Cambridge University Press, 1981).

Cabrera, G., "Migración y actividad económica en México," *Cahiers des Amérique Latines* 12, 1975.

Cardona, R., and A. Simmons, "Toward a Model of Migration in Latin America," in B. M. Dutoit and H. I. Safa, eds., *Migration and Urbanization* (Paris: Mouton Publishers, 1975).

Castro, M. G., et al., *Women and Migration—Latin America and the Caribbean: A Selective Annotated Bibliography*, Center for Latin American Studies, Paper No. 4 (Gainesville: University of Florida, 1984).

Chaney, E., "Women Who Go and Women Who Stay Behind," *Migration Today* 10, nos. 3–4 (1982):6–14.

Cornelius, W., and F. M. Trueblood, eds., *Urbanization and Inequality, The Political Economy of Urban and Rural Development in Latin America* (Beverly Hills: Sage Publications, 1975).

Corona Vásquez, R., and C. Ruíz Chiapetto, "Migrantes internacionales con y sin antecedentes de migración interna: algunas características socioeconómicas" (Mexico: CENIET [Centro Nacional de Información y Estadísticas del Trabajo], 1981).

Crummett, M., "Agrarian Class Structure and Migration: A Comparative Regional Analysis from Aguascalientes, Mexico," Ph.D. dissertation, New School for Social Research, New York, 1984.

Deere, C. D., "Rural Women's Subsistence Production in the Capitalist Periphery" *Review of Radical Political Economics* 8, no. 1 (spring 1976):9–15.

————— , "The Development of Capitalism in Agriculture and the Division of Labor by Sex: A Study of the Northern Peruvian Sierra," Ph.D. dissertation, University of California, Berkeley, 1978.

de Janvry, A., *The Agrarian Question and Reformism in Latin America* (Baltimore: Johns Hopkins University Press, 1981).

Díaz Ronner, L., and M. E. Muñoz Castellanos, "La mujer asalariada en el sector agrícola," *América Indígena* 38, no. 2 (1978):327–339.

Dinerman, I., *Migrants and Stay-at-Homes: A Comparative Study of Rural Migration from Michoacán, Mexico*, Monograph Series, No. 5. Center for U.S.-Mexican Studies (La Jolla, Calif.: University of California, 1982).

Elizaga, J. C., "A Study of Migration in Greater Santiago, Chile," *Demography* 3, no. 2 (1966):352–377.

————— , *Migraciones a los áreas metropolitanas de América Latina* (Santiago, Chile: CELADE, 1970).

Fei, J.H.D., and G. Ranis, "A Theory of Economic Development," *American Economic Review* 51, no. 4 (1961):553–565.

Fernández-Kelly, M. P., *For We Are Sold, I and My People: Women and Industry in Mexico's Frontier* (Albany: State University of New York Press, 1983).

García, B., et al., *Migración, familia y fuerza de trabajo en la ciudad de México*, Cuadernos del CES 26 (Mexico: El Colegio de México, 1979).

Garrett, P., "Some Structural Constraints on the Agricultural Activity of Women: The Chilean Hacienda," Land Tenure Center, University of Wisconsin, Madison, 1976.

Goldsmith, M., "Trabajo doméstico, asalariado y desarrollo capitalista," *Fem* 4, no. 16 (1981):10–20.

Harkness, S., "The Pursuit of an Ideal: Migration, Social Class and Women's Roles in Bogotá, Colombia," in A. Pescatello, ed., *Female and Male in Latin America* (Pittsburgh: University of Pittsburgh Press, 1973).

Jelin, E., "Migration and Labor Force Participation of Latin American Women: Domestic Servants in the Cities," *Signs: Journal of Women in Culture and Society* 3, no. 1 (1977):129–141.

Laquian, A., and A. B. Simmons, "Public Policy and Migratory Behavior in Selected Developing Countries," unpublished manuscript, IDRC, Canada, 1975.

Lattes, A. E., "Territorial Mobility and Redistribution of the Population: Recent Developments," *Population Distribution, Migration and Development*, International Conference on Population, New York, United Nations, 1984.

Long, J., "Economic Outcomes for Women Migrants to Mexico City," paper presented at Conference on Women and Industrialization, Bellagio, Italy, 1983.

Margolis, J., "El papel de la mujer en la agricultura del Bajío," *Iztapalapa* 1, no. 1 (July–December 1979):158–169.

Marshall, A., "Inmigración, demanda de fuerza de trabajo y estructura ocupacional en el área metropolitana," in *Migración y Desarrollo* (Mexico: CLACSO and El Colegio de México, 1980).

Muñoz, H., et al., *Migración y desigualdad social en la ciudad de México* (México: UNAM and El Colegio de México, 1977).

Oliveira, O. de, *Migración y absorción de mano de obra en la ciudad de México: 1930–1970*, Cuadernos del CES 14 (Mexico: El Colegio de México, 1976).

————, and B. García, "Urbanization, Migration and the Growth of Large Cities: Trends and Implications in Some Developing Countries," in *Population Distribution, Migration and Development*, International Conference on Population (New York: United Nations, 1984).

Orlansky, D., and S. Dubrovsky, *The Effects of Rural-Urban Migration on Women's Roles and Status in Latin America*, Reports and Papers in the Social Sciences, No. 41 (France: UNESCO, 1978).

Pereira Reis, E. M., "Migração rural urbana e política agrária na América Latina: Notas para uma investigação," IUPERJ, No. 13, Rio de Janeiro, Brazil, 1976.

Pessar, P., "Kinship Relations of Production in the Migration Process: The Case of Dominican Emigration to the United States," New York University, 1982, unpublished manuscript.

Prates, S., "Organización de la producción rural y emigración," in *Migración y Desarrollo* (Mexico: CLASCO and El Colegio de México, 1980).

Ramos, J., "Urbanización y mercado de trabajo," *Revista de la CEPAL*, No. 24, Naciones Unidas, 1984.

Rutte García, A., *Simplemente explotadas: el mundo de la empleadas domésticas de Lima* (Lima: DESCO, 1973).

Schmink, M., "Household Economic Strategies: Review and Research Agenda," *Latin American Research Review* 19, no. 3 (1984):87–101.

Sen, G., "Capitalist Transition and Women Workers: A Comparative Analysis," paper presented at the Fifth Berkshire Conference on Women's History, Vassar College, Poughkeepsie, New York, 1981.

Singer, P. I., "Migraciones internas, consideraciones teóricas sobre su estudio," in H. Múnoz et al., eds., *Las Migraciones internas en América Latina* (Buenos Aires: Editorial Nueva Visión, 1974).

Smith, M. L., "Domestic Service as a Channel of Upward Mobility for the Lower Class Woman: The Lima Case," in A. Pescatello, ed., *Female and Male in Latin America* (Pittsburgh: University of Pittsburgh Press, 1973).

Stern, C., *Las migraciones rural-urbanas*, Cuadernos del CES 2 (Mexico: El Colegio de México, 1979).

Tadesse, Z., *Women and Technological Development in Agriculture: An Overview of the Problems in Developing Countries*, Science and Technology Working Papers Series 9 (New York: UNITAR, 1979).

Thadani, V. M., and M. P. Todaro, *Female Migration in Developing Countries: A Framework for Analysis*, Center for Policy Studies, No. 47 (New York: Population Council, 1979).

Todaro, M. P., "A Model of Labor Migration and Urban Unemployment in Less Developed Countries," *American Economic Review* 59, no. 1 (1969):138–148.

UN Secretariat, "Population Distribution, Migration and Develoment: Highlights of the issues in the context of the World Population Plan of Action," in *Population Distribution, Migration and Development*, International Conference on Population (New York: United Nations, 1984).

Vásquez de Miranda, G., "Women's Labor Force Participation in a Developing Society: The Case of Brazil," *Signs: Journal of Women in Culture and Society* 3, no. 1 (1977):261–274.

Wainerman, C., and Z. R. de Lattes, *El trabajo femenino en el banquillo de los acusados* (San Francisco: The Population Council and Editorial Terra Nova, 1981).

Weist, R. E., "Wage-Labour Migration and the Household in a Mexican Town," *Journal of Anthropological Research* 29, no. 3 (1973):180–209.

Whiteford, M., "Women, Migration and Social Change: A Colombian Case Study," *International Migration Review* 12, no. 2 (1978):236–247.

Wood, C., "Structural Change and Household Strategies: A Conceptual Framework for the Study of Rural Migration," *Human Organization* 40, no. 4 (1981):338–344.

————, "Equilibrium and Historical-Structural Perspectives on Migration," *International Migration Review* 16, no. 2 (1982):298–319.

Young, K., "Economía campesina, unidad doméstica y migración," *América Indígena* 38, no. 2 (1978):279–302.

Youssef, N., et al., *Women and Migration: A Third World Focus* (Washington, D.C.: International Center for Research on Women, 1979).

Conclusion

Carmen Diana Deere
and Magdalena León

Over the course of the UN Decade for Women, a significant body of research on women's productive and reproductive roles was amassed, and the many ways in which state policy affects women's position and gender relations were demonstrated. At the same time, the economic crisis focused increased state attention on women's multifaceted roles. Changed economic conditions offered rural women new possibilities while imposing new constraints, both on the development process and on the possibilities for gender equality.

In our view, the eventual outcome will largely depend on the possibility of rural women's organizations becoming a political force and on the ability of the various national and the international feminist movements to articulate a clear vision of what we want for women and what we want society to be like if the goals of the UN decade—equality, development, and peace—are in fact to be achieved.

This process did begin at the end of the decade conference at Nairobi with the presentation and discussion of the report by the Third World women's group, Development Alternatives with Women for a New Era (DAWN). As it so eloquently argues, an alternative vision of development must begin by questioning "developmentalism" and its assumption that social change and, hence, state intervention are neutral with respect to gender and class. For the problem is not simply that women have been marginalized by the development process—a finding that leads to the solution that women need to be integrated into development. It is also important to question the central thesis with which the UN Decade for Women began (DAWN 1985).

In the marginalization perspective, it was thought that by increasing women's access to resources such as land, employment, income, education, and health the necessary and sufficient conditions were being created to bring about dramatic changes in women's position in society. But in societies where growth produces absolute and relative inequality, it is

261

impossible to create the preconditions required for *all* women's equality. The transformation of women's position fundamentally challenges the very logic of capitalist development.

As demonstrated in Chapters 1 to 4 and Chapter 6 on Chile, the Dominican Republic, Brazil, Mexico, and Ecuador, incorporating women into the wage labor force does not automatically bring about an improvement in the quality of women's lives or their social position. Although both men and women often work in exploitative conditions, the terms of women's employment continue to be much more unfavorable than those faced by men. Even though capitalism did not invent women's subordination, its need to maintain a cheap labor force is a powerful inducement to the reproduction of the structures and mechanisms that subordinate women to men.

The subordination of women is complexly related to a number of factors. Patterns of growth and distribution that systematically produce social inequality are just one element. Just as important is the social construction of gender and gender relations based on patriarchal structures and ideology. Although class and gender can be separated analytically, in practice they are difficult to distinguish for they articulate in all instances of social life. Women's subordination is also integrated to other relations of domination and subordination such as race, ethnicity, and age. As a result, class and gender have to be treated simultaneously as part of the struggle to change both the model of development and women's subordination.

The experiences of transition to socialism are particularly instructive in that they highlight the complex overdetermination of women's social position. Although in both Nicaragua and Cuba the importance of state policy is demonstrated in overcoming the constraints of capitalist inequality with regard to class privilege and gender inequality, the case studies of those countries illustrate the deep roots of cultural, ideological, and material factors that perpetuate women's subordination. Even socialist states or those in transition cannot will away the association of the female gender with reproduction or male privilege within the domestic unit or society. Nevertheless, they have accomplished a lot in the material realm.

The organization of women into their own autonomous organizations must be the focal point for any process of feminist social transformation. Most important, the development of gender consciousness among women is a precondition for women to become a political force—to challenge state policy by becoming the subject of development—and to challenge gender relations in daily life, particularly within the domestic unit.

For a state to formulate a macro policy designed to favor rural women requires political will. In the absence of an ideology of social equality, the likelihood that Latin American states will target gender equality will largely depend on instrumental goals or the development problems women may help to solve. For example, as León argued in Chapter 5 on Colombia, rural women may be integrated into rural development policy when that is the only approach that will make possible a solution to the food crisis. As pointed out by various authors in Part 2, this strategy has characterized most "Women in Development" efforts.

But this approach is not the only one by which to create a dynamic and commited governmental policy toward rural women. The organization of rural women and their pressure upon the state could be even more important factors in the short term and guarantee in the long term the political will of states—capitalist or socialist—to prioritize gender equality.

The organization of rural women is not only important for fundamental political change, but it is also essential for the transformation of gender relations in daily life. The household or family—the domestic unit—is a contradictory site where different individual and collective interests are expressed, imposed, and negotiated. Here women's process of re-negotiation must initially center. Changes in gender relations challenge patriarchal authority within the domestic unit, inevitably producing tensions and conflict. Women's organizations can provide the forum from which to seek collective solutions to seemingly individual problems.

Policies aimed at rural women in future decades should continue to be designed to open up new opportunities for women and provide services that mitigate the harsh conditions of daily life, enhancing the material conditions of poor rural households. But at the same time, they must have an organizational component so that material factors (land, employment, income) and ideological factors (values, consciousness, empowerment) are integrated aspects (León 1986). In a similar manner, just as poor rural women themselves have to integrate their productive and reproductive roles, actions aimed at enhancing women's gender position must take their multifaceted roles into account.

The central element of every strategy of intervention, whether public or private, should focus on raising women's consciousness, so that rural women are empowered to generate new and creative development solutions. As part of this process, as feminist researchers, we should continually strive to develop new and better techniques of participatory research. By providing women with a new and different vision of themselves, we will guarantee that they develop an understanding of the conditions that reproduce their subordination—only in this way can they begin to change them.

In sum, we must seek that rural women become new social actors who will at the same time implement the construction of a different model of development. In this perspective, the organization of women becomes a means and an end—the formative process for the development of new forms of participation, which will engender the new actions and attitudes of mobilized women.

References

DAWN (Development Alternatives with Women for a New Era), *Development Crises, and Alternative Visions: Third World Women's Perspectives,* Norway, 1985.

León, Magdalena, "Informe de la Consultoría 'Participation in Action Programme for Latin America and the Caribbean' (PAPLAC) of UNIFEN," United Nations, Bogotá, 1986, mimeo.

About the Editors
and Contributors

Mavis Alvarez, a Cuban agronomist, has been a staff member of the Cuban National Association of Small Farmers (ANAP) since its founding. She specializes in the economic and technical problems of peasant farming and is currently completing a Ph.D. in economics at the University of La Habana.

Lourdes Arizpe received her Ph.D. from the London School of Economics. A Mexican social anthropologist, she has written numerous books and articles on rural and urban women, migration, and the peasantry. Over the past decade, she has been one of the intellectual leaders in fostering research on women in Latin America. Formerly a professor at the Colegio de Mexico, she is currently director of the Museo Nacional de Cultura Popular in Mexico City.

Carlota Botey, a Mexican social anthropologist, is director of the Centro de Estudios Históricos del Agrarismo in Mexico City. She is an expert on Mexican agricultural development and peasant organizations.

Elsa M. Chaney earned her Ph.D. in political science from the University of Wisconsin, Madison. Formerly a professor at Fordham University, she now works as an independent social policy analyst for development agencies. A pioneer in the field of women in development, she recently coauthored *Sellers and Servants: Working Women in Lima*.

Ana Criquillon, a French researcher, has resided in Nicaragua since before the revolution. She works at the Asociación de los Trabajadores del Campo (ATC), the rural worker's union. She participated in the national-level study of rural women wage workers in Nicaragua.

María de los Angeles Crummett received her Ph.D. in economics from the New School for Social Research in New York. She has carried out fieldwork in Mexico and has written numerous articles on the Mexican agrarian structure, rural women, and migration. She has been a Fellow at the Kellogg Institute at the University of Notre Dame and currently is a consultant to the United Nations Voluntary Fund for Women.

Carmen Diana Deere is professor of economics at the University of Massachusetts, Amherst. Her Ph.D. is in agricultural economics from the University of California, Berkeley. She has carried out research and advised studies on rural women in Peru, Colombia, Nicaragua, the Dominican Republic, and Cuba. Her most recent book is the coedited collection *Transition and Development: Problems of Third World Socialism*.

Cornelia Butler Flora is professor of sociology at Kansas State University. She received her Ph.D. in development sociology from Cornell University. Her publications include numerous articles on rural women and popular culture in Latin America. She is the author of *Pentecostalism in Colombia: Baptism by Fire and Spirit*. She is researching agricultural development and farming systems in the United States and Latin America.

Lydia Grant, a Puerto Rican anthropologist, received her degree from the Universidad Autónoma de Santo Domingo. She was a researcher on the first national-level study of rural women in the Dominican Republic carried out by the Centro de Investigación para la Acción Femenina (CIPAF).

María Soledad Lago, a Chilean sociologist, is a researcher at the Grupo de Investigaciones Agrarias (GIA) in Santiago, Chile. She has carried out extensive fieldwork in the agrarian sector and is the coauthor of a forthcoming book on rural women in Chile.

Magdalena León is director of research at the Asociación Colombiana para Estudios de Poblacion (ACEP) in Bogotá, Colombia. A Colombian sociologist, she holds a master's degree from Washington University, St. Louis. She has published *Mujer y Capitalismo Agrario*, the first national-level study of rural women carried out in Latin America, edited the three-volume collection *Debate sobre la Mujer en America Latina y el Caribe,* and is coauthor (with Deere) of *Women in Andean Agriculture.*

Belkis Mones, a Dominican economist, has been a researcher with the Centro de Investigaciones para la Acción Femenina (CIPAF) since 1983. She participated in the national-level study of rural women and on an earlier study of women workers in the free trade zones of the Dominican Republic. She was recently the coordinator of the CIPAF training course on research on rural women held in conjunction with the National University of Honduras.

Clara Murguialday was born in the Basque country of Spain, where she received her degree in economics. She has lived in Nicaragua since 1979, working as a researcher at the Instituto Nacional de Estadísticas and at the Asociación de los Trabajadores del Campo. She participated in the national study of rural women wage workers.

Martha Luz Padilla, a Nicaraguan researcher, was one of the founders of the rural women's research team at the Centro de Investigaciones y Estudios de la Reforma Agraria (CIERA) of the Nicaraguan ministry of Agricultural Development. She was a coauthor of *Las Mujeres en las Cooperativas Agrarias en Nicaragua* and participated in the national study of rural women wage workers.

Lynne Phillips received her Ph.D. from the University of Toronto. A Canadian anthropologist, she has carried out extensive fieldwork in coastal Ecuador. She has been affiliated with the Center for Research on Latin America and the Caribbean (CERLAC) at York University and has also taught at the University of Toronto.

Cheywa R. Spindel, a Brazilian sociologist, received her Ph.D. from the University of São Paulo, Brazil. She is a professor in the Department of Economics, Pontifícia Universidade Católica, and senior researcher at the Instituto de Estudios Económico, Politicos e Soçais in São Paulo. She is the author of numerous articles on rural women and is researching the role of women in the Amazonian free trade zone.

Jean Stubbs, a British social historian, received her Ph.D. from Oxford University, England. She has resided in Cuba for many years, researching the island's agrarian history. Among her published works is *Tobacco on the Periphery: A Case Study in Cuban Labour History, 1860–1958.*

Index

Absolute marginalization, 2
Aconcagua, Chile, 26
ACs. *See* Cuba, farmer's associations
Agrarian reform, 196
  and agricultural policy compared, 81–82
  beneficiaries, 60, 67, 99, 112–113, 117, 128, 165–166, 171, 173–181, 186, 213, 247
  and capitalist development, 170
  and import substitution processes, 38
  and industrial development, 6
  land distribution, 117
  migration processes, 246–247
  state policies, 11, 93–95, 165, 183, 186
  women's component, 8, 26, 67–68, 179–181
  See also Cooperative movements; Credit and technical assistance; Income generation projects; Integrated rural development projects; *See also under individual countries*
Agricultural development
  and agrarian policy compared, 81–82
  state intervention, 67
  women's participation in, 23, 61–64, 89, 171, 212, 263
  See also Agrarian reform
Agricultural extension services. *See* Extension services
Aguascalientes, Mexico, 251, 253
Alcoholism, 80

Allende, Salvador, 21, 170, 178–179
Alliance for Progress, 85, 112, 169–170, 174
ANAP. *See* Cuba, National Association of Small Producers
Animal husbandry. *See* Small animal and livestock production
APP. *See* Nicaragua, Area of People's Property
Appropriate Technology for Rural Women Project (PTAMC)
  community development model, 222–225
  welfare model, 226–228
Argentina, 140, 242
Artisan activities, 27, 114, 117, 204
Association of Nicaraguan Women (LAE), 139
ATC. *See* Nicaragua, Association of Rural Workers

Bakery cooperative, 226
Balaguer, Joaquín, 37–38, 46
Balmaceda, Manuel, 25
Banana production, 110–111, 113
Barley production, 23, 108
"Bartolina Sisa." *See* Bolivian National Peasant Women's Federation
Bean production, 29, 39, 43, 90, 146
Beet production, 23
Belaunde, Fernando, 180
Beneficiaries of reform. *See* Agrarian reform, beneficiaries; Credit and technical assistance, beneficiaries
Bogotá, Colombia, 47